BEN NEVIS AND GLEN COE

BEN NEVIS AND GLEN COE

100 LOW, MID AND HIGH LEVEL WALKS

by Ronald Turnbull

JUNIPER HOUSE, MURLEY MOSS,
OXENHOLME ROAD, KENDAL, CUMBRIA LA9 7RL
www.cicerone.co.uk

© Ronald Turnbull 2017
Second edition 2017
ISBN-13: 978 1 85284 871 2
Reprinted 2020, 2022 (with updates)
First edition 2007
Printed in China on responsibly sourced paper on behalf of Latitude Press Ltd

© Crown copyright 2016 OS PU100012932
All photographs are by the author unless otherwise stated.

Updates to this Guide

While every effort is made by our authors to ensure the accuracy of guidebooks as they go to print, changes can occur during the lifetime of an edition. Any updates that we know of for this guide will be on the Cicerone website (www.cicerone.co.uk/871/updates), so please check before planning your trip. We also advise that you check information about such things as transport, accommodation and shops locally. Even rights of way can be altered over time. We are always grateful for information about any discrepancies between a guidebook and the facts on the ground, sent by email to updates@cicerone.co.uk or by post to Cicerone, Juniper House, Murley Moss, Oxenholme Road, Kendal, LA9 7RL.

Register your book: To sign up to receive free updates, special offers and GPX files where available, register your book at www.cicerone.co.uk.

Warning

Mountain walking, and particularly scrambling or winter walking, can be dangerous activities carrying a risk of personal injury or death. It should be undertaken only by those with a full understanding of the risks and with the training and experience to evaluate them. While every care has been taken in the preparation of this book, the user should be aware that conditions can be highly variable and can change quickly, materially affecting the seriousness of a mountain walk. Therefore, except for any liability that cannot be excluded by law, neither Cicerone nor the author accept liability for damage of any nature (including damage to property, personal injury or death) arising directly or indirectly from the information in this book.

To call out the Mountain Rescue, phone 999 from a landline. From a mobile, phone 999 or 112: these should connect you via any available network. Once connected to the emergency operator, ask for Police Scotland.

Front cover: Arriving on Clach Leathad (Route 85) with Bidean nam Bian behind

CONTENTS

Stob Coire nan Lochan (Routes 61, 62) and the top of its northwest ridge from Coire nan Lochan in early May

N

Map Key

☐ ground above 1200m / 4000ft

☐ ground above 1050m / 3500ft

☐ ground above 900m / 3000ft

☐ ground above 750m / 2500ft

☐ ground above 600m / 2000ft

☐ ground above 450m / 1500ft

☐ ground above 300m / 1000ft

☐ ground above 150m / 500ft

☐ ground below 150m / 500ft

Contour intervals chosen to feature the Munro and Corbett levels at 3000ft and 2500ft

▲ Munro

△ Other summit of interest: on overview maps, the Corbetts

P Parking (typically at walk start)

V visitor centre

▫ building

⌂ bothy or the CIC Hut, Ben Nevis (private)

♜ castle

loch

river, stream

major road

minor road

unsurfaced track

 The route start ◄ finish (if different)

 Variants, and adjacent routes

Overview maps (pages 12–15)

estate boundaries (see access section)

27 the through routes (long daywalk
or backpacking)

53 route location

⚪● town, village

Route symbols on OS map extracts

 route 1
alternative route 1
route 2
alternative route 2
linking routes

 start point

 finish point

 start/finish point

 direction of walk

For OS symbols key see OS maps

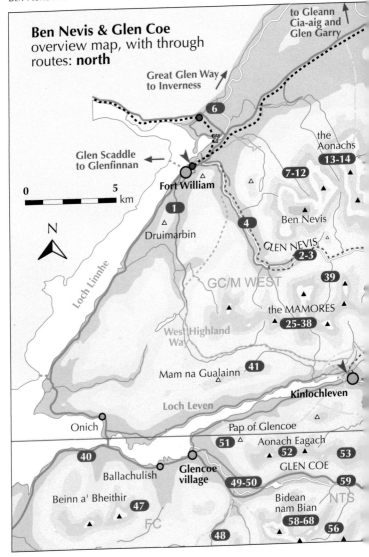

Ben Nevis & Glen Coe
overview map, with through
routes: **north**

to Gleann
Cia-aig and
Glen Garry

Great Glen Way
to Inverness

the
Aonachs
13-14

6

Glen Scaddle
to Glenfinnan

7-12

Fort William

0   5
km

1

4

Ben Nevis

Druimarbin

GLEN NEVIS
2-3

N

GC/M WEST

39

Loch Linnhe

the MAMORES
25-38

West Highland
Way

Mam na Gualainn   41

Kinlochleven

Loch Leven

Pap of Glencoe

Onich

51   Aonach Eagach
52   53

40

GLEN COE
59

Ballachulish   **Glencoe
village**   49-50

NTS

Beinn a' Bheithir   47

Bidean
nam Bian
58-68   56

FC

48

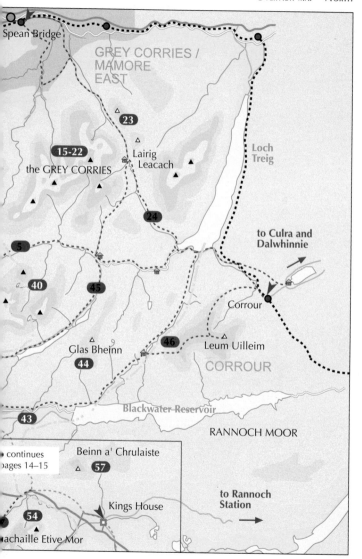

Spean Bridge

GREY CORRIES / MAMORE EAST

23

15-22

the GREY CORRIES

Lairig Leacach

Loch Treig

24

to Culra and Dalwhinnie

5

40

45

Corrour

Leum Uilleim

Glas Bheinn

46

CORROUR

44

43

Blackwater Reservoir

RANNOCH MOOR

continues
pages 14–15

Beinn a' Chrulaiste

57

Kings House

to Rannoch Station

54

achaille Etive Mor

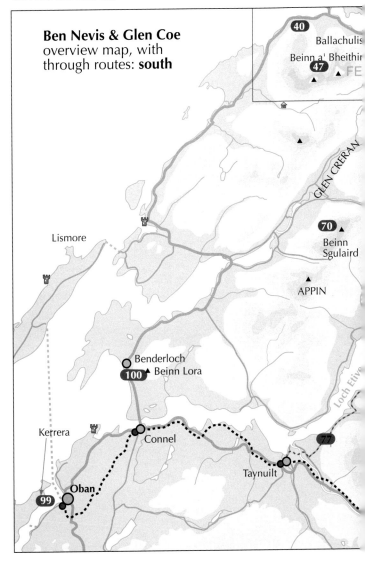

Ben Nevis & Glen Coe
overview map, with
through routes: **south**

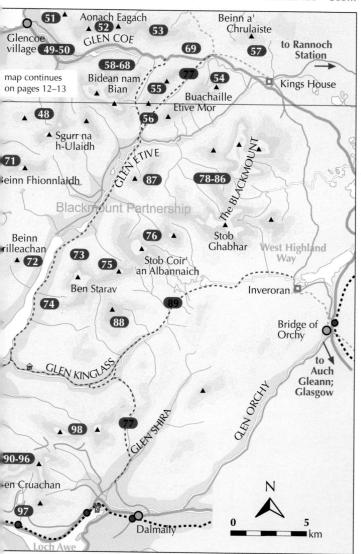

Coire nam Beitheach (Route 59), the western one of the three craggy valleys leading between the Three Sisters to the high ridgelines of Bidean nam Bian

INTRODUCTION

Bidean nam Bian (Section 7),
seen across Loch Leven

'GLEN COE, GLEN COE,
IT'S THE PLACE TO GO...'

The best of walking is ridge walking. Swoop downwards from the peak, level off along a rocky crest, then rise again to another summit; and then do the same thing again, four or five or even eight times over. Let the ridge sides drop steeply 900m to a green valley where a river gleams among the alder trees; and beyond the valley another steep ridge, and another, and the sea reaching silver-grey into the furthest west. For added interest let the ridge top be composed of three different sorts of stone. And you've started to understand why the area from Ben Nevis southwards to Glen Coe is some of the finest mountain walking there is in the UK.

I put 'some of' so as not to annoy the lovers of Snowdonia, or the English Lakes, or Skye, or Torridon. There's a lot more of Lochaber than there is of Snowdonia; it's one and a half times as large as Lakeland. It's a whole lot easier to get to than Skye. Still not convinced? In that case...

Follow me first onto one of the less celebrated summits, Ben Starav at the bottom of Glen Etive. Its long ridge (Route 73) is stony with moss, and leads into an easy scramble over blobby boulders of grey granite. But now drop into the green valley on the left and enjoy another aspect of it all. Steep grass and granite slabs shut out the sky. Below the path a gloomy ravine, with the flash of a waterfall. And at the valley foot, under green

17

Clockwise from left: dwarf cornel, golden saxifrage, dwarf azalea

birch and dark pine, the cuckoo calls, and white water slides over granite that mysteriously is now coloured pink.

Next, let's visit Bidean nam Bian. The rocks now are volcanic, grey-blue andesite and pinky-grey rhyolite, all of it great to climb on if you're a rock climber. Enter Bidean up one of its three ravines, each with some of that great climbing rock hanging impressively overhead. It's steep, and it's gloomy, and it gets steeper, until all at once you emerge onto Bidean's ridge, with bright sky around you.

Granite and volcanic rock; the third rock is called quartzite. It's flat but cracked, like a city pavement after earthquakes. Follow it along the Grey Corries, where its sharp edges will slash your boots, but its flat slabs give almost-easy walking above the precipices.

By now you're getting tired. So take a break; and come back in February or March. The eroded path along the Mamores is gone, and instead a snow edge swoops like a breaking wave, the snow crisp and crunchy for your crampons. In the clear cold air of a classic winter day, views are southwards over half a dozen ranges to the dome of Ben Lomond.

At the bottom of every steep-sided ridge there's a steep-walled valley. Some of those valleys contain the A82 (alas, how even lovelier would be Glen Coe without its busy road). But the others offer long through routes, with rugged paths and smooth Landrover tracks. A comfortable track leads between the jaws of the Lairig Leacach, and down past small waterfalls while looking up at Ben Nevis and the Mamores. Then it's down a river whose alder-shaded bank has green levels for the tent. An even lonelier glen – but still with a good footpath – leads you to a lochan and bothy that are completely out of it. And however bleak the Blackwater, the last 4 miles, through a deep, steep glen of beautiful birchwoods, will leave you at Kinlochleven longing for the next really long walk with the big rucksack. Just as soon as your feet and shoulders have recovered from the first one.

GETTING THERE, GETTING ABOUT, FOOD AND SHELTER

The Nevis Glencoe area is perhaps Scotland's best for real walks reached without the use of a car.

Travellers from afar should aim for Glasgow Airport, which has direct bus links by Citylink coach to Glencoe village and Fort William. From within the UK, aim for Glasgow rail or bus station. The Citylink coach is particularly useful, a lovely run past Loch Lomond to serve Bridge of Orchy (for Inveroran Hotel), Kings House, Glencoe village, Fort William, and Spean Bridge on its way towards the Isle of Skye. The West Highland Railway is even more beautiful, its crossing of Rannoch Moor featuring in various Harry Potter films.

Accommodation is widely available, from cosy old inns to both SYHA and independent hostels, bunkhouses and camp sites. There is also a right of responsible wild camping anywhere in the countryside.

For those visiting without the benefit of a nasty tin box on wheels, I commend Kinlochleven. Reasonably easily reached by bus, and with useful facilities such as shops, it has a wide range of good walks, from riverside to mountaintop, right from the village edge. From there a short bus ride lets you relocate to Fort William or Glen Coe.

The alternative, for those with strong shoulders, is to arrive

Buachaille Etive Mor (Route 55)

somewhere in the south (Dalmally, Bridge of Orchy) and trek north along the valleys – stopping off at Kinlochleven for a hot bar meal and a night in a bed – then onwards for Spean Bridge or Fort William. Such adventurers will note the quite frequent bothies, marked on the overview maps with a small hut symbol.

Details of local food, transport and information are in Appendix C.

OH, SIR HUGH MUNRO

An oddity of hillwalking in Scotland is that it takes place almost entirely above the 900m contour line. Sir Hugh Munro in 1892 listed the hills above 3000ft (914.4m) – after revisions there are currently 282 of them, of which 44 are in the area of this guidebook. Many hillwalkers are engaged in

visiting these 282, and they are indeed worthwhile hills to visit. But the consequence is that the well-trodden ways and rebuilt paths are on these, rather high, hills. The heights of 914.3m and below are largely pathless, and their lesser altitude usually means denser and tougher vegetation. Accordingly, the lower hills are interesting, and unfrequented; but they are not easy. The less difficult of them, and the most interesting, are included here.

The 'standard routes' up the Munros are detailed in several existing guidebooks, including Steve Kew's *Walking the Munros Vol 1* (Cicerone). So, while I have described them here briefly, I have also sought out the interesting ways around the back, the unfrequented corries, the more demanding rugged ridgelines from the less convenient car parks.

Easy rocks above the Zigzags of Gearr Aonach, Bidean nam Bian (Route 63), one of three scrambles that sweet-talked their way into this walking guide

But on the finest of them all I've left the choice to you. Bidean is a hill to visit many times by many different routes; and so, in the south, is Ben Cruachan. The Mamores is one great ridge of many mountains: where you go up and come down depends on how much of it you want to do on a given day. The Black Mount's great complex sprawl also deserves to be explored in detail.

I have included various tough walking routes involving rock, but just two of the easiest and most spectacular scrambles: the magnificent Ledge Route on Ben Nevis, and the Zigzags onto Bidean nam Bian (Routes 9 and 63). Here is also the harder, but unmissable, scramble of the Aonach Eagach ridge above Glen Coe (Route 52).

For **low-level walking**, Scotland used to offer only the plod through the bog or the smooth and stultifying forest road through the spruce. The south of the area is still like that. However, Kinlochleven has an excellent little network of scenic paths; Glen Nevis has a more variable selection. Some are waymarked and signposted, some not; it's a good idea to carry a compass and keep a general idea of which way is the road and which way is vast and pathless wilderness.

The **mid-level hills** are more demanding. They tend to offer arduous half-days, somewhat tougher but less rockily rewarding than the higher ground. Chase after them though for good views achieved in solitude, or

Walking above raised beaches on the west coast of Kerrera island (Route 99)

on a windy day or one with poor-quality soggy snow on the bigger hills.

On **mountains** of 900m and upwards, bare rocks and stones replace the clinging heather or grassy tufts. Or else you're on a path; popular ways lead to all the Munro summits. The high ground may be comparatively easy but it is also serious. On the ridges of Bidean nam Bian you're several hours' walk from any shelter, and that walk will involve finding your way down between crags.

Fancy backpacking, but not sure how it all fits together? Worried you might pack too little gear into the big rucksack – or, even worse, too much? The **treks and through routes** are full-on in terms of big scenery, lochs and rivers, and real remote country. But at the same time they are fairly easy-going in terms of tracks and footpaths, and a couple of bothies just in case you did manage to lighten your pack by leaving behind the tent poles.

But let's be hopeful and suppose you remember the tent poles (and even the tent itself), get the weight below 25lb/12kg without leaving out anything that really matters, start early, and keep the speed sensibly low. Then Glen Coe and Glen Nevis could turn you from a boring Munro-bagger into a backpacker for ever.

Within the various sections, the through routes are described from south to north so as to get the bad weather beating on your back. In the northern part of the area, routes web in and out around Corrour station at the edge of Rannoch Moor. The overview maps let you link them into expeditions of up to a week.

These overview maps also mark deer-stalking estates. In Scotland there is a legal **right of access** to virtually all open country, provided that access

Wild camping below Castle Ridge on the exciting side of Ben Nevis (Route 10)

is taken responsibly. In certain areas, responsible access means – during three months of autumn – adapting your walking so as not to disturb deer stalking. Over Ben Nevis itself, and in Glen Coe, there is free access year-round; in places like Black Mount and Etive, where deer are hunted for sport, helpful phone lines or agreed routes are available. Full details are in Appendix B.

WHEN TO GO

April is still winter on the summits, but low-level routes already offer good walking then and in May. The leaves are breaking and birds are at their noisiest. Low-level routes are also excellent in October as the birch leaves turn gold.

May and June are enjoyable at all altitudes. July and August can be hot and humid, with less rewarding views and midges infesting the glens. West Highland midges can be pretty grim; the trick is to keep moving, and when you stop, stop high.

Midges hang on until the first frost, normally some time in September. October often brings clear air and lovely autumn colours. In between times there'll be gales. Deer stalking (mid-August to mid-October) causes only minor disturbance to hill-walking in this area; with a little care and consultation, you can have hill days here during the stalking season more readily than anywhere else in Scotland (see Appendix B).

Winter is a time of short days and often foul weather. Snow often lies on the high tops from December to April, with patches in the corries obstructing some routes even into June. Well-equipped walkers skilled in navigation and with ice axe love the winter most of all, for the wonderful crisp

The grand winter ridge of Ben Starav (Route 73)

WEATHER AND SNOW CONDITIONS

The most useful and accurate Internet forecast is at Mountain Weather Information Systems www.mwis.org.uk. This site has links to snow reports from various Fort William climbers and guides. The Scottish Avalanche Information Service issues forecasts of snow conditions and avalanche risk daily for Glencoe and for Lochaber (Ben Nevis area) from December through to Easter at www.sais.gov.uk, or the BAA (Be Avalanche Aware) app for phones.

A webcam for Ben Nevis is at aboutfortwilliam.com. For Glen Coe, see the Meall a' Bhuiridh ski area (or not, if the cloud's down) at Glen Coe webcams, www.glencoemountain.co.uk/webcams/.

snow along the ridges of Bidean and the 100km views through the winter-chilled air.

SAFETY IN THE MOUNTAINS

In Glen Coe and Lochaber you're usually within a few hours of a road; but the downward ground may be steep with crags. Safety and navigation in the mountains is best learnt from companions, experience, and perhaps a paid instructor; such instruction is outside the scope of this book. Those experienced in smaller, less steep hills will need some extra fitness and endurance, and a level of map expertise that enables you to get away safely when the headwind that's cutting you off from your descent route is also going to shred your map should you attempt to unfold it.

The international mountain distress signal is some sign (shout, whistle, torch flash or other) repeated six times over a minute, followed by a minute's silence. The reply is a sign repeated three times over a minute, followed by a minute's silence. To signal for help from a helicopter, raise both arms above the head and then drop them down sideways, repeatedly. If you're not in trouble, don't shout or whistle on the hills, and don't wave to passing helicopters.

To call out the rescue, phone 999 from a landline. From a mobile, phone either 999 or the international

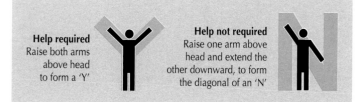

Help required
Raise both arms above head to form a 'Y'

Help not required
Raise one arm above head and extend the other downward, to form the diagonal of an 'N'

emergency number 112: these will connect you via any available network. Reception is good on most summits and ridges, but absent in places without direct sightlines to Fort William, Glencoe village or the mast behind Kings House. Sometimes a text message can get through when a voice call can't. For this you must pre-register your phone with the emergencySMS service (text the word 'register' to 999). The 'OS Locate' app, if preloaded on your phone, will give a precise grid reference you can pass on to the rescue team.

Given the unreliable phone coverage, it is wise to leave word of your proposed route with some responsible person (and, of course, tell that person when you've safely returned). Youth hostels have specific forms for this, as do many independent hostels and B&Bs. You could also leave word at the police stations at Glencoe or Fort William.

Being lost or tired is not sufficient reason for calling the rescue service, and neither, in normal summer weather, is being benighted. However, team members I've talked to say not to be too shy about calling them: they greatly prefer bringing down bodies that are still alive…

There is no charge for mountain rescue in Scotland – teams are voluntary, financed by donations from the public, with a grant from the Scottish Executive and helicopters funded by the Department for Transport. You can make donations at youth hostels, tourist information centres (TICs) and many pubs.

MAPS

The mapping used on lower walks in this book is from the Ordnance Survey's Landranger series at 1:50,000 (enlarged in Routes 49 and 58). For high mountain walks, too, these maps

Heading south along Beinn Fhada (Route 65)

were for about 40 years the only ones available, and are perfectly satisfactory: Sheet 41 is Ben Nevis and Glen Coe with part of Black Mount and Glen Etive; the rest of Black Mount and Glen Etive, southwards to Ben Cruachan, are on Sheet 50 (Glen Orchy) – annoyingly, the two sheets don't overlap.

The Harveys Ben Nevis British Mountain Map, at 1:40,000 scale, covers the whole area as far south as Loch Tulla and the head of Loch Etive. Just 15 of the routes here (notably, Cruachan) aren't on it. It is beautifully clear and legible, marks paths where they actually exist on the ground, and is made of plastic so robust that one lightweight gear guru uses it as his groundsheet.

For detailed exploration of crags and corries and pathless boulder slopes, you will be helped by the extra contour detail at 1:25,000 scale. The two Harveys Superwalker XT25 maps 'Ben Nevis' and 'Glen Coe' score very highly. They cover much the same ground as the Mountain Map, and overlap conveniently, so that Kinlochleven is on both. Also at 1:25,000 is the Explorer series of the Ordnance Survey. These maps have excellent contour detail on the lower ground, but many of the summits are so obscured with crag-marks that the contour detail is almost illegible. Harveys also offer an A4-sized Ben Nevis summit map at 1:12,500. This is equivalent to the summit enlargement on their 1:25,000 map with its useful

addition of 100-metre grid lines for GPS users.

I'd suggest the Ben Nevis Mountain Map, with Landranger Sheet 50 (Glen Orchy) for the far south around Cruachan. But for ambitious mountain explorations, the Harvey Superwalker is preferable.

COMPASS, GPS AND PHONE

A compass is a very useful aid in mist, even if your skills extend only to 'northwest, southeast' rather than precision bearings. Magnetic deviation is about 2° west (2020), decreasing to zero around 2030. To convert a map bearing to compass, add 1. No magnetic rocks have been found in this area; it's you that's wrong, not the compass!

For users of old-fashioned GPS devices, I have given 8-digit (10m accuracy) grid references at various tricky points, such as where you turn down off a ridge. The GPS readings are supplementary; this book is designed to be used without a GPS. Many walkers use a smartphone app for navigating. Batteries run down, especially in cold weather, so a paper map is a desirable backup. The antique compass is also a very useful supplement to the phone. Equally, maps can blow away – a smartphone app is a desirable backup!

Note that without a phone signal your mapping can go disconcertingly blank. Work out how to download the necessary map chunks via Wi-Fi the night before. OS Maps and

Meall a' Bhuiridh (Route 82)

Outdooractive are two apps offering fairly cheap subscriptions to all OS mapping – and if you pay extra, Outdooractive offers Harveys as well.

USING THIS GUIDE

A glance ahead into the book will show two different sorts of mapping. The **low-level** and **mid-level** routes have 1:50,000 mapping; this scale is large enough for use on the actual walk. The **linear through-route** walks are on the overview maps at the beginning of the book; the **mountain** routes have similar hand-drawn sketch maps at a larger scale. These sketches are not sufficient for route-finding on the actual mountaintop. A full-sized walkers' map is needed so that you know not just the route you're walking, but also the bad-weather escape route which may take you into a different glen altogether.

Each of the **Munros** (3000ft/914m mountains) has its well-worn 'standard route'. That will be the quickest and most convenient – and fairly straightforward – route, but usually not the most interesting. I have pointed out those routes in the preambles, and they are listed in several guidebooks, including Steve Kew's *Walking the Munros Vol 1*. However, I've concentrated on what I consider the most rewarding routes for each hill. These may also be a little more demanding, as they seek out the steeper scenery and avoid the flat Landrover track.

But for the very finest hills I have left the choice to you. **The Grey Corries, the Mamores**, and the **Black Mount**; **Bidean** and **Ben Cruachan**: these are hills you will want to ascend lots of times, by many different routes, or ranges where only you can decide how much to do, once you're up. For these I have given a **summit**

27

The type of walk is indicated as follows:

Low level
Forest and riverside walks, below 600m

Mountain
Mountain walks above 900m

Mid level
Moorland and foothills, below 900m

Treks and through routes
Bothy or tent, or using rail/bus

summary, with the standard route and the adventure around the back, the slightly rocky scramble and the long, long walk in from somewhere else altogether.

Many of the mountain routes start off along one of the low or mid-level ones. Accordingly, the starts of high-level routes are marked (in green) on the 1:50,000 mapping of the lower ones.

At the start of each walk there is a route information box, with an icon showing the type of route: low-level, mid-level, mountain or trek. The difficulty indicators are explained in the panel below. The length indicators correspond to the **approximate times**

given in the route information box: one square is up to 4 hours, two squares up to 6 hours, with the full five squares for walks of over 10 hours – those could also be enjoyed over two days using a tent or bothy. The approximate times are based on 1 hour for 4 horizontal km or for 400m of height gained, with extra time where the ground is particularly steep or rough. They'll be about right, including brief snack stops, for a moderately paced party. (Note there are no timing indicators in the summit summary routes as they are uphill only.)

On the treks and through routes, I've used the same calculation of 4km per hour for the 'going time'.

Slabby granite below Meall Tarsuinn (Route 76)

These walks can sometimes be done as day walks with a light pack. When done with a load, the calculated time should be considered to exclude lunch and other stops. The length in days supposes 8 hours of actual walking.

Where a bus or train can be used to link the two ends of a linear route, or to go up one route and come down another, I've noted this at the routes concerned. Other public transport information is in Appendix C.

In old numbers, 600ft was a vertical distance, while 200yds was horizontal. I've used a similar convention, so that 600m is an altitude or height gain, while 600 metres is along the ground. I use 'track' (rather than 'path') for a way wide enough for a tractor or Landrover; the exception here is the Mountain Track on Ben Nevis, as this new name for the

The **difficulty ratings** are on a rough scale of 1 to 5:

■□□□□ Clear smooth paths, with no steep sections

■■□□□ Small rough paths, some steep ground

■■■□□ Short steep climbs or long gentle ones, pathless ground with clear ridgelines

■■■■□ Some boulderfields, steep rough ground, navigation at the level of 'northwest, southeast'

■■■■■ Featureless plateau requiring compass bearings in mist or pathless forest; heather tramping; remote high ground; long steep rough ascents and descents; rocky ground and scrambling

Pony Path appears on many maps and leaflets.

Finally, the 'standard route' up a hill is the convenient and well-trodden one featured in guidebooks like Steve Kew's *Walking the Munros*. Thus the Mountain Track is the 'standard route' up Ben Nevis. The ranger for Blackmount has determined that 90 per cent of walkers would be content to be restricted to such routes and no others. If that figure drops as a result of this book, the Blackmount ranger may not like it – but I shall be very pleased.

Aonach Dubh from Clachaig Inn (Route 59)

1 FORT WILLIAM AND GLEN NEVIS

Fort William, below the Aonachs and Ben Nevis

Fort William is a prettier place than Aviemore (the entry point for the Cairngorms) or Chamonix (the entry point for Mont Blanc). This still doesn't make it very pretty. It is, however, very useful, with its supermarket and street full of gear shops, its hostels both independent and SYHA, its rail and coach links, and its charming little museum for a wet day.

For a slightly less wet day, or for a half-day, this section rounds up some walks that don't go up Ben Nevis. The highlight here is the Nevis Gorge (Route 2): the shortest walk in this book, but on its wide path possibly Britain's most spectacular stroll.

ROUTE 1
Cow Hill and Druimarbin

Length

Difficulty

Start/Finish	Fort William south end (NN 098 736)
Distance	14km/8½miles
Total ascent	500m/1700ft
Time	4½hr
Terrain	Smooth paths
Max altitude	Druimarbin 287m

A gentle exploration of Fort William and lower Glen Nevis; but with a touch of mountain ground, plus Linnhe views, on Druimarbin.

Start at the car park at the Ballachulish end of Fort William. Follow the loch-side pavement northeast around the town to a roundabout with the old fort, the start of the Great Glen Way, on the left. GGW waymarkers lead along tarred path to left of McDonalds, then through a warehouse area. Dogleg right then left among houses to a road bridge across River Nevis.

Cross, and ignoring a track beside the river, turn right up a fenced path beside houses for 300 metres. Keep ahead along Dubh MacDonald Road, then bear right to the A82. Cross into a street signposted for the Ben Nevis Inn, but after 100 metres turn right on a stone bridge over River Nevis. Turn left on pavement for 400 metres, until a track forks down left to another crossing of River Nevis, a metal footbridge.

Turn right to a small car park, where a good path continues ahead along the river. After 1.2km, cross a footbridge into the car park of the **Nevis Visitor Centre** (Ionad Nibheis). Pass along riverbank to left of the visitor centre, onto a path through trees to the Glen Nevis road. Continue for 50 metres, to a path on the right signed as the Peat Track to Cow Hill. Head up the wide path; as you enter trees, a gate on the right leads to a footbridge to the nearby **burial ground**, a place of not terribly antique gravestones and beech trees. Return to the Peat Track and continue up.

At a forest road crossing, right is signed for Fort William, but keep ahead up the steep but good path for Cow Hill. At the top of the trees, keep ahead on the path to meet a track. Turn right, for 1.5km to **Cow Hill**. At the radio mast, keep ahead for a few steps for a view down onto Fort William.

Return along the track. After it passes the path you came up on, it bends round to the

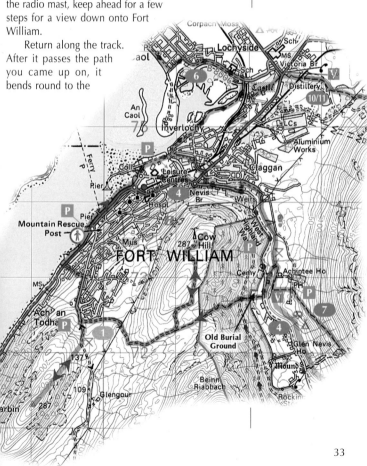

On Druimarbin, view to Fort William and Great Glen

right. Follow the track down to a road at the edge of Fort William.

Turn left up to a car park viewpoint and picnic place. Opposite this, go through a rusty metal gate. Head up, with a fence on the right to start with, to a second rusty red gate onto open hill. A peaty, heathery path leads uphill and follows the rounded crest to the trig point on **Druimarbin**, with a lovely view along Loch Linnhe.

Turn round – the views now are along the Great Glen – and head back to the road at the viewpoint. Turn left, downhill, past the end of the Peat Track and into **Fort William**. Keep ahead down Lundavra Road for 500 metres. Just after a bridge over a stream, at a waymark post, turn left down a tarred lane. After it recrosses the stream, turn right down steps then a tarred path. Keep ahead down Ashburn Lane to the A82.

Cross the main road and take paths past flowerbeds along the lochside, to the walk start.

ROUTE 2
Nevis Gorge

Start/Finish	Glen Nevis top car park (NN 168 691)
Distance	3km/2 miles
Total ascent	150m/500ft
Time	2hr
Terrain	Choice: a wide smooth path, or a slippery scramble
Max altitude	285m on upper path

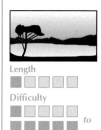

Length

Difficulty

to

The Nevis Gorge has high, steep slopes where 1000 pine trees cling to ledges between glaciated slabs. Below, the river rushes under house-sized boulders, and at its head is the 90m-high Steall waterfall.

A deservedly popular path leads up the gorge. It is smooth and engineered, but even so has warning notices because of the drops alongside. However, two older and disused paths, one above and one below, offer slightly better views and a much wilder experience. The lower path, in particular, crosses damp and rather slimy rocks in an exposed position. All three options are given here: my preference is take the lower path up the gorge, and the high one back again.

Start along the big, level main path out of the car park end, with signs for Corrour, and another warning about exposure to come. This path leads straightforwardly up the wooded gorge side to the meadow below **Steall Falls**.

There are two alternative paths that are much less comfortable.

Lower path
The lower path gives a more intimate acquaintance with the river below. Its untrodden rocks are damp and slippery; there are drops below, so the path in its current condition must be considered a mild scramble (Grade 1).

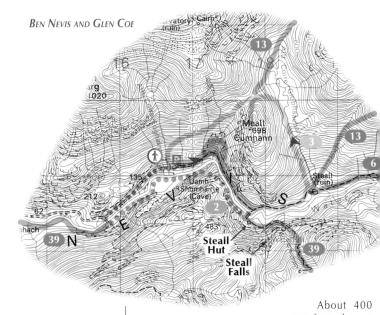

About 400 metres from the car park, the main path becomes a gangway carved out of pink rock to cross a stream. In another 20 metres, just round a left bend, a small waymark points left along the main path. This is where the lower path forks down right.

The small path drops close above **River Nevis**. Then it ascends again on a ledge around a craggy slope. There are old iron posts and ringbolts. After its rocky section, the path ascends gently over large stones. It rejoins the main path at another small waymark, at the foot of a grey rock gangway on the main path.

Upper path

The upper path is very small and needs some care to follow, especially in reverse at the Steall end. It is rough but not rocky, and leads to a splendid little shelf below the crags of Meall Cumhann.

About 400 metres from the car park, the main path becomes a gangway carved out of pink rock to cross a stream. It bends left, past the waymarker at the start of the lower path, then rises for 100 metres across a pitched section and then between sheep-sized grey boulders. As it levels, three stream culverts cross it in quick succession. The middle culvert is where the upper path forks up left. It slants gently uphill, but with a couple of little zigzags to look out for. It emerges onto open hill at a grassy platform below crags of **Meall Cumhann** (small cairn, NN 1751 6896).

The path slants down, to left of a large boulder, then zigzags south down a spur with some birch trees, to join the main path just above the top of Nevis Gorge.

All three routes arrive in the meadow above the gorge, dominated by the high **Steall waterfall** on the right. At the meadow's end the path forks, the right branch leading to a bridge over the Water of Nevis marked 'dangerous bridge' and consisting of three steel cables. According to your temperament, this crossing is either terrifying or terrific. It is not necessary – return is by the same side of the river – but it does let you reach the foot of the Steall Falls by a muddy path.

Return is by any of the three paths. Below is given the upper path, as its start is not clear. Should you cross

Steall Falls

the wire footbridge and find you prefer not to come back over, there's also a very rough descent by the south side of the river (see variant below). Meanwhile, those unsatisfied by Scotland's finest 2-mile walk can explore Meall Cumhann on the following Route 3.

Upper path (return)

For every 100 people who come up the main path and return the same way, approximately zero people take this stimulating alternative path back. From the Steall meadow, the path dips to the first trees at the entrance of the gorge. Immediately before this short descent, turn uphill, right, towards a ruined stone terrace among the bracken. From the left-hand end of this, the path heads up left in its first zigzag. Once found, the zigzags rise north up a spur with a few birch trees, towards a boulder visible on the skyline. The viewpoint terrace is just above; there's an old cairn on the left and a view down lower Glen Nevis.

Contour forward for 20 metres to find the beginning of the descent path. It is small but clear; just watch out for a couple of zigzags where it doubles back on itself as it slants down through the wood to join the main path.

South riverside variant

Across the three-wire bridge, head downstream above a rocky knoll, then find a small path along the riverside meadow. Just upstream from the gorge entrance, the path turns left, and climbs a steep grass slope in two zigzags to a wide shelf of grass and glacier-smoothed rocks.

Head northwest across the rocks, with an ancient deer fence on the left. At the shelf end, follow the fence down to the right into a grassy wooded gully. There are traces of a rough, steep path. In steep woodland below, keep downhill near the fence (avoiding steeper ground on the left). As the ground gets less steep there is a small rough path just above the fence.

As the fence joins the river, pass through it to find a well-used path. Follow this downstream along beautiful riverbank, with river roar drowning any traffic sounds from the other side. Just before the path suddenly becomes well made, cross a footbridge on the right to join the road. Head up right for 1.2km to the car park, taking care as the road has blind corners and is busy.

ROUTE 3
Meall Cumhann

Start/Finish	Glen Nevis top car park (NN 168 691)
Distance	6.5km/4 miles
Total ascent	600m/2000ft
Time	3½hr
Terrain	Rough hillsides
Max altitude	Meall Cumhann 698m

Length
■ □ □ □ □

Difficulty
■ ■ ■ ■ □

If Nevis Gorge on its own isn't magnificent enough, take in this viewpoint 500m higher up. Meall Cumhann (Hill of the Gorge) is a fine little top in its own right, and if you can bring yourself to turn round has views eastwards up Glen Nevis as well as down onto the gorge and across to Steall Falls.

▶ Start along Route 2 to the meadow below **Steall Falls**. After playing around on the wire footbridge (but returning

For map see Route 2.

Nevis Gorge and Polldubh Crags

to the original side), take the path that continues up Glen Nevis. After 1km, just before a footbridge, turn up left into **Coire Giubhsachan**, on a rough path to left of its stream. After 1.5km it reaches a flat, boggy section of valley. Here turn up left, slanting right to avoid outcrops, to the summit of **Meall Cumhann**.

Head north along a fine little ridge and down to Bealach Cumhann col. Head southwest, slantwise down a steep slope towards the long waterslide of **Allt Coire Eoghainn**. The slabs of the waterslide itself are smooth and slippery, and there have been accidents there, so take care. A path runs down on the near side of the waterslide, to the car park.

ROUTE 4
Down Glen Nevis

Start	Glen Nevis lower falls, 300 metres up-valley from Achriabhach (NN 145 683)
Finish	Fort William station (NN 105 741)
Distance	11.5km/7 miles
Total ascent	Nil
Time	3hr
Terrain	Small paths
Max altitude	Upper fall 55m
Transport	Stagecoach bus 41 serves the youth hostel: there have been buses to the Lower Falls – check with Tourist Information

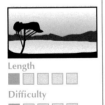

Length

Difficulty

The Glen Nevis road hardly intrudes on this at all, and enables an outward journey on the Glen Nevis bus – that's unless you make it the second half of the walk from Corrour station (Route 5) or a backpack trek from Kinlochleven, Rannoch, or elsewhere.

Start by turning right out of the car park, to cross two bridges, under the second of which are the Lower Falls. Beware of inaudible traffic coming round the blind bends. A stile on the left is for canoeists and photographers – pass it to a track just beyond. Follow this past **Polldubh** cottages, to find a faint path. After 400 metres along the foot of the hill slope, the path joins the river; then follows it downstream, past the square wooded enclosure of an old burial ground. After crossing the two branches of the Red Burn (no footbridges), you reach a long bridge on the left that would lead to the youth hostel.

Keep going on a good path still to right of the stream. Pass another bridge into the car park at **Nevis Visitor Centre**. After another 400 metres the path is

Meal an t-Suidhe, Burial Ground east of River Nevis, Ben Nevis

map continues on page 42

41

about to join the Achintee Road.

To avoid this, fork left on a path under trees, still alongside the river, to join the road further down. After 200 metres cross a green footbridge over the **River Nevis**, then turn right to join the pavement of the Glen Nevis road. At the roundabout by the Nevis Bank Hotel, turn left to the town centre.

ROUTE 5
Corrour Station to Glen Nevis

Start	Corrour station (NN 355 664)
Finish	Fort William station (NN 105 742)
Distance	33.5km/21 miles
Total ascent	150m/500ft
Time	1 long or 2 short days (9hr walking time)
Terrain	Small, rough paths
Max altitude	Tom an Eite 375m
Transport	Train (Scotrail) Fort William to Corrour. No road access to Corrour

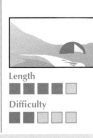

Length

■ ■ ■ ■ ☐

Difficulty

■ ■ ☐ ☐ ☐

The long valley starts at Corrour, a place reached by railway but by no road, with a restaurant and a youth hostel, and runs for 30km between two of Scotland's highest mountain ranges. Along the way it passes a couple of handy bothies. At last it emerges round the back of Ben Nevis by a huge waterfall and a gorge: this is where, if anywhere, Scotland becomes Himalayan.

While it's the last day of long backpack trips from almost anywhere, the early train (7.40am) from Fort William lets you do this as a day walk. Route 4 allows you to walk the riverside for those last 10km, but you may prefer the road, where any passing car will be a climber or walker and might offer a lift, even to the muddy. (You can't phone for a taxi on your mobile; mobiles won't work.)

▸ Start from **Corrour station** on the west side of the railway, where a well made path runs to left of the railway line. As this bends up left away from the railway, keep ahead on a faint, soggy path. After 1.5km, the firm track from Loch Ossian emerges from under the railway.

See overview map Ben Nevis & Glen Coe north.

Start from Loch Ossian youth hostel
Turn right on the track towards Corrour station, then right on a side track at a waymark arrow. In 200 metres the track bends left; at once, turn off left on a rugged old

*Loch Ossian
youth hostel*

track. After 400 metres this joins a much newer one, running west to pass under the railway in the bed of a stream.

Follow the track down to **Loch Treig**, and then around it; at the foot of Gleann Iolairean it reverts to its rough state. The track ends at Abhainn Rath near **Creaguaineach Lodge**. ◄ Cross the slippery wooden bridge and turn left upstream, on a path that's sometimes a delight on firm green riverbank and sometimes less pleasant. After 2km you pass the charmingly situated **Staoineag** bothy on the opposite bank; with normal summer water levels you can cross to it on large stones. The better path continues to right of the river. After another 3km the valley floor levels, and the path bears away from the river across bog to visit **Meanach** (Meannanach) bothy (see Route 45). It regains the riverbank opposite Luibeilt.

If you're heading for Staoineag bothy, and if the river under the bridge is in spate, don't cross but head upstream to left of the river.

The OS map marks the path continuing on the southern bank of Abhainn Rath. However, the crossing can be awkward, and I've always kept my feet dry and stayed on the path on the northern bank. After 2.5km, the river turns up in front of you, so now you must cross it to the small landmark knoll Tom an Eite. The best

Steall Falls

crossing is 100 metres north of the knoll (NN 241 695; 15km, 4hr).

A new path heads downstream then turns right, passing immediately to left of Tom an Eite. The path is clear, and mostly not boggy, as it heads down to right of a small stream that gradually develops to become the **Water of Nevis**.

After 7km the path gets much better, as you cross a footbridge to emerge onto the level meadow with the high Steall Falls on the opposite side of the river. Here the three-strand wire bridge across Water of Nevis does not need to be crossed (Steall hut, on the further side, is a private and locked club hut). Continue to right of the river, into the narrows at the top of Nevis Gorge. ▶ The path now is very well built, but with steep drops on the left to the roaring river: in the dark this section is spectacular. After 1km the path reaches the car park at the top of Glen Nevis.

From here it's 12km mostly tarmac to **Fort William**, or 7km if you cleverly booked into Glen Nevis youth hostel. After 1km, take a footbridge onto a well made and pretty path to left of the river, to rejoin the road near the Lower Falls. ▶

See Route 2 for exciting side-paths here.

From the Lower Falls, Route 4 offers a riverside alternative, which is delightful if you have the energy – start by turning right, back across the river.

ROUTE 6
Caledonian Canal

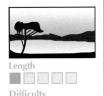

Length

■ ▢ ▢ ▢ ▢

Difficulty

■ ▢ ▢ ▢ ▢

Start/Finish	Fort William, old fort (NN 104 742)
Distance	14.5km/9 miles
Total ascent	30m/100ft
Time	3½hr
Terrain	Smooth paths and pavements
Max altitude	Neptune's Staircase 33m

A flat walk at Fort William? Well, you only need the cloud to rise 35m to enjoy this one. It explores the seaside, the canal side and a ruined castle, as well as some less interesting back streets of Inverlochy and Caol. The surprise bonus is the underwater section at the halfway point.

Start at the old fort, which is on the shoreline at a roundabout 100 metres west of Fort William station. A stone marks the start of the Great Glen Way; and GGW markers will guide for the first part of the walk. Follow them along pavement north to a second roundabout, and take a tarred path to left of McDonalds. It runs through scrubby industrial waste ground, then to left of the shinty pitch. At a housing estate, dogleg right then left to a disused road bridge.

Across it, the path on the left is signposted GGW. It runs around a wood to the shoreline by the tidal **River Lochy**. Follow the path next to the river, then through a wood, then again alongside the river past a football pitch. At the field end the path heads right but keep ahead to a narrow footbridge over a tailrace, then to a stile beside a long footbridge beside the railway – Soldiers' Bridge.

◄ Cross Soldiers' Bridge, and turn left along Glenmallie Road. The street runs down by River Lochy, then turns right into **Caol**. The first street left is signposted GGW. At its end, take a gravel path alongside

Before crossing Soldiers' Bridge, take the track on the right under the railway to visit Old Inverlochy Castle.

46

Caledonian Canal at Corpach

the salt waters of Loch Linnhe towards the imposing (but scarcely attractive) Wiggins Teape factory. After a football pitch, a footbridge crosses an overflow stream out of the **Caledonian Canal** and rises to its towpath.

Now the GGW turns right, but turn left to the canal's end, and cross the lock gate between salt water (left) and fresh (right). Turn back along the northern towpath for 1km to the bridges at **Banavie**. Take a level crossing beside the railway's swing bridge, then cross the road, and go up steps along- side **Neptune's**

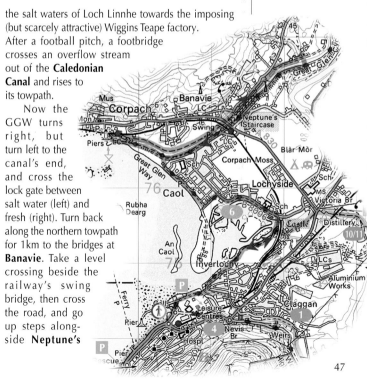

Staircase. Continue along the towpath for 1km around a right-hand bend. Now a track forks down left to the base of the canal banking. Pass under the canal by a dripping tunnel, and turn up right to a path along the wooded canal bank. Soon it returns via a grey field gate to the towpath.

Turn left along the southern towpath, passing a tearoom alongside Neptune's Staircase. GGW markers divert left, but you can simply cross the road and railway ahead. Follow the towpath for another 1km. With Loch Linnhe visible ahead, turn down left on a broad path to join a street near its end. From the street end, cross grass between houses (left) and a football pitch (right), to rejoin the outward route alongside **Loch Linnhe**.

2 BEN NEVIS AND THE AONACHS

Ben Nevis half-way plateau (Route 7)

Ben Nevis is a hill of two halves – except that the northern half has been carried away by a glacier and isn't there. Instead there's the hollow of the Allt a' Mhuilinn burn, and the biggest crag in Britain.

The very popular Mountain Track, on the mountain's western side, misses all that. It's a harsh trudge on a stony path, and Ben Nevis being the biggest, it's the harshest trudge in all UK hillwalking. If you enjoy the Mountain Track, then every one of Scotland's remaining 281 hills will be even better! Round the back, however, there's the Carn Mor Dearg Arête. Not quite a scramble, it's a spectacular granite ridge, with an outstanding view of the northern crags. Meanwhile the Ledge Route, which is a scramble (albeit a fairly easy one), gets right in among those crags.

On either of those routes, the sudden arrival at the summit, with its crowds, its cairns, and its litter, comes as a horrid shock – so avoid the top altogether. The Half Nevis takes you instead into the fine northern valley; and Meall an t-Suidhe, as a stand-alone or as a side-trip on the descent, has views of Loch Linnhe better than you get from the big Ben itself.

SUMMIT SUMMARY: BEN NEVIS

BEN NEVIS ROUTES

Route 7 Ben Nevis by the Mountain Track
Route 8 Carn Mor Dearg Arête
Route 9 Ledge Route
Route 10 Half Ben Nevis (CIC Hut)
Route 11 Meall an t-Suidhe
Route 12 Carn Mor Dearg East Ridge

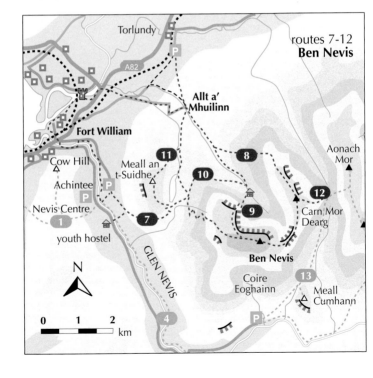

ROUTE 7

Ben Nevis by the Mountain Track

Start/Finish	Achintee (NN 125 730)
Distance	14.5km/9 miles (up and down)
Total ascent	1300m/4400ft
Time	7hr
Terrain	Path well built below, then stony
Max altitude	Ben Nevis 1344m

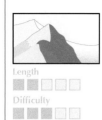

Length
■■□□□

Difficulty
■■■□□

Even for experienced hillwalkers, the ascent of the Mountain Track, from barely above sea level to Scotland's highest point, is tough and tiring. As hillwalks go, it's not wonderful; relentlessly uphill for 1200m on a stone-built path, and with no view at all of the mountain's exciting northern side. The summit is in cloud more often than not. Still, Ben Nevis has to be done, and this is the convenient way to do it. Less experienced walkers should bear in mind that on the summit the weather will usually be two clothing-layers colder than at the start, and that for sore legs the rather steep downhill is almost as arduous as up.

A more serious problem can be the leaving of the summit. The path is unclear on the stony plateau, and doglegs between crag drops. Mostly, the way down is obvious because of the other walkers coming up; but the slowest person up, who may also be injured and exhausted, has no such guide. It's worth picking up one of the detailed summit maps handed out in Fort William's shops and information outlets. Compass bearings and GPS references are also in a box below. There is an emergency shelter on the summit; if the Mountain Rescue is alerted to your non-return, this is the first place they'll look. Mobile phone coverage on the upper Mountain Track is good.

ALTERNATIVE START POINTS

This walk can also be started from the Nevis Visitor Centre (NN 123 730) or the informal roadside parking near Glen Nevis youth hostel (NN 128 718). The youth hostel route is shortest, but gives a steep stone-surfaced descent right at the end when you really don't want it.

See Ben Nevis summit summary map.

Turn off here for Route 11, Meall an t-Suidhe.

Pony Path, Ben Nevis, above Red Burn

You may now refer to this hill as 'The Ben'.

◄ Start from the road end at Achintee. At the car park end, ignore a small stile but take a gate onto a track, to a signpost just ahead. Now the wide, well-built path slants up the side of **Meall an t-Suidhe**, with a couple of zigzags and crossing two little aluminium footbridges, into the hollow of the lower Red Burn. At the top of this it makes a zigzag to the left to arrive on the halfway plateau above **Lochan Meall an t-Suidhe** (the Halfway Lochan). ◄

The wide path slants uphill northeast above the lochan. After 400 metres a path ahead starts to run gently downhill: here turn back sharp right up the main path. (Or keep ahead for a nicer walk altogether, the Half Nevis, Route 10).

After this sharp right turn, the path slants back across the hill to cross the **Red Burn** below a waterfall, and rises in wide zigzags. The rebuilt path is clear to follow, except when snow covered. As the slope starts to ease at 1100m, unseen drops into Five Finger Gully are on the right; occasional glances backwards will help memorise the path line for the descent. At 1200m the slope eases further, and the path runs just south of east to a steepening, MacLean's Steep. At this point you become aware of the tops of the great northern crag nearby on the left.

The path, marked by cairns but still not very clear, continues in the same direction to pass the head first of Tower Gully (with a small pinnacle on its left wall) and then of Gardyloo Gully. It bears left beyond, to the **summit** with its observatory ruins, shelter, large cairn and trig point. ◄

In normal conditions, the descent is easily made by passing the stream of people coming up. In mist (or if you happen to be the tired and damaged last person up) it requires care. In a winter (or spring, or autumn) whiteout, this can be a life-threatening place. In falling snow it may be impossible to see cliff edges until you're already standing on the unstable and overhanging snow cornice. The summit shelter was provided for such situations.

From the summit cairn head past the memorial cairn to the top of Gardyloo Gully that falls to the right, and turn half-right (see bearings in box 'Getting off

Ben Nevis summit

Ben Nevis') on a wide path which is cairned, and clear enough in snowless daylight. After 400 metres is the top of MacLean's Steep. In mist, take the direct downhill path (north of west) rather than the gentler zigzag leading out left, as the latter path flirts with top of Five Finger Gully.

In another 500 metres you reach the cairn at the top of the zigzags (see GPS ref in box below). The well-built but stony path descends in broad sweeps, the last one heading rightwards to cross the **Red Burn**. In another 600 metres you reach the path junction above the **Halfway Lochan**. ▶

For the North Face car park, continue ahead now on Route 8; or a crossing of Meall an t-Suidhe on Route 11.

Turn sharp left, on the well-reconstructed smooth path. It leads over the plateau edge to a zigzag, then down right, around the flank of **Meall an t-Suidhe**. Just after another small zigzag is the junction with the path down left for the footbridge to the **youth hostel**, or keep ahead for the gentler descent to **Achintee car park**. Just before that one, a signpost points down left for the car park at the **Nevis Centre**.

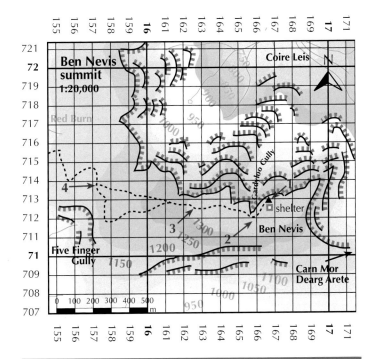

GETTING OFF BEN NEVIS

Using **GPS and compass**:

1 NN 1668 7128 Nevis summit
   Southwest 150 metres to
2 NN 1658 7117 Turning point opposite Gardyloo Gully
   282° (just north of west) 400 metres to
3 NN 1625 7125 Top of MacLean's Steep
   Same bearing 282° (just north of west) 500 metres to
4 NN 1572 7137 Top of zigzags (you have now avoided Five Finger Gully)
   Down path, or else:
   282° (just north of west), directly downhill, to
   NN 1467 7165 Mountain Track at foot of zigzags

Path, north, 200 metres to
NN 1474 7186 Path crosses Red Burn
Using **compass** alone, the bearings are:
From the summit to clear the head of Gardyloo Gully: pass to right of the observatory ruins, bearing 231° (roughly southwest) for 150 metres (roughly 100 double steps).

Thus having passed to left of the head of Gardyloo Gully: take a careful bearing 282° (slightly north of west) for 400 metres to the top of MacLean's Steep, and the same bearing for another 500 metres to the top of the zigzags. If the zigzags are invisible (for example under fresh snow) the same bearing, which should be directly downhill, will eventually lead down steep soggy grass into the lower hollow of the Red Burn.

Bearings are magnetic 2022: subtract 1° for every six years after 2022.

ROUTE 8
Carn Mor Dearg Arête

Start/Finish	North Face car park at Torlundy (NN 145 763)
Distance	16.5km/10½ miles (up and down)
Total ascent	1500m/4900ft
Time	8hr
Terrain	Hill paths and a bouldery arête
Max altitude	Ben Nevis 1344m
Access	At Torlundy 3km northeast from Fort William, turn right off A82, signed 'North Face Car Park'. Cross a narrow railway bridge, then turn right onto a track to the car park.

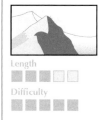

Length
Difficulty

The Pony Path, now renamed the 'Mountain Track', misses out all the exciting side of the mountain. The route by Carn Mor Dearg ('carn more jerrack', big red stonepile) and its arête gives all the excitement you want (and if there's a wind or some old snow, rather more excitement than that). It's more of a clamber than a scramble, over a ridge of granite blocks. The slopes falling either side are steep, and ahead is the whole of the magnificent northern crag. Or else it's misty, which is even more atmospheric.

This grander route is usually started from Glen Nevis. (Start as Route 10, Half Nevis; arriving at Allt a' Mhuilinn, cross the stream and slant up left to join the rounded crest running up east to Carn Beag Dearg.) But this start from Torlundy keeps you mostly off the Mountain Track, and gives a gentler ascent of Carn Mor Dearg.

See Ben Nevis summit summary map.

◀ Start along the track, then on a wide path signed for Allt a' Mhuilinn. It rises to cross the former aluminium tramway. A wide path slants up through the plantations, roughly south. The older route by the old tramway and Allt a' Mhuilinn is prettier but is now disused and overgrown.

The path winds up through woods to meet a track. Keep on up the track, ignoring a side-track on the right, and as it bends left, cross a ladder stile ahead. A well-built path leads up to the left of **Allt a' Mhuilinn** stream, with great views of crags ahead. After about 1km a small path forks off left to climb the broad spur of **Carn Dearg Beag**. It does not actually visit this first top but skirts to its right, running high along the slope, opposite the great northern crags on Nevis.

Far below you may see the CIC Hut; directly above it the path turns uphill to the crest of the ridge, then turns right and soon reaches the summit of **Carn Dearg Meadhonach**. Down left you can see the top tower of its east ridge, a rather scrappy scramble.

A brief dip and rise lead to **Carn Mor Dearg** (CMD). One clear sharp ridge runs down left (Route 12, for the Aonachs); the one for the arête is equally clear, forking right, slightly west of south.

The CMD Arête is narrow but well trodden. The crest becomes a line of piled boulders, which can be crossed without hands for the first two-thirds of the way. As the

On the Carn Mor Dearg Arête, with the Northeast Buttress of Ben Nevis (Photo S Warren)

ridge bends right, southwest, and starts to rise, the final crest will require handholds, but there's a small path down on the left.

Where the crest joins the main mountain there is a marker for the abseil posts into Coire Leis. A few more steps and the rock changes from the pale granite to darker volcanic andesite, with a broad boulderfield rising ahead. Head up beside the fierce drop on the right that's the top of Northeast Buttress (snow here may form cornices along the right-hand edge), to join the crowds among the various junky structures at **Nevis summit**.

For precision bearings, and grid refs for GPS, see Route 7.

From the summit, descent is obvious in normal conditions. Using the arriving people as live waymarks, pass left of the head of Gardyloo Gully and then bear right, just north of west. In mist (or worse mist and snow) getting off the plateau is more serious as there are sudden gully tops, with snow cornices, both to left and right, and a dogleg course is required. ◄

Once over the rim of the plateau, the Mountain Track zigzags down a broad, steep slope. (Old snow in the hollow of the Red Burn, over on the right, can give easy descent, but stay in control as there's a waterfall lower down). The path takes a final 'zag' to the right, to cross the **Red Burn** below its waterfall. After another 500 metres the Mountain Track turns sharply back left. ◄

Here you could switch to Route 11 below – the crossing of Meall an t-Suidhe.

Keep ahead, on a well built path that runs down to the outflow of **Lochan Meall an t-Suidhe**. Do not cross this stream, but descend rough grass to right of it. Posts mark a faint path used by quad bikes.

Join a ruined deer fence down to the **Allt a' Mhuilinn**. Cross this at a metal mesh barrier below a deer fence, to join the track used for the ascent just above its ladder stile. If the stream is too full, there's a track bridge 200 metres downstream. Reverse the ascent route, back down the track, to Torlundy.

Descent from Nevis to CMD Arête

Head southeast, down quite steep stonefield, with the way well trampled. If heading northeast down a narrowing ridge, this is the top of Northeast Buttress! Contour off right (or return to the summit and start again).

A spur descends bending left (east) to the stony cairned col at the start of the CMD Arête (NN 1708 7098, 1150m). The ridgeline is slightly uphill, the rock changes to rounded granite boulders, and a metal triangle marks the top of some abseil posts down left into Coire Leis.

Scramble along the ridge, cross **Carn Mor Dearg** to **Carn Beag Dearg**, and drop northwest down grassy slopes to join the **Allt a' Mhuilinn**.

ROUTE 9

Ledge Route

Start/Finish	North Face car park at Torlundy (NN 145 763)
Distance	7km/4½ miles (up only)
Total ascent	1100m/3600ft
Time	5½hr up
Terrain	Scramble Grade 1 on ledges and ridge

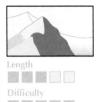

Length
■■□□□

Difficulty
■■■■□

(scramble Grade 1)

This is just magnificent. The scrambling reaches Grade 1 only at a couple of points, but the route is still serious because of its length and situation. It is fairly easy to find and follow, even in mist. However, snow lingering often to midsummer in Number 5 Gully requires a diversion (left of Moonlight Gully Buttress, not described here) which is rather trickier to find – or an ice axe, and possibly crampons. Snow can be observed from the CIC Hut, or in advance on the Internet (for details of webcams, see Appendix C).

For confident scramblers it's a feasible descent route, provided you start from the correct cairn on Carn Dearg – coming from Ben Nevis it's the second one, at 1214m (NN 1585 7210).

▶ Start as for Route 8, onto the path beside **Allt a' Mhuilinn**. Carry on up this path, which is well built up to the stream junction below the **CIC Hut**. Cross one stream to reach the hut.

From here, the way up ahead into Number 5 Gully should be visible. Directly opposite the hut, ascend a steep bank above the stream onto the toe of a long slope of gentle slabs. These can be walked up, with perhaps a little scrambling if wet. The slabs run up to big boulders at the foot of the imposing **Carn Dearg Buttress**. Here turn left up the crag base, then straight up on rough scree paths alongside the crag, into Number 5 Gully.

Clamber up the bouldery gully bed with stream for 100 metres. Above here, the gully steepens, divides, and

See Ben Nevis summit summary map.

59

Number 5 Gully and Carn Dearg Buttress, Ben Nevis

becomes gently rocky; don't continue up it, but head to the right up a grassy terrace onto a gentle but somewhat exposed slab. This is ascended on the footholds provided by a crack slanting right.

At its top, follow a small path to the right along a grass ledge, with big drops below, for 30 metres. Now a grassy groove slants back up left; the groove itself is eroded to loose stones, so the easy scrambling on its left is preferable. After 30m of height gained you emerge at the top of the groove, and look down a steep slope back into Number 5 Gully.

Turn right up the ridgeline formed by the slope top, to pass to right of a tottery rock pillar, to a stony ledge with a viewpoint boulder.

Head straight up the ridgeline above, which is bouldery with easy scrambling. After 100 metres or so, the ridgeline has a vertical wall dropping on its left. Gradually you are forced nearer to the brink of this wall as the ridgeline narrows. This narrowing ends with a drop to a small notch. The obvious way is to follow the narrowing arête to its very end, becoming somewhat exposed, to descend down right, into the notch (see photo – upper scrambler in dark top); but if you don't fancy that, there are easier ways (see box).

Notch on Ledge Route, Ben Nevis

ROUTES AVOIDING THE NOTCH DROP

Harder but less exposed
Five metres before the notch, take a groove down right: it's steep, but with good well-worn holds. Reach the gravel gully below the notch.

The easiest option
Ten metres before the notch, descend to the right to find a narrow ledge with good handholds, traversing right, to the foot of the steep groove just described (see photo – lower scrambler in blue top).

Continue up the blocky bouldery ridge. Rocky steepenings can be avoided on the right if desired, but always return to the crest. The crest levels, then a final tower is scrambled direct (good Grade 1) with a photogenic little arête to finish, or else bypassed on the left.

Arrive on the plateau at the 1214m cairn on **Carn Dearg**. This is the main cairn but not the main summit. Pass south around the head of Number 5 Gully, to the higher but less cairned 1221 summit. ▸

Descend south around the plateau rim – the Mountain Track is visible to the right with its procession of folk. Pass the head of Number 4 Gully (which has a cairn with marker post), then ascend gently to pass the

Strictly, this is 'Carn Dearg North' as Nevis has two tops called Carn Dearg. A shelter marked on old maps here has been removed.

2

head of Number 3 Gully (which has a pinnacle in the top and a view down to CIC Hut), then trend right to join the Mountain Track just below MacLean's Steep. Follow it past the head of Gardyloo Gully to **Ben Nevis summit**.

What next? Simplest is to descend the top part of the Mountain Track (Route 7) then past Lochan Meall an t-Suidhe's outflow (Route 8). You could incorporate **Meall an t-Suidhe** (Route 11). More ambitiously, go down by way of the **Carn Mor Dearg Arête** (end of Route 8).

ROUTE 10
Half Ben Nevis (CIC Hut)

Length

Difficulty

Start/Finish	Glen Nevis Visitor Centre (NN 123 730)
Distance	17.5km/11 miles
Total ascent	700m/2300ft
Time	6hr
Terrain	Paths, rough for 4km
Max altitude	Ben Nevis (CIC) Hut 670m

Half Ben Nevis actually gives you more of the mountain, as it takes you into the grandeur of the northern corrie. It also includes 3km of the Nevis riverbank, as well as some less lovely back corners of Fort William. Walkers halfway up the Mountain Track who can't face another 600m of straight 'up' can switch into this route, with its much better balance of pleasure and effort. ('CIC' stands for Charles Inglis Clark, a climber who died in World War I.)

Start at the Visitor Centre. At the downstream end of the car park cross the footbridge signed for Ben Nevis and turn upstream, but where the Mountain Track turns off left, continue along the riverside. In 1.5km you reach the footbridge to **Glen Nevis youth hostel**. Don't cross it, but turn up left on the rebuilt path that climbs steeply beside a plantation to join the Mountain Track.

Turn right, uphill. The wide, well-built track slants up the side of **Meall an t-Suidhe**, with a couple of zigzags and crossing two little aluminium footbridges, into the hollow of the lower Red Burn. At the top of this it makes a zigzag to the left to arrive on the halfway plateau above **Lochan Meall an t-Suidhe**.

The wide path slants uphill northeast above the lochan. After 400 metres, the path divides: here walkers for Ben Nevis summit would make a sharp right turn. But keep ahead on a smooth rebuilt path. As it bends down left towards the outflow of Lochan Meall an t-Suidhe, fork off right on a faint, unbuilt path. This bends around a spur, and becomes rugged as it contours into the valley of **Allt a' Mhuilinn**. (In winter, note that the slope crossed here is susceptible to avalanches – check the avalanche forecast.)

As you reach the stream, your eventual descent path is opposite, but continue upstream for 600 metres through scenes of increasing grandeur to the Ben Nevis hut, formally the Charles Inglis Clark or **CIC Hut**. ▶

Cross the stream 100 metres below the hut, and head down the well built path to its right (east). After 3km, a

If it was in Austria, the hut would serve gassy beer and herbal tea on red-chequered tablecloths. Being in Scotland, it is owned by the Scottish Mountaineering Club and is locked up.

Heading up Allt a' Mhuilinn to Ben Nevis

wide ladder stile leads to the top of a forest road. After 200 metres fork down left, and follow the road left over a bridge. It contours southwest for 1km, with fine views, until you can take the main track forking

down to the right.

At the slope foot it joins another track. Turn left for 200 metres, under power lines, until an overgrown stony path turns off right (NN 133 752). It is signed for the **Distillery**. It leads to a stream, and follows its left bank, under the railway. Then it runs along to the right of a whisky shed. Head out though the distillery's main gate to the A82.

Cross the A82 but not the Lochy Bridge ahead; instead turn sharp left onto a well-made path between the golf course (left) and the River Lochy (right). At a car park, bear right along the riverbank to **Old Inverlochy Castle**. Turn left, pass through the castle and back to the riverbank.

Ahead, a lane takes you under the railway. Just past the end of the long Soldiers' Bridge

(footbridge) take a stile on the right, to reach a narrow bridge over a tailrace stream. Cross grass to join the smooth gravel path of the Great Glen Way. It runs near the wide, tidal river, then through woodland; then is again beside the Lochy for 400 metres. Finally it bends left around a wood to a tarred street.

Turn left for a few steps, ignoring a rough riverside track to find a gravel path alongside houses. After 300 metres it drops to join Dubh MacDonald Road. At this street's end, turn right in Earl of Inverness Road to the **A82**.

The street opposite is signed for Ben Nevis Inn. Follow it for 100 metres, then cross a stone bridge on the right. Turn left, up Glen Nevis, and follow the pavement for 500 metres until a track forks off left to another footbridge, a green-painted metal one. Recross the **River Nevis** and turn right, upstream. In 300 metres the street bears left; here keep ahead on a riverside path. After 1km it brings you to the footbridge at the **Visitor Centre**.

ROUTE 11
Meall an t-Suidhe

Length
■ ■ □ □ □

Difficulty
■ ■ ■ □ □

Start/Finish	Glen Nevis Visitor Centre (NN 123 730)
Distance	14.5km/9 miles (for circuit)
Total ascent	700m/2300ft
Time	5½hr
Terrain	Paths, grassy hillsides
Max altitude	Meall an t-Suidhe 711m

As an alternative to visiting the northern corrie on Route 10, you can top out on Meall an t-Suidhe, a hill half as high as Ben Nevis but with rather better views as it's out of the cloud more often and also closer to the rest of the scenery. It's pronounced and sometimes spelt Melantee, the Hill of the Seat. The summit is grassy and peaceful and it is indeed comfy to sit down on. It can be done when you change your mind halfway up the Mountain Trail, or as a warm-down summit when descending the Ben towards the North Face car park (adding 1.5km, 150m, and 40mins to the descent from Ben Nevis).

▶ Start as for Route 10 from the Nevis Visitor Centre, and follow the Mountain Track until it levels onto the halfway plateau. At once turn off left.

See map in Route 10.

If descending from Ben Nevis
Come down the zigzags of the Mountain Track and across the Red Burn, and at the path junction above the halfway loch turn back sharp left (all as Route 7). Before the path drops off the edge of the plateau, turn off right.

Cross grassland past the head of **Lochan Meall an t-Suidhe** to cross the trickle flowing out of the loch (a proper stream flows from the other end, which is accordingly the foot of the loch). Head up the grassy and somewhat wet slope beyond, then turn right along the rounded crest, which dips then rises to the cairned summit of **Meall an t-Suidhe.**

Descend northeast, on a rounded spur, with a small path vanishing. At the spur foot continue northeast, crossing a stream then following it down, to find the metal posts of an old deer fence (marked on Harveys map). A small path and quad-bike wheelmarks run alongside this.

On Melantee (Meall an t-Suidhe), view to Loch Linnhe

Follow it down north, to reach the **Allt a' Mhuilinn** at the 300m contour. Cross the stream at the metal grating underneath a deer fence, to reach a ladder stile on the upward path – or if the stream is full, continue downstream for 150 metres to a bridge.

Head down the track and path to the **North Face car park**, if that's where you started, or else follow Route 10 through Fort William for the **Nevis Visitor Centre**.

ROUTE 12
Carn Mor Dearg East Ridge

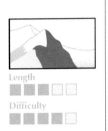

Length

Difficulty

Start/Finish	End of public road, Glen Nevis (NN 167 691)
Distance	7km/4½ miles (to Nevis summit)
Total ascent	1100m/3600ft
Time	4½hr up
Terrain	Small paths, grassy ridge, stony plateau

This sharp and stony ridge is used by those ambitiously linking the Aonachs with Carn Mor Dearg (combining Routes 8 and 14), or the even more ambitious joining Nevis with the Grey Corries in one over-the-top hill day. It's also a logical descent for anyone who ascends Nevis from the south, via Coire Eoghainn and Carn Dearg South (1020m) – the third-best Nevis route, not included here.

See Ben Nevis summit summary map.
See Route 2 for an exciting scrambly diversion off this path.

◄ Start from the far end of the car park, where a wide smooth path is signed for Kinlochleven and other distant places. ◄ At the head of the gorge the path emerges suddenly into a narrow meadow; above on the right are the spectacular Steall Falls. Keep to left of the river for 1km to a small footbridge over Allt Coire Giubhsachan. Just before this, turn up left on a rough path, and follow the stream up to the col at the head of Coire Giubhsachan.

Turn up left, on a fairly steep rocky spur with a rough path. The spur narrows attractively in its upper part, to the summit of **Carn Mor Dearg**. Continue on Route 8 to the Nevis summit.

ROUTE 13

Aonach Beag from the Back

Start/Finish	End of public road, Glen Nevis (NN 167 691)
Distance	14.5km/9 miles
Total ascent	1350m/4500ft
Time	7hr
Terrain	Small paths, grassy ridge, stony plateau
Max altitude	Aonach Beag 1234m

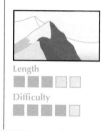

Length
▪ ▪ ▪ ▫ ▫

Difficulty
▪ ▪ ▪ ▪ ▫

Do the ethics of Munro-bagging allow the Nevis Range gondola? Do you even want to, if it means a trudge up Aonach Mor under the chairlifts, and a simple plateau walk to Aonach Beag? For more mountain fun, take the back way, by Glen Nevis. You'll come through the magnificent Nevis Gorge, and pass the Steall waterfall. You'll go between great mountains, and head up Aonach Beag by the way that actually feels like the seventh highest in the land. Then you'll descend by the grim and granitty bealach beside Carn Mor Dearg. (If you don't despise the gondola, there's a nice way up Aonach Mor on that side as well – see Route 14.)

Start from the far end of the car park, where a wide smooth path contours through beautiful woodland above the Nevis Gorge. At the head of the gorge the path emerges suddenly into a narrow meadow. ▶ Above on the right is the spectacular Steall waterfall. Keep to left of the river, and after 1km cross a small footbridge over **Allt**

This was a lochan until the river broke through the rock bar at the top of the gorge.

Aonach Mor (Nevis Range) from Aonach Beag

Coire Giubhsachan. Straight after the footbridge, strike left (northeast) on a small path to right of Allt Coire nan Laogh stream, then up a steepening grassy hillside to a shoulder at 800m. A gentler ridge leads up east, to the minor top **Sgurr a' Bhuic**.

Now the going gets more interesting, as well as rather more horizontal. Head east of north along the top of steep rocky slopes falling to the right. The ridge drops to a col at 895m, then rises to a corner above steep spurs descending east and north. The ridgeline turns left, first west then northwest, to the summit of **Aonach Beag**. The view across the Carn Mor Dearg Arête to the great north face of Ben Nevis is compelling.

Head north beside drops on the right for 150 metres, then head down northwest on rough path to a col. Now a broad slope of short grass, with a path, leads gently upwards for 1.2km to the summit of **Aonach Mor**, the lowest of Scotland's nine 4000ers.

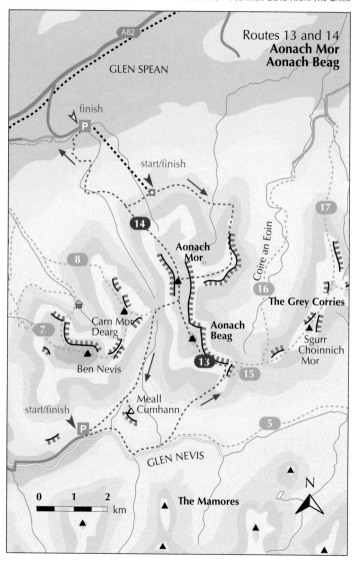

Routes 13 and 14
**Aonach Mor
Aonach Beag**

A82

GLEN SPEAN

finish

P

start/finish

14

8

Aonach Mor

Coire an Eoin

17

16

The Grey Corries

7

Carn Mor Dearg

Aonach Beag

13

15

Sgurr Choinnich Mor

Ben Nevis

start/finish

P

Meall Cumhann

5

GLEN NEVIS

0   1   2
km

The Mamores

N

71

Now you need to find the descent point for Bealach Giubhsachan, the pass 300m below. In clear weather, return southwards down the gentle grassy plateau, looking for a small path soon forking off right. In mist, the easiest way is to follow the top of the steep slope that forms the right (west) edge of the grassy plateau. Where this edge bends back to the left (NN 1915 7219) is the top of a zig-zag path heading directly down the steep slope below. This slope can hold steep, hard snow, even into early summer. If you're unhappy about that, or if you fail to find the drop-off point, it's safest to retrace the outward route over Aonach Beag. This only adds 30mins to the walk.

Having found the steep little path, descend it. The gritty granite soil is fragile so stick to the zigzags; any short-cutting will worsen the erosion. At the bottom, the deep and wide pass **Bealach Giubhsachan** has a few little pools.

Meall Cumhann means the Hill of the Gorge; and indeed, the Nevis Gorge is directly between your toes. However, the horizontal views up and down Glen Nevis are equally spectacular.

Descend to the left (south) into **Coire Giubhsachan**. A small path forms to right of the stream. If time or energy are short, this path leads right down to the Glen Nevis path, passing some waterfalls low down. However, the more interesting continuation heads out to the right at about the 600m contour, to the col Bealach Cumhann. Turn left up a gentle ridge of grass and rock to **Meall Cumhann**'s summit. ◄

Return north to Bealach Cumhann, and slant down across a fairly steep and pathless slope towards the long waterslide of the **Allt Coire Eoghainn**. Beware of the waterworn slabs alongside the watersplash, the site of accidents. A small path runs down the near side of the stream to the car park.

ROUTE 14

Aonach Mor by Gondola and Stob an Cul Choire

Start	Gondola top station (NN 187 756)
Finish	Same, or gondola foot (NN 172 774)
Distance	13.5km/8½ miles (to gondola top finish)
Total ascent	850m/2800ft
Time	5½hr
Terrain	Pathless but comfortable, with a steep grass ascent to the plateau
Max altitude	Aonach Beag 1234m
Parking	Park at the Nevis Range bottom station and take the gondola up

Length
⬛⬛⬜⬜⬜

Difficulty
⬛⬛⬛⬛⬜

Aonach Mor is odd as being the 4000er that wasn't. When hills were measured imperially, Aonach Mor was 3999ft. It was only when they remeasured it in metric that it rose to 1221m, which is 4006ft. The names also are confused, in that Aonach Mor, the Big Ridge, is 13m lower than Aonach Beag, the Small Ridge. But in a sense they are both small hills, as the Nevis Range gondola lifts you up and over the unexciting spruce to visit two 4000-footers with a total climb of less than 3000ft. So it creates what is rare here, a real mountain walk in under 6 hours.

Mountain walks don't have to be severe and strenuous, but they are supposed to be fun; and for me, up and down Aonach Mor under the ski tows isn't. But there's a splendid side-ridge where instead of looking up at dangling metalwork you look down from a great height on deer. Cul Choire is the Back Corrie, a name that invites any adventurous hill-goer.

▶ Start underneath the Great Glen Chairlift out left, only very slightly uphill. (On some summer weekends you can ride this first kilometre of the walk as well.) Pass a café hut and carry on contouring into the valley of **Allt Choille-rais**. Cross the stream and slant left up the slope beyond onto the north ridge of Tom na Sroine. Go up the

See map in Route 13.

Schist (grey, flaky) interchanges with Nevis outer granite (rounded lumps, pinkish where unweathered).

ridge, which becomes more defined with drops on the right. Across the valley is the black-run area of the Nevis Range ski slopes.

Cross the hummocky top of Tom na Sroine (**918m**, a Munro Top) and continue south along a pleasant ridge, with big drops now on the left to Allt Coire an Eoin. ◄ On the right, now, you are opposite the winter climbing ground of Coire an Lochan.

The ridge curves right – follow the crest or use a grass path down right – to a second Munro Top, **Stob an Cul Choire**. On the left now is the rocky face of Aonach Beag, with its classic North-East Ridge showing well (Diff, with pinnacles, popular in winter with those undiscouraged by the long walk in).

A rocky but not difficult ridge leads down west to a col. The slope ahead looks intimidating but is OK. Fairly steep grass heads straight up towards a tower of reddish granite. Either head up this grass, or find some easy, scrappy scrambling (Grade 1) immediately to the right.

On Stob an Cul Choire, approaching Aonach Mor

Once at the base of the reddish tower, head round to its right, then slant back up left to reach its top. Now

a small zigzag path heads up the spurline, reaching the plateau about 50 metres east of the summit cairn on **Aonach Mor**.

SAFETY NOTE OF DESCENDING THIS ROUTE

The spur top is only visible from the plateau edge, so in mist take a bearing from Aonach Mor's cairn or use the GPS reading: NN 1944 7295.

From the summit of Aonach Mor, a path runs south down the grassy plateau. ▸ The main path descends gently south to the narrow neck joining Aonach Mor to Aonach Beag. It heads on up through rocks, then becomes a scree path with drops on the left. At the slope top the drops are also ahead. Turn right alongside them, over stony ground without path, for 150 metres to the smallish cairn of **Aonach Beag**. There's a very fine view across Carn Mor Dearg and its arête to Ben Nevis, which looks like a pointy crag mountain from here.

Ignore a much smaller path soon forking off right (descent towards Bealach Giubhsachan, Route 13).

Aonach Mor, from the Great Glen

Meall Beag means, simply, Small Hump.

The mountain bike path under the gondola is closed to walkers during biking hours, and unattractive at any time.

Return to **Aonach Mor**. Continue ahead with steep drops on your left, north to a very slight rise and then downhill roughly northwest. Pass the top of a ski tow and then of a chairlift. At a levelling at 650m, you reach a well-built path leading to Meall Beag just ahead. ◄

After visiting the viewpoint, you could head back along this path to the gondola top station. However, if the gondola has closed or you just fancy a stroll, from Meall Beag head on northwest down pathless ridge, zigzagging carefully down a steep descent, then heading down left to join a rough path alongside **Allt Daim**. It runs down to an intake, with a footway across a dam and a track beginning beyond.

The track recrosses the stream at another dam and enters forest. Immediately bear right and follow a track down northeast for 1km to another junction. Here turn left, curving downhill. The third turning left, a mountain-bike path, short-cuts a bend in the track. At its foot continue to a horizontal track below, where you turn right to the **car park** at the gondola foot. ◄

3 GREY CORRIES AND SPEAN BRIDGE

East along the Grey Corries ridge to Stob Coire Claurigh

Quartzite is quite different. It's not the usual rocky grey, but a pale yellowish-white that under sunlight shows an evil gleam. It's not lumpy but flat and smooth, and when it breaks it breaks in sharp edges and cubes. The three grey corries are flat-bottomed and green, but rise to bleak fields of blocks and boulders. The tops of the corries are fringed with crags, and the hill range that takes its name from them is a long wiggly ridge. The rock underfoot is sometimes smooth as a pavement, but the sharp edges will slash your gaiters.

Rising between a wide, dreary spruce wood in the north and the remote top end of Glen Nevis to the south, the Grey Corries are slightly awkward to get at. This adds a certain solitude to their other excellent qualities. To make things even more strenuous, you really want all of this ridge, from Sgurr Choinnich Beag in the west right along to Stob Coire na Ceannain. So make an expedition of them, using handy bothies to the east and south. Make it more than an expedition by adding Ben Nevis, Carn Mor Dearg, and both of the Aonachs – a big hill day that even so is just the first half of the ultimate in such things: Tranter's Walk around the Nevis Watershed.

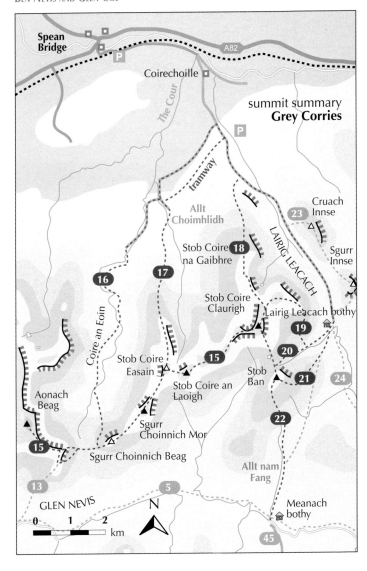

SUMMIT SUMMARY: GREY CORRIES

Though overshadowed by its big neighbours to the west, the ridge's main mountain, Stob Coire Claurigh, is actually Scotland's 15th-highest mountain (1177m/3862ft). Route 15 follows the entire main ridge westwards; Routes 16–18 join that ridgeline from the north. The routes are described, and measured, to the summit of Stob Coire Claurigh and timings are up only.

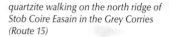

GREY CORRIES ROUTES
Route 15   Grey Corries Ridge
Route 16   Coire an Eoin
Route 17   Stob Coire Easain North Ridge
Route 18   Stob Coire Claurigh North Ridge
Route 19   Cul Coirean
Route 20   Lairig Leacach and Lochan Rath
Route 21   Lairig Leacach to Stob Ban
Route 22   Meanach Bothy to Stob Ban

quartzite walking on the north ridge of Stob Coire Easain in the Grey Corries (Route 15)

ROUTE 15
Grey Corries Ridge

Start	Aonach Beag summit (NN 197 715)
Distance	8.5km/5½ miles
Total ascent	900m/3000ft
Time	4½hr up
Terrain	Mostly paths but with scrambling, boulderfields, and very steep descent off Aonach Beag

Difficulty

■ ■ ■ ■ ☐

If you like your ridges rocky but not scrambly, this is the place to be. For the seriously ambitious, the description begins at Aonach Beag, with various side-routes joining in as we go along the ridge to Stob Coire Claurigh.

See Grey Corries summit summary map.

◀ From **Aonach Beag** descend following big crag drops on the left, first south, then east over a minor hump. After another 500 metres the ridge turns sharply right, south-east, steepening down to the ridge corner at NN 207 708.

A steep zigzag path leads down to a narrow rib, then down a grassy gully on the right; then keep down to right of broken quartzite outcrops to the wide col at the head of Coire Bhealaich. However, if the steep spur is snow-covered, an easier descent can be made from the col north of Sgurr a' Bhuic, turning down a gully then contouring left to the wide col.

Route 16 joins here.

A small path leads up grass to the top of **Sgurr Choinnich Beag**. ◀ The path continues on pleasant grass through a col and up **Sgurr Choinnich Mor**.

Descend a sharp grass ridge northeast. It levels, then drops steeply with a small path. The south ridge of Stob Coire Easain is quartzite slabs and stones, one of the best parts of the ridgeline. Stob Coire Easain, though named on Landranger, is not the local Munro. ◀

Route 17 joins here.

Head down southeast, over stones and small quartzite outcrops. The ridge of rocks and stones rises to **Stob Coire an Laoigh** (1116m, a Munro but unnamed on older Landranger maps). Here the ridge turns northeast, over three more minor tops and much pleasant rocky ground. In mist, at the first of these tops, Caistell, careful compasswork is required to avoid a wrong ridge northwards; at the second, Stob Coire Cath na Sine, the main ridge itself turns north; at the third, Stob a' Choire Leith, again you must avoid a wrong ridge northwards. In clear weather just enjoy the ridge and its views all the way to **Stob Coire Claurigh**.

Stob Coire an Laoigh from Stob Coire Easain

ROUTE 16

Coire an Eoin

Start	Forest edge above Corriechoille (NN 255 788)
Distance	18.5km/11 miles (to Stob Coire Claurigh)
Total ascent	1450m/4800ft
Time	8½hr up
Terrain	Pathless rough valley, with quad-bike wheelmarks higher up
Access	The route could also be started, ideally with bike, from Spean Bridge station.
Parking	Pull-offs for about eight cars above the farm at Corriechoille (park with care, as timber lorries use the track); otherwise go back to Cour bridge (NN 248 810), adding 3km, 120m and 2hr to the return journey, or to the car park at Coille Anachain, adding a further 2km and 1hr.

Difficulty

■ ■ ■ ■ ■

This rock-ringed, empty corrie under the Aonachs sees far more deer than people. Being pathless, it's rather tough uphill, but makes a good, wild descent route; survey ahead from Sgurr Choinnich Beag to work out the best line. The valley is bog and bare rock – walk the rock rather than the bog. The old tramway makes for a rough but quick start, with some views; the forest road is trouble-free but dull, and might be preferred by weary descenders.

See Grey Corries summit summary map.

◀ Directly opposite the parking pull-in, the green track of an old railbed contours west across grassland, marked with occasional wooden sleepers. In places this track is swampy, but the mire is only a couple of inches above a hard surface. There are wide views over the Great Glen to start with. After 800 metres, cross a new forest road, and continue now in forest. After 1.5km in the trees, you arrive on a forest road. Turn down right for 200 metres, then sharp left across the top of a large quarry.

Forest road start
A drier but longer option goes up a forest road. Take the track back towards Corriechoille for 800 metres, and turn left ('Spean Bridge') into plantations. After 2.5km, ignore a smaller track down right (again 'Spean Bridge') and follow the main track uphill for another 700 metres, then forking right around the top of a quarry.

Either way, cross the Cour stream and keep ahead under tall trees (soon due for felling). The track emerges from plantations at a bridge over **Allt Coire nan Eoin**. Just before the bridge, turn off through a gate on the left.

Ahead, the valley is divided by the rocky knoll An Guirean. The small, green track runs up to left of the stream then zigzags up the left wall of the valley to a T-junction. Turn right, up into the wide gap to left of An Guirean. The track fades away, but keep ahead, slightly downhill, to rejoin the main valley, which is wide and wet with a winding stream.

Follow the left edge of the level ground, finding traces of quad-bike track, to cross the river at a pebbly ford (NN 2203 7455). Here is the start of a helpful quad-bike track that sweeps out right then back to the river at a solitary birch below two fine pools (NN 2213 7429). The track runs south up a spur with grey schist boilerplates, to pass a small cairn at 470m (NN 2186 7343). It gently descends to the valley floor at the foot of Creagan na Gaibhre. It rises gently across the spur foot to fade at **Allt a' Chuil Choire** just down from a clump of boulders from a rockfall (NN 2156 7245). These fallen rocks are marked on Harvey map and visible, for descenders, from the hills above.

Cross the stream to head southwest along the top of a river-moulded moraine hump. Cross a smaller

In mist, it's simpler to head upstream, south, through the damp corrie to the col at its head.

side-stream, then go up a spur of schist boilerplates to right of the main stream (the one out of Coire Bhealaich). At the corrie rim, cross that stream and head up a spur of bare rock slabs that now are of whitish quartzite. ◄ A low crag at half-height is bypassed on either side. At the top of the quartzite slabs, below the final steepening of **Sgurr Choinnich Beag**, contour to the right (south) for 400 metres, to reach **Choinnich Beag**'s southwest ridge at the foot of its steep section (800m, NN 2174 7055; so far 10.5km/6½ miles with 550m/1800ft of up, about 4hr).

Continue along the whole of the main ridge to **Stob Coire Claurigh** (see Route 15).

ROUTE 17
Stob Coire Easain North Ridge

Start	Corriechoille (NN 255 788)
Distance	10.5km/6½ miles (to Stob Coire Claurigh)
Total ascent	1200m/4000ft
Time	5½hr up
Terrain	Steepish pathless grass, then pathed ridge

Difficulty

The gentle ridge is another great descent, after achieving most (but not quite all) of the Grey Corries ridgeline. Uphill, it's a bit of a trudge.

See Grey Corries summit summary map.

◄ Start as Route 16 (see information box for advice on parking). If using the **tramway**, then at its end turn up left on forest road. If using the drier but longer forest road option, then at the quarry bend (NN 238 771) keep ahead up the smaller forest track.

The track runs above **Allt Choimhlidh** stream, to a concrete culvert leading to an intake dam. Cross a ladder stile onto a rough path down to the little reservoir.

Descending towards the Great Glen from Stob Coire Easain

Cross the stream above it onto a steep grass slope with an eroded little path. ▶

Now it's just a long slog up a grass slope. Helpful quad-bike wheelmarks are easier to find when descending the route. At 750m a definite ridgeline starts to form, and at 850m you're on a very enjoyable ridge with great views of quartzite across the Grey Corries to Stob Coire Claurigh. The ridge underfoot, though, remains schist almost to the summit cairn of **Stob Coire Easain**.

Before the summit, you could use a path left **below crags**, then up scree to the col west of Stob Coire Easain. But if you like hills, why skip SCE – which is a nice one? And if you don't like hills, what are you up to attempting 282 of them?

At the summit, turn left along the main ridge (Route 15) to **Stob Coire Claurigh**. Alternatively turn right, cross **Sgurr Choinnich Mor**, and descend by Route 16 (8hr circuit, 21km/13 miles, 1150m/3800ft of ascent).

If streams are full, it's better to cross it in the forest (Route 16) for a gate at the forest top NN 235 764.

ROUTE 18
Stob Coire Claurigh North Ridge

Start	Corriechoille (NN 255 788)
Distance	5.5km/3½ miles (up)
Total ascent	1000m/3300ft
Time	4hr up
Terrain	Ridge grassy then stony with path
Parking	See Route 16

Difficulty

This is the easiest route onto the Grey Corries ridge. It is also a good way of descending from the ridge, as it has gentle grassy terrain and great views north.

See Grey Corries summit summary map.

Inconvenient to bypass in mist, and with fine views if mistless.

◄ Head south up the track to the gate at the top edge of the forest, and once through it, turn off right alongside the forest fence. Ascend beside the fence for 1km, to its corner, then head straight up grass slopes south. The wide ridge leads up to **Stob Coire na Gaibhre**. ◄

A small path follows the steep edge southwest across a col, then disappears. Head up the ridge, with drops on the left, passing to left of a stony ridgetop hollow to the minor top where the ridge joins from Stob Coire na Ceannain. Ahead the ridge sharpens: bypass on the right, or cross, some little quartzite towers to the summit of **Stob Coire Claurigh.**

Descending from Stob Coire Claurigh
Head down north over or around some little quartzite towers and along the right-hand rim of a strange stone hollow to the little North Top. Head down northwest on a ridge that's stony then grassy, before a steeper descent leads into a slight col. A small path leads right, to **Stob Coire na Gaibhre**.

Descend broad slopes north. A short stretch of path rounds the head of Allt Coire na Gaibhre. Carry on north down broad slopes. Resist temptation to slant down right towards the top of an invisible crag (Ruigh na Gualainn), instead easing left to join the top edge of forest. Follow the forest fence down northeast to join the Lairig Leacach track.

ROUTE 19

Cul Coirean (east corrie of Stob Coire Claurigh)

Start	Corriechoille (NN 255 788)
Distance	9.5km/6 miles (up)
Total ascent	1000m/3300ft
Time	5hr up
Terrain	Pathless hillside and ridge
Parking	See Route 16

Difficulty

A remote and indirect route onto the splendid sub-summit of Stob Coire na Ceannain, the true start of the Grey Corries Ridge. From the parking spaces at the track top, a cycle to Lairig Leacach bothy knocks about 2hr off the round trip, most of the saving being on the return.

▶ Start up the track, passing through a gate into forest. After 1.3km pass out again by another gate with a kissing gate alongside. The track continues through the beautiful **Lairig Leacach** (Lairig means pass) to the small **Lairig Leacach bothy** (6km, 300m, 2hr).

Turn upstream behind the bothy on a peaty path that stays close to, and to right of, Allt a' Chuil Choirean, with waterfalls heard below. The path stays to right of the stream, to a stream junction, where the bigger stream tumbles down in waterfalls out of Cul Choirean.

Turn right, up this stream, through quite deep heather at first. As the ground steepens, a sheep or deer path is alongside the stream, initially on its right (east) side. Pass

See Grey Corries summit summary map.

Dwarf willow, Cul Choirean

lots of little waterfalls, and small ravines colourful with roseroot and cranesbill. A crag outcrop defends the corrie above. Follow the stream up to left of this crag, then strike up onto its top, and cross the corrie's rim onto the ridgeline beyond. This runs up north, then west, onto **Stob Coire na Ceannain**.

A sharp little ridge runs to the north top of Stob Coire Claurigh. Turn up left, around the rim of a strange stone hollow reminiscent of limestone country in Europe, following the ridgeline with big drops on the left. Bypass or cross some little quartzite towers to the summit of **Stob Coire Claurigh**.

ROUTE 20
Lairig Leacach and Lochan Rath

Start	Corriechoille (NN 255 788)
Distance	9.5km/6 miles
Total ascent	1000m/3300ft
Time	5hr up
Terrain	Small rough paths

See Grey Corries summit summary map.

Difficulty

A beautiful route of ravine and ridge, and one that cleverly avoids any steep climbs.

See above

Just ahead now is the stack of quartzite slabs and crags that make the Giant's Staircase scramble (Grade 2, very enjoyable, see Noel Williams' Scrambles in Lochaber).

◀ Start by following Route 19 to **Lairig Leacach bothy** (2hr).

Turn upstream behind the bothy on a peaty path that stays close to, and right of, **Allt a' Chuil Choirean**, with waterfalls out of sight below. The path stays to right of the stream, crossing the sidestream from the Cul Coirean, to a stream junction at NN 270 731. ◀

Bear left across grass below the quartzite slabs and then below the ravine that bounds them on the left, onto the wide spur beyond. The path reforms, heading up the left side of this spur, then up right, onto its crest. It keeps

up the spur to 800m, where it turns right and contours across the rock-floored terrace between the middle and the uppermost of the Giant's three Stairs, to reach the col beyond. This is the lowest point between Stob Ban and Stob Coire Claurigh.

Coire Claurigh and Stob Ban

Keep ahead (north) across the col, past its small pool **Lochan Rath**, and head straight up the grassy slope to **Stob Coire Claurigh**.

STOB BAN OUTING

Those based at Lairig Leacach bothy could turn left at the col, reversing Route 21. Steep scree path leads up Stob Ban. Take a small path down the ridge east, then northeast. The 2½hr circuit of 5km/3 miles with 500m/1700ft of ascent turns Stob Ban from a nuisance Munro into a handy evening outing.

ROUTE 21
Lairig Leacach to Stob Ban

Start	Corriechoille (NN 255 788)
Distance	10km/6½ miles
Total ascent	1200m/4000ft
Time	5½hr up
Terrain	Track and path, rough off Stob Ban

Difficulty

This route is gentle onto Stob Ban, and harsh off it, so more comfortable in reverse.

See Grey Corries summit summary map.

◄ Start by following Route 19 to **Lairig Leacach bothy** (2hr).

Just beyond the bothy, a footbridge crosses Allt a' Chuil Choirean. Follow the good stalkers' path beyond for 200 metres, to turn off up the spur of Stob Ban. A path passes along the right-hand (northwest) slopes of the minor knoll at 770m, then follows a pleasant ridge to the summit of **Stob Ban**.

Descend northwest on a scree path, becoming loose and steep down to the col above Coire Rath. Pass the pool there, **Lochan Rath**, and head straight up the grassy slope opposite to **Stob Coire Claurigh**.

ROUTE 22
Meanach Bothy to Stob Ban

Start	Meanach (Meannanach) bothy (NN 266 685)
Distance	4.5km/3 miles
Total ascent	600m/2000ft
Time	3hr up
Terrain	Pathless but grassy up Stob Ban, then rough stony descent
Access	Meanach bothy is reached from Glen Nevis or Corrour station (Route 5), from Coirechoille (Route 24), or from Kinlochleven (Route 45)

Difficulty
◼◼◼◼☐

A pathless but reasonably comfortable line, used to link Grey Corries with Mamores on Tranter's Walk, or as an end-of-day descent to the bothy.

▶ Start from the riverbank opposite Luibeilt, taking the stalkers' path up beside **Allt nam Fang**. At a stream junction at 500m, leave the path and follow the main Allt nam Fang upstream, due north. Its grassy banks give a way up through the heather, onto open grass high on the side of **Stob Ban**.

Reach Stob Ban's south ridge at about the 900m level and follow it to the summit. Continue as Route 21 to **Stob Coire Claurigh**.

See Grey Corries summit summary map.

ROUTE 23
The Innses

Length

■ ■ □ □ □

Difficulty

■ ■ ■ ■ □

Start/Finish	Above Coirechoille (NN 255 788)
Distance	13km/8 miles
Total ascent	900m/3000ft
Time	5½hr
Terrain	Rough hillsides
Max altitude	Cruach Innse 857m

'Sgurr' is the generic name of only the finest mountains, such as the Cuillin. Among Corbetts south of the Great Glen, just two receive this top designation (and Sgor Mor on Deeside doesn't deserve it!). Sgurr Innse is an impressive cone of crag and heather; this route, while remaining on the heather, takes you right in among the crag.

Sgurr Innse from Lairig Leacach bothy; Route 23 follows the shadow-edge spur

Start by following Route 19 towards **Lairig Leacach bothy** (2hr). From the bothy itself, there's a good view of the ascent route. But 300 metres before it, turn off left on a rough track fording the stream. Head up grassy slopes with

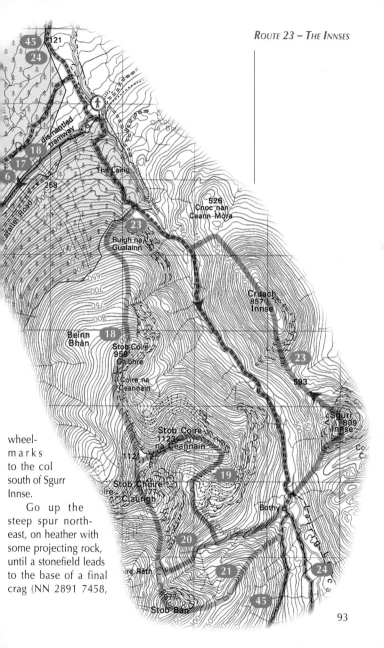

wheel-
marks
to the col
south of Sgurr
Innse.

Go up the
steep spur north-
east, on heather with
some projecting rock,
until a stonefield leads
to the base of a final
crag (NN 2891 7458,

675m). Turn right, along the crag base, on a heathery shelf with deer path, and more big crags below. After 100 metres, with stonefield ahead, turn up left to the knolly summit plateau. Head uphill to pass a small pool to the summit of **Sgurr Innse.**

Direct descent northwest leads to crags, so head down north for 200 metres. As the slope gets steep, slant down left, northwest, with traces of path, into the broad **593m col** (589m on old maps). A small path winds up peat and outcrops to the plateau, where ground of compact quartzite, like the Grey Corries opposite, leads to the summit of **Cruach Innse**.

Descend gentle grassy slopes northwest, steepening towards a col. Before reaching this, turn down left, west, to reach the track of the outward walk.

ROUTE 24

Lairig Leacach: Corrour to Spean Bridge

Start	Corrour station (NN 356 664) (or Loch Ossian youth hostel)
Finish	Spean Bridge (NN 221 814)
Distance	24.5km/15½ miles
Total ascent	200m/700ft
Time	1 short day (6½hr walking time)
Terrain	Tracks and paths, quite rough by Allt na Lairige
Max altitude	Lairig Leacach 510m
Transport	Spean Bridge to Corrour, trains evening (for Loch Ossian overnight) or early morning

Length
■ ■ ☐ ☐ ☐

Difficulty
■ ■ ■ ■ ☐

Shorter than the Glen Nevis trek (Route 5), this takes in the fine and historic Lairig Leacach pass. Alternatively, a night in Lairig Leacach bothy could prelude a romp along the Grey Corries.

▶ Start along the tracks of Route 5 to the head of Loch Treig (6km, 1½hr). Cross Abhainn Rath to the boarded-up **Creaguaneach Lodge** and follow the loch shore to the next **river**, Allt na Lairige, where the path rises through a gate into a small enclosure.

Of the paths up-valley, the one west of the river, which happens to be the right-of-way, is clearer. ▶ Ignore a footbridge down right, but climb slightly through a col behind a small knoll and then drop right, to the riverbank.

The path runs up-valley, mostly alongside the river. After 3.5km the valley levels and the path gets boggier, to a footbridge over Allt a' Chuil Choirean near **Lairig Leacach bothy**.

See overview map Ben Nevis & Glen Coe north.

The path east of the river is very narrow and vague but has great views of the waterfalls Easan Dubh. To reach it, drop right to a footbridge among the first trees.

The abandoned Creaguaneach Lodge

A good track runs north through the Lairig Leacach pass and down through forest into cattle pastures. From here the quickest route to the finish continues past Coirechoille to the lane below, which runs pleasantly alongside River Spean to **Spean Bridge**, while a more convoluted but no less pleasant route takes in some woodland (see below).

Way of plantations and woodland

About 800 metres below the forest foot, turn left, signed 'Spean Bridge'; this forest route is signposted 'Spean Bridge' throughout. Follow the new track into the plantation for 2km (ignoring side tracks up left then down right), then turn down right on a smaller grassier track. After 700 metres, as the track bends right, a path down left leads to a footbridge under birches. Turn right on a cycle path, which after 2km becomes a mossy old track.

Ignore a side-track down right (leading to Killiechonate). After 1km the track ahead reverts to cycle path, which descends to cross a track (NN 228 808). Take the path down ahead until it bends right, then on a track immediately below, turn left. After 200 metres, a path forks down right, signed 'station'. It slants through woods to emerge above **Spean Bridge station**.

4 MAMORES

Mamores: Am Bodach, Stob Coire a' Chairn, from pipeline path

Sgurr a' Mhaim, Stob Ban, Am Bodach: their shapes alone send a tingle into every limb. Link them along a ridge that's steep-sided and sometimes rocky, that swoops westward over 5 hours of walking and six Munros – and you have hillwalking perfection.

The two sides of the range represent two different sides of hillwalking. Glen Nevis is slightly gloomy, unless you follow it right up into the Nevis Gorge, when it's seriously gloomy, grand and grim. Above Glen Nevis steep paths lead up to the northward spurs of Sgurr a' Mhaim and An Gearanach, or the north ridge of Stob Ban. Each offers scrambling that's technically easy, but still serious and exposed.

With most of this north side so steep, it's tempting to flop down the gentle grass into Coire a' Mhail, with its little river winding out towards Glen Nevis. A mistake: that little river drops over the famous waterfall at Steall. The circuit of the deceptive corrie links the ridges of An Gearanach with the Devil's Ridge to Sgurr a' Mhaim. It's the 'Ring of Steall', one of the classic hard hillwalks. I've lifted this out of the summit summary as the separate Route 39.

Walkers from Kinlochleven have the opposite approach, literally but also metaphorically. Instead of the concrete malls of Fort William they have a peaceful little village. Instead of spruce trees and gloom, they have birchwoods, and sunset all the way along Loch Leven. Instead of Steall Falls they have the green splashiness of the Grey Mare's Tail. When it's time to head uphill, instead of steepness they have well-graded stalkers' paths.

But once you're up, it doesn't matter which way you got there. Between Binnein Mor and Mullach nan Coirean, 12 wonderful kilometres await you. You get all the variety of quartzite, schist and granite; but always the same narrow and shapely ridgelines, the same views of Ben Nevis hanging above you, and Bidean peering over the jagged wall-top of the Aonach Eagach. Ahead is the Atlantic, going golden under the sunset.

All this is pretty popular, and some paths are wide and eroded. So do the Mamores in winter, cramponing all day from peak to peak before leaping down some accommodating snowslope into the darkening glen.

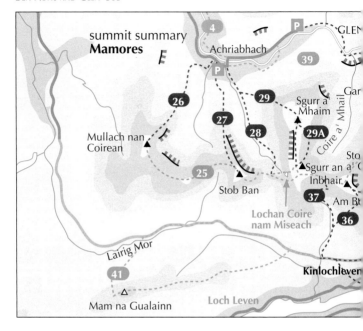

SUMMIT SUMMARY: MAMORES

Route 25 is the entire main ridge, eastbound. Route 38 is the same main ridge in the westbound direction. The classic Ring of Steall (Route 39) is a separate stand-alone, as is Route 40 which visits the two eastern outliers, Sgurr Eilde Mor and Binnein Beag.

MAMORES ROUTES	
Route 25	Mamores Main Ridge Eastbound
Route 25A	Bodach Bypass: Eastbound
Route 26	Mullach nan Coirean North Ridge
Route 27	Stob Ban North Ridge
Route 28	Coire Mhusgain
Route 29	Sgurr a' Mhaim and Devil's Ridge
Route 29A	Escaping the Devil

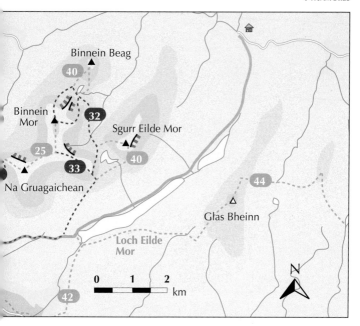

ROUTE 25
Mamores Main Ridge Eastbound

Start	Mullach nan Coirean (NN 122 662)
Finish	Binnein Mor (NN 212 663)
Distance	11.5km/7½ miles
Total ascent	4300ft/1300m
Time	6hr end-to-end
Terrain	Paths, some quite steep and eroded

Difficulty

A fine varied ridge, over many peaks.

See Mamores summit summary map.

Route 27 joins here.

Route 28, the one comfy descent into Glen Nevis, goes off here.

Route 29, and its bypass, 29A, also arrive here.

The Bodach bypass (Route 25A) bears off left at the lowest point of the col.

◄ From **Mullach nan Coirean**, steep drops on the left guide eastwards over two minor tops. The path then skirts right of the small grass top above Stob Ban's north ridge and climbs stony slopes southeast to the summit of **Stob Ban**. ◄

Head south along crag tops for 30 metres, then down a ridge that curves left to display Stob Ban's eastern crags. Just before the ridge tip, the path drops off right (east). The slope eases, and a small hummock is crossed to the col with cairn at the top of Coire a' Mhusgain. ◄ The better path now contours along the northern (left) side, just below the crest, to the outflow of **Lochan Coire nam Miseach**. Cross the stream, and take a zigzag path up the steep slope to the col at the base of the Devil's Ridge. ◄ Turn right, up stony slopes, to the summit of **Sgurr an Iubhair**.

The pathed ridgeline runs down southeast to a long, level col. ◄ Keep ahead up the pleasant ridge onto **Am Bodach**.

Head down northeast, on steep rocky scree with various nasty paths. At the foot of the steep quartzite summit cap, keep to the right of the small crest outcrop, for the

less uncomfortable path. The ridge continues over a narrow top, then rises to **Stob Coire a' Chairn**. Pathed ridge continues to the northern top of Na Gruagaichean, with a drop into a spectacular notch before the southern and main summit.

On the south ridge of Binnein Mor

Ignore the apparent ridge continuing ahead south, as the true ridgeline turns down left, east. An attractive sharp ridge leads to the next col, then a wider one runs up to the 1062m south top of Binnein Mor. ▶ Head north up the ridge to the main top of **Binnein Mor**. A rocky crest leads onwards for 100 metres to a lower sub-summit: anyone who likes scrambling will decide that must be the true ridge end and so require a visit, but it's not needed for Munro-bagging purposes.

Route 33 from Kinlochleven arrives here.

ROUTE 25A
Bodach Bypass: Eastbound

Start	Col west of Am Bodach (NN 169 652)
Distance	1km/¾ mile
Warning	This path could be strayed off in mist, and dips into Coire a' Mhail, which runs down not to safety but to the top of Steall Falls – see Route 31.

Difficulty

See Route 38A for the same route westbound.

At the lowest point of the ridge west of **Am Bodach** (NN 1688 6522), a grassy notch crosses the ridgeline. Here look over the left-hand (northern) edge to see the path slanting down across chunky scree. At the scree foot continue on the same line; the grass path is hard to see, as it passes below a strip of stonefield. The path becomes clear again, crossing a mossy stream, then contouring below a large stonefield with a prominent outcrop at its head.

At the end of this stonefield, with the path unclear again, slant up the grassy slope ahead (east) to reach the col east of **Am Bodach**.

ROUTE 26

Mullach nan Coirean North Ridge

Start	Achriabhach (NN 145 683)
Distance	4.5km/2½ miles (up)
Total ascent	900m/2900ft
Time	3½hr up
Terrain	Path, rough path under trees, pathed ridge

Difficulty

Nice once you're out of the forest, and makes a fairly comfortable descent.

▶ Start from the car park by taking the road down-valley for 300 metres to the corner of plantations. Take a path under the trees just inside the forest, up to a bend in a forest road. Turn right on the higher, uphill, branch for 800 metres. A steep, rough path heads up left under the trees – the **Allt a' Choire Riabhaich** (stream) is heard nearby to the right.

See Mamores summit summary map.

Walkers on East ridge, Mullach nan Coirean

A ladder stile (NN 132 681) leads out of the trees. A small path leads ahead, with a deer fence nearby on its left for 1km. By the time the fence turns away, the ridgeline ahead is well defined and clear all the way to **Mullach nan Coirean** summit.

In descent

From the summit, start down north but bend to the right along the tops of crags dropping to the right, to find the ridgeline running down east. The ridge bends left, north-east, and soon has a deer fence along the crest. Follow the path and fence down to the ladder stile at NN 132 681.

A path runs down between the trees to a forest road. Turn right to a hairpin bend, and then take a downhill path close to the forest edge and a stream.

ROUTE 27
Stob Ban North Ridge

Start	Achriabhach (NN 145 683)
Distance	3.5km/2 miles (up)
Total ascent	950m/3200ft
Time	3½hr up
Terrain	Steep grass, ridge, a little scrambling (Grade 1)

Difficulty
▨ ▨ ▨ ▨ ▨

A fine ridge with some easy scrambling.

See Mamores summit summary map.

◀ Start from the car park and head down-valley on road for 250 metres, then take a gate on the left just before the road bridge over **Allt a' Choire Dheirg**. Cross swampy ground near the river on your right (with forest beyond it). Level with a forest road bend within the forest, slant

Stob Ban, its north ridge forming the right skyline

away left towards the first steep rise. A wooded rock band obstructs the slope above; near its right end is a grassy gap. Head into this to find a path starting. Above the rockband this path slants leftwards to a cairn at the ridge tip (Sron Dearg).

The ridge now runs almost level, with a path and remains of a fence. Where it steepens, the rocky crest can be avoided by a path just to right of the crest. The crest rocks are crampon-scratched and have good holds. However they are lichened, and being schist are slippery when wet.

A spectacular tower leads to the final crest, almost level but narrow, with a small path. It finishes at a triangular summit just northwest of **Stob Ban**.

ROUTE 28

Coire Mhusgain

Start	Achriabhach (NN 145 683)
Distance	4.5km/2¾ miles (up)
Total ascent	950m/3100ft
Time	3½hr up
Terrain	Good path

Difficulty

■ ■ ■ □ □

A scenic and easy path with trees and waterfalls; good also in descent.

See Mamores summit summary map.

◄ Start by turning right out of the parking area across one road bridge to the bridge over the Polldubh lower falls. Just before this bridge, take a stile on the right (not the gate beside it onto a riverside path). Follow a good path left of the stream up **Coire a' Mhusgain**.

After 2km, at 400m, you're crossing a steep slope with waterfalls around. Here a small wrong path runs ahead, but the clearer main path zigzags up left before heading back right towards the stream. The path remains mostly good right up to the main ridge.

In descent

At the lowest point of the ridge between Stob Ban and Sgurr an Iubhair, a cairn (NN 156 653) marks the top of the clear path down **Coire Mhusgain**. This has one steep zigzag section but is mostly comfortable walking, with waterfalls below. It reaches the Glen Nevis road beside the Achriabhach **car park**.

ROUTE 29
Sgurr a' Mhaim and Devil's Ridge

Start	Achriabhach (NN 145 683)
Distance	4km/2½ miles (to Sgurr an lubhair)
Total ascent	1100m/3700ft
Time	4½hr up
Terrain	Steep climb, then narrow grass ridge with a scrambling moment (Grade 1)

Difficulty
▪ ▪ ▪ ▪ ▪

A fine, narrow ridge with some easy scrambling.

▶ Start by turning right out of the car park to cross Allt Coire a' Mhusgain. Just before the next bridge over the River Nevis (with the waterfalls underneath), take a stile on the right (not the gate beside it onto a riverside path). Follow a good path to left of the stream up **Coire Mhusgain** for 1km. As the main path starts to contour above the stream, fork off left, up a spur. The path is steep, relentless, and rather eroded, on grass to a slight

See Mamores summit summary map.

The footbridge of Allt Coire Giubhsachan below Sgurr a' Mhaim

flattening at 850m; then up quartzite stones to the summit of **Sgurr a' Mhaim**.

A good path heads quite steeply down south from Sgurr a' Mhaim, first on rocky stony ground, then on grass. ◄ The path bends a bit west of south to where the ridge levels and narrows into the **Devil's Ridge**. There is one rocky gap to scramble down into (slightly right of the crest) and then a spectacular grass knife-edge. After the drop to a final col, either climb steep stony ground ahead to **Sgurr an Iubhair** or else turn down right on zigzags to **Lochan Coire nam Miseach**.

For descent see Route 39.

Devil's Bypass (Route 29A) turns off at the top of the grass.

ROUTE 29A
Escaping the Devil

Difficulty
■ ■ ■ ■ □

Start	Sgurr a' Mhaim (NN 164 667)

This route avoids the exposed, windswept ridge. It is indistinct in mist, and escape into Coire a' Mhail below is a bad idea (see Route 31).

See Mamores summit summary map.

◄ From **Sgurr a' Mhaim,** the good path (towards Devil's Ridge) heads quite steeply down south over rocky stony ground. After about 5mins the angle eases and the path is on grass. Here leave it to head left, pathless, across a grass dip and over a grass knoll (NN 1652 6656), then down southeast on a grass spur. An unused zigzag stalkers' path could soon be discovered underfoot. Follow it down to just above where the ridge angle eases at 930m (NN 1664 6638).

Here the path turns right (south) to contour above a grassy hollow with the headwaters of a stream. It becomes indistinct, but is clear ahead and somewhat lower down, as it passes the toe of an outcrop (NN 1650 6599). It then slants gradually up below the **Devil's Ridge**, steepening in zigzags to reach the Devil's col.

Turn left up **Sgurr an Iubhair**, or directly ahead across the col is the path descending to **Lochan Coire nam Miseach**.

ROUTE 30

Gearanach and Garbhanach

Start	End of Glen Nevis road (NN 167 691)
Distance	5km/3 miles (to Stob Coire a' Chairn)
Total ascent	1000m/3300ft
Time	4½hr up
Terrain	Steep climb, then narrow stony and rocky ridge with a scrambling moment (Grade 1)

Difficulty

A steep climb onto a fine ridge with scrambling.

This is the uphill section of Route 39 (Ring of Steall).

ROUTE 31

Escape from Coire a' Mhail

Start	Coire a' Mhail

Difficulty

If you have, by design or accident, descended into the trap of Coire a' Mhail, continuing downstream will lead onto crags on either side of Steall Falls. To escape, at the point where the valley narrows (NN 179 675) head up northeast, to right of the hump **Cnoc Reamhar**, to reach the northwest ridge of An Gearanach at a levelling (NN

Steall Falls. From above, gentle Coire a' Mhail looks like a way down off the Mamores. The slopes either side of these falls are the reason why it isn't

184 677). Contour onwards to join the steep, zigzag descending path (Route 39) to Glen Nevis.

ROUTE 32

Round the Back to Binnein Mor

Start	Grey Mare's car park, Kinlochleven (NN 187 622)
Distance	8.5km/5½ miles (up)
Total ascent	1300m/4300ft
Time	5½hr up
Terrain	Paths and tracks, pathless stony and grassy ridge

Difficulty

Remote and romantic. To bag Sgurr Eilde Mor or Binnein Beag on the way, switch into Route 40.

See Mamores summit summary map.

◀ Start as for Route 33, onto the steep southeast spur of Sgor Eilde Beag. At the first zigzag, ignore a peaty path ahead (it's heading to Sgurr Eilde Mor) but zig back left and then zag right, two little zigzags. Keep ahead on a clear path that contours north, to pass left of a large **lochan** (Lochan Coire an Lochain).

The path then drops steeply into the hollow of Coire a' Bhinnein. It follows a stream down for 30 metres, then crosses it and contours north around the base of Binnein Mor. It climbs slightly to reach the outflow of a narrow lochan on the plateau between the two Binneins. ▶

The easy way up Binnein Mor from here is southwest up grass into the corrie with the two high lochans, then onto the north ridge. Also, immediately ahead is the northeast ridge, which starts steep, levels, then rises again in a rock arête that looks to offer some easy scrambling (the author hasn't yet been up this ridge).

The preferred route contours out to the left, south, to a little ravine. Go up to right of this into Binnein Mor's hidden little northeast corrie. Cross its floor to its bounding ridge, which is gently angled with quartzite outcrops. This ridge goes up, southwest then bending south, becoming fairly steep and sharp to reach **Binnein Mor** summit.

To bag Binnein Beag now, see Route 40. Or for a fine through-route to Fort William, traces of path lead north, to left of the lochan and Binnein Beag, for a rough descent into Glen Nevis – Route 5.

Binnein Beag seen from the east ridge of Binnein Mor

ROUTE 33

Sgurr Eilde Beag to Binnein Mor

Start	Grey Mare's car park, Kinlochleven (NN 187 622)
Distance	7.5km/4½ miles (up)
Total ascent	1200m/4000ft
Time	4½hr up
Terrain	Paths, one steepish ascent
Parking	There used to be parking at Mamore Lodge, then a hotel (NN 185 629), saving 200m of ascent. This estate track is now closed to other vehicles, and the gate at its foot is sometimes locked without warning. The Kinlochleven start is more tiring, but very beautiful.

Difficulty

The easternmost of the attractive 'mix and match' routes onto the Mamores from Kinlochleven. See Route 42 and its map for more details of the woods above the village.

See Mamores summit summary map.

Cables crossing the stream are the start of a commercial via ferrata course, which climbs the crags up left of the falls.

◀ Leave the car park on a wide, smooth path, turning left (sign for Grey Mare's waterfall). The path soon drops to a footbridge where you can turn left down the side-stream for 100 metres to view the waterfall. ◀ Return and continue past the footbridge for 100 metres, where the path bends back left, steeply uphill. At the top of trees, with two low-voltage power lines above, fork right (yellow, green arrows). The path follows a spur to a gate in a deer fence (NN 192 629), then contours along the spur's left side under birches across three streams to a final path junction. Turn up right (yellow arrow).

The path rises between two streams to join the track above. Cross to pass a stone bench and rejoin the track.

Follow the track for 1km, to just before its highest point, where a cairned path turns off left (in a few steps more, another path turns off right for Kinlochleven). The peaty/stony well-used path crosses Allt Coire nan Laogh and turns uphill beyond it for 200 metres. Then it slants up the face of **Sgor Eilde Beag** in a climb that's been visible for much of the walk so far.

Once on the steep southeast spur of Sgor Eilde Beag, the path rises in steep zigzags to a cairn at its top. A gentle ridge runs up to Point 1062 (Binnein Mor South Top), then a fine sharp one rises north to **Binnein Mor**.

On Sgurr Eilde Beag, looking back across Loch Eilde Mor to the Blackwater Reservoir

ROUTE 34

Coire na Ba to Stob Coire a' Chairn

Start	Grey Mare's car park, Kinlochleven (NN 187 622)
Distance	6km/3¾ miles (up)
Total ascent	950m/3200ft
Time	4½hr up
Terrain	Good paths
Parking	See Route 33

Difficulty

A good, comfortable path with an attractive wood and waterfall to start. You will follow green waymarks for the first part of the walk as far as the high track.

See Mamores summit summary map.

◀ Start from the car park on a wide, smooth path, turning left. The path rises to the right, then drops to a footbridge where you can turn left for 100 metres to view the Grey Mare's Waterfall. Return and continue past the footbridge for 100 metres, where the path bends back left, steeply uphill. At the top of trees, with two low-voltage power lines above, fork right. The path follows a spur to a gate in a deer fence (NN 192 629), then contours along the spur's left side under birches across three streams. At the next junction keep ahead (the final green arrow) on a smaller path to arrive at a track above. Turn left for 200 metres; just before a stream there's a track with gate on the right.

Go up the rough track into **Coire na Ba**. This high valley is pleasingly wooded beside its stream, with a big cirque ahead around Am Bodach by the two tops of Stob Coire a' Chairn to Na Gruagaichean. The track degenerates to a path, which after 1km crosses a stream and 200

Here Route 35 turns off.

metres later turns uphill alongside a second stream. ◀ The path ahead goes up a wet slope where it may be lost. It reappears slanting right to pass a small pool. After 100 metres it turns sharp left, and contours across the steep slope of **Na Gruagaichean**, going gently downhill for a while. Finally it climbs in zigzags to the main ridge at the col southeast of **Stob Coire a' Chairn** (NN 1939 6559).

Mamores: Am Bodach, Stob Coire a' Chairn, from the Pipeline Path

ROUTE 35
Am Bodach East Corrie

Start	Grey Mare's car park, Kinlochleven (NN 187 622)
Distance	5.5km/3½ miles (to Bodach summit)
Total ascent	1000m/3300ft
Time	4½hr up
Terrain	Steep pathless grass
Parking	See Route 33

Difficulty

A dramatic and little-used back way in to Am Bodach.

▶ Follow Route 34 into the cirque between Am Bodach and Na Gruagaichean. Where the path turns uphill by a second stream, leave it and contour left, then slant up to join the ravine that emerges from the eastern corrie of Am Bodach.

At 540m altitude the ravine splits. Continue up to right of the right-hand branch to cross its head (with the stream steepening in further falls above), or else cross the right-hand branch above its lowest waterfall and go up the spur between the two branches, then switch into the left-hand ravine branch (bouldery but otherwise easy). At 600m the left-hand branch peters out. Here (NN 182 650) bend up left, following the remaining stream southwest into a grassy hollow, with an imposing crag up left.

In the broken ground on the right is a gully with a weathered rockfall emerging from its foot. From under the rockfall, a grassy old path slants across the grassy hollow. Take this path up left, to reach grassy slopes immediately above the imposing crag. Head straight up south onto a narrow grass ridge. This bends to the right around the head of the grassy hollow to a small summit on Am Bodach's southeast ridge (NN 179 645). Cross the small summit, to find the ridge path beyond, and turn right on

See Mamores summit summary map.

this. Follow it to the summit levelling, with a preliminary cairn and 50 metres later the summit of **Am Bodach**.

ROUTE 36
Sgurr an Fhuarain: Descent

Start	Am Bodach summit (NN 176 651)
Finish	Grey Mare's car park, Kinlochleven (NN 187 622)
Distance	5.5km/3½ miles (from Am Bodach summit)
Total descent	1000m/3300ft
Time	4hr (up), 2hr (down)
Terrain	Rough grass

Difficulty
■ ■ ■ ■ □

This would be a grassy trudge up, but makes a comfortable descent, especially when holding snow.

See Mamores summit summary map.

◄ Descend Am Bodach's south ridge, on a small path, to a slight rise at 900m, or else right down to **Sgurr an**

Mamore Lodge and Am Bodach

116

Fhuarain. Turn down right wherever good snow overlies the rough grass. Cross Allt Coire na h-Eirghe to join the path beyond and follow it down to the West Highland Way track. Turn left, back across the stream, to where the West Highland Way forks down right to **Kinlochleven** (see Route 41).

ROUTE 37
Coire na h-Eirghe
(southwest corrie of Am Bodach)

Start	Grey Mare's car park, Kinlochleven (NN 187 622)
Distance	5km/3 miles (to Sgurr an Iubhair)
Total ascent	1000m/3300ft
Time	3½hr
Terrain	Good paths

Difficulty

A comfortable ascent on path all the way.

▶ Start by taking the West Highland Way out of Kinlochleven along the Fort William road, forking up right at the village edge on a signposted path. The path crosses the Mamore Lodge access lane, to reach a high track. Turn left for 400 metres to cross Allt Coire na h-Eirghe, then continue for 100 metres to the highest point of the track.

Here a path turns up right just behind some bare, glacier-scratched slabs. It heads up to left of the stream, crosses it above a waterfall, then continues up to its right. In the upper corrie the path zigzags towards the summit of Am Bodach, thinks better of this, and swings left to the Bodach/Iubhair col. Turn left on the wide ridge path to Sgurr an Iubhair.

See Mamores summit summary map.

ROUTE 38
Mamores Main Ridge Westbound

Start	Binnein Mor (NN 212 663)
Finish	Mullach nan Coirean (NN 122 662)
Distance	11.5km/7½ miles
Total ascent	1100m/3700ft
Time	6hr end-to-end
Terrain	Paths, some steep and eroded

Difficulty

Eastbound is Route 25. This direction looks at the sea and the sunset.

The cairn of Binnein Mor lies just before a narrow rocky ridge running north; the further, lower, cairn does constitute the true start of the Mamores ridge.

◀ From **Binnein Mor**, a shapely ridge descends south to Point 1062 (Binnein Mor South Top). This enjoyable ridge, not as narrow as it looks, continues southwest to **Na Gruagaichean**; the path, down left of the crest, misses out a little of the fun.

From Na Gruagaichean a sharp descent north into a spectacular little col leads to Gruagaichean's lower northwest top (between the two tops you pass over three different rocks: white quartzite, grey schist and pinkish

Ridge to Na Gruagaichean

granite). Easier ridge continues northwest to **Stob Coire a' Chairn** (981m, this Munro is among several unnamed on old Landranger maps).

Head down southwest, across a sharp narrow hump, to the following col. ▶ Ahead, now, the climb to Am Bodach is rather steep, and the path zigzags up loose scree, seeking the firmest footing. In winter patches of hard snow are much nicer. Quite soon the ground eases to the stony top of **Am Bodach**.

Here a cairn (NN 178 654) marks the start of the Bodach Bypass (Route 38A).

The descent is on a gentle ridge westwards, with a short climb to **Sgurr an Iubhair** (1001m). This used to be the 11th Mamores Munro, but was downgraded in 1997. Its stony top doesn't show much path: there are two descent routes westwards, with the first option being steeper but more sheltered.

Lochan route down Iubhair

Make a short steep descent northwest into the col at the south end of the Devil's Ridge. Here turn down left, soon to find a zigzag path to the small **Lochan Coire nam Miseach**. Contour westwards for another 400 metres, to right of the ridge crest, to regain the crest at the cairn marking the top of the path down Coire Mhusgain (Route 28).

Ridge route down Iubhair

Descend southwest, to arrive at crag tops. Turn left along them. As they turn downhill, nearby on the left is a lightly used stalkers' path that zigzags off southwest before returning to the col above Lochan Coire nam Miseach. Continue ahead on a path just to left of the crest to the low point of the col, with the cairn at the top of Coire Mhusgain's path (Route 28).

Cross a small rise, then head up steeply onto a ridge curving left, with big drops on the right, onto **Stob Ban**. Head down northwest, passing left of a stony sub-summit, to a grassy col. Ahead is a triangular grass summit (the top of Route 27). The main path contours to left of this grass summit to regain the ridgeline, and follows drops on the right over two minor summits to **Mullach nan Coirean**.

ROUTE 38A

Bodach Bypass: Westbound

Start	Col north of Am Bodach (NN 178 654)
Note	This path could be strayed off in mist, and runs around the top of Coire a' Mhail, which runs down not to safety but to the Steall Falls – see Route 31.

Difficulty
■■■□□

Route 25A is the same route eastbound.

From the col with cairn to east of Am Bodach (NN 178 655) slant down roughly west. Ahead is a prominent little outcrop, and below it a stonefield: at the toe of the stonefield the good path will be found. It contours below the stonefield, crosses a mossy stream, then slants slightly uphill on grass with small strip of stonefield directly above. On the dry grass it becomes unclear but can be seen ahead, still on the same line, as it slants up chunky scree to the col west of Am Bodach.

ROUTE 39

Ring of Steall

Start/Finish	End of Glen Nevis road (NN 167 691)
Distance	14.5km/9 miles
Total ascent	1600m/5300ft
Time	8hr
Terrain	Long, steep ascent and descent, small ridge paths, easy scrambling
Max altitude	Sgurr a' Mhaim 1099m

Length
■■■□□

Difficulty
■■■■■

120

Link the ridges of An Gearanach with the Devil's Ridge to Sgurr a' Mhaim, and you have the 'Ring of Steall'. With its narrow ridges, scrambling sections, and four Munro summits, this is one of the classic hard hillwalks. So I've lifted it out as a stand-alone from the Mamores summit summary where it belongs. Once up on Stob Coire a' Chairn, you can switch into previous routes for half a dozen different continuations, even if none will be quite as airily inspiring as the Devil's Ridge.

The name comes from the 'Ring of Steel', the Soviet tanks that surrounded General Paulus' Sixth Army at Stalingrad in the winter of 1942. The Stalingrad campaign left the German army shattered and destroyed. The Ring of Steall can have a similar effect on the walker of today. It's best done clockwise, starting up An Gearanach. The descent off Sgurr a' Mhaim is slightly less steep; more importantly, that direction allows an escape from the start of the Devil's Ridge down Route 28. There are **no earlier escapes**, as the route circles Coire a' Mhail with its waterfall exit (see Route 31).

▶ Start from the end of the car park, along the wide, smooth path above Nevis Gorge.(See Route 2 for an exciting variant here.) At the top of the gorge, the path emerges suddenly onto a flat riverside meadow. Cross it to the footbridge below the huge Steall Falls. As noted above and very visible here, there is no descent line alongside the waterfall: so, later on in the walk, don't be tempted to descend into Coire a' Mhail above it.

The footbridge is three steel cables, giving a wobbly crossing. Make things easier by crossing one at a time, and by placing feet along the cable rather than sideways across it. Bear left past the Steall hut, to cross the stream below the Steall Falls.

Continue up the valley for 300 metres, then turn right up a steep path alongside a scoured-out earth gully. This erosion feature appeared during a single storm several years ago. The path beside it is quite good, but the climb is steep. At the top of the steep valley (Coire Chadha Chaoruinn) the path contours right, onto the ridgeline alongside. ▶) Now the climb is less steep and the views wider. Follow the pathed ridge to the summit of **An Gearanach** (982m, unnamed on old maps).

See Mamores summit summary map.

If you do later end up in Coire a' Mhail, you'll have to climb back out to this point.

The so-called footbridge below Steall Falls is just the first of the challenges on the Ring of Steall

From An Gearanach the sharp ridge runs south to the rocky summit of **An Garbhanach**. After the summit comes a moment of easy scrambling (Grade 1). There's a choice between an exposed downward step left of the crest, or a short groove descent right of the crest. Continue down an eroded path or rocks alongside, over a subsidiary hump, to a wide col, then easily up the walk's second Munro, **Stob Coire a' Chairn** (983m).

From here you could take the Bodach bypass path, around its northern flank (Route 38A).

The ridge path runs down southwest, rises over a sharply defined bump, then drops to the col before Am Bodach. ◄ The climb ahead to Am Bodach is rather steep, and the path zigzags up loose scree, seeking the firmest footing. If you're not used to such ground look for rock handholds, and spend some time picking out the most comfortable line. But quite soon the ground eases to the stony top of **Am Bodach**.

The descent is on a gentle ridge westwards, with a short climb to **Sgurr an Iubhair** (1001m, unnamed on older maps). This used to be the walk's fourth Munro, but was downgraded in 1997. From its top, make a short steep descent northwest into a col. (From here, if time is short, you could escape left down to Lochan Coire nam Miseach, to descend the good path of Route 28.)

Ahead, a path leads up onto the start of the **Devil's Ridge**. ▶ This is grassy, but astonishingly sharp. At the end of the narrow crest is a notch, which requires a few steps of scrambling, just left of the crest. Less exposed ridge runs downhill to the steep cone of **Sgurr a' Mhaim**. The path leads straight up, north, onto stony ground and the summit.

Bear left to descend a worn scree path northwest, to a slight flattening at 850m at the foot of the screes. Crossing this flattening the path is briefly invisible, but reforms on a grassy spur below. At this steepens (NN 1587 6722) the main path turns down left, onto a spur descending northwest. (A smaller path north, down the apparent spurline ahead, soon turns left to rejoin the proper, main path.) Steep and rather eroded, the path descends the spur to Allt Coire a' Mhusgain, where an easier path leads downstream to the Glen Nevis road near **Polldubh**.

As your foot touches the road, turn back sharp right, through a gate, onto a fenced riverside path. Follow this, to right of the Water of Nevis, for 1.5km. After a downhill section, look out for a footbridge down on the left. Cross it to rejoin the road, and turn right for 1km to the **car park** at the walk start.

It'd be mere Munro-bagging to reach Sgurr a' Mhaim without the Devil's Ridge: Route 29A reversed.

ROUTE 40
The Back of the Binneins

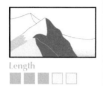

Length

◼◼◼◻◻

Difficulty

◼◼◼◼◻

Start/Finish	Grey Mare's car park, Kinlochleven (NN 187 622)
Distance	18km/11 miles
Total ascent	1500m/5000ft
Time	8hr
Terrain	Paths, but rough up and down Eilde Mor
Max altitude	Sgurr Eilde Mor 1010m
Parking	See Route 33

This walk takes you into some wonderfully remote country at the eastern end of the Mamores, to bag a pair of out-of-the-way Munros. The return is by the same route; however, if energy levels and clouds are high, then cross Binnein Mor (Route 32) for a fine ridgewalk over Na Gruagaichean and a descent to Coire na Ba (Route 34). That full day, the back *and* the front of the Binneins, gives 11½ miles/6000ft of serious hill (18.5km/1800m of ascent).

See Mamores summit summary map.

◀ Leave the car park on a wide, smooth path, turning left (sign for Grey Mare's waterfall). The path soon drops to a footbridge where you can turn left down the sidestream for 100 metres to view the waterfall. Return and continue past the footbridge for 100 metres, where the path bends back left, steeply uphill.

At the top of trees, with two low-voltage power lines above, fork right. The path follows a spur to a gate in a deer fence (NN 192 629), then contours along the spur's left side under birches across three streams to a final path junction. Turn up right to a contouring track. Cross it to pass a stone bench and rejoin the track.

Follow the track for 1km, to just before its highest point. A cairn on the left marks the start of a rough, well-used path, which crosses Allt Coire nan Laogh and turns uphill beyond it for 200 metres. Then it slants up the face

of **Sgor Eilde Beag** in a climb that's been visible for most of the walk so far.

At the first zigzag, where the main path heads on up towards Sgor Eilde Beag, keep ahead on a small peaty path. It contours round to the flat wet plateau south of the lochan that's presumably called Lochan Coire an Lochain. Continue northeast across flat ground to cross the outflow of the lochan, onto the southeast spur of **Sgurr Eilde Mor**. Follow it up, with some loose blocky quartzite scrambling if wished, to the summit.

A clear path heads west down a well-defined spur. But before the spur end, the path heads down right, on eroded scree zigzags, then down northwest on steep-ish grass until below the steep ground on the left (800m altitude approx, NN 2280 6586). Here the path turns abruptly to contour left for 200 metres before descending between the small lochans north of Lochan Coire an Lochain to join the stalkers' path opposite. ▶

Turn right, as the new path zigzags down steep grass into the hollow of Allt Coire a' Bhinnein. After descending briefly beside the stream, the path crosses it and contours out north along the slope of Binnein Mor. It rises gradually to reach the plateau between the two Binneins.

Sgor Eilde Beag and Mor

Here you could turn left to contour the slope foot above Lochan Coire an Lochain and rejoin the outward route – leaving Binnein Beag inconveniently unbagged.

125

Turn off right, to cross the outflow of a long lochan and follow a low ridge containing it on its right. This flat ridge leads to the steep southern spur of **Binnein Beag**. Go up this on bits of path and block-field to the summit.

Descend the same way: or, from the summit, return for 50 metres to where the path starts to descend. Here turn off right down an eroded hollow leading to the top of a long scree slope, which can be descended fast by those who can fast descend scree. Either way, return to the long lochan's outflow.

Here you decide whether to continue onto Binnein Mor by Route 32. Otherwise, return along the path through Coire a' Bhinnein. Having climbed up the zig-zags from the stream, keep ahead on the main path. This takes you above, and to right of, **Lochan Coire an Lochain** along the slope of Sgor Eilde Beag, to rejoin the outward route.

5 KINLOCHLEVEN

Pap of Glencoe, Loch Leven, and Beinn na Caillich of Mam na Gualainn

Kinlochleven is all that Fort William isn't. Where the Fort is big and busy, Kinlochleven, bypassed by the Ballachulish Bridge, is quiet. The Fort has great rail and coach links; Kinlochleven is reached by the occasional bus, or by the West Highland Way. Above all Kinlochleven, between the waterfalls and the sea, fringed by birchwoods, is a pretty place to be. And while it's a great jumping-up point for the Mamores,

it also has – rare in this big-hill district – a network of attractive low-level walks.

Kinlochleven's independent hostel and campsite, pubs and late-opening shop make it a comfortable place to stay, and a welcome staging-point on various long-distance routes to north and east, as well as the West Highland Way. For wet days its unique feature is indoor ice-climbing in the former aluminium factory, the Ice Factor.

ROUTE 41

Mam na Gualainn

Length
■ ■ ■ □ □

Difficulty
■ ■ ■ □ □

Start/Finish	Grey Mare's car park, Kinlochleven (NN 187 622)
Distance	19km/12 miles
Total ascent	1000m/3300ft
Time	7hr
Terrain	Track and path, sometimes rough
Max altitude	Mam na Gualainn 796m
Parking	See Route 33

Mam na Gualainn breaks my rule that small hills are tougher. It may not have the trampled paths of the main Mamores, but the West Highland Way and an old stalkers' path make for comfortable walking. A shortish day on the hill lets you choose among all the interesting ways down through the woods at day's end.

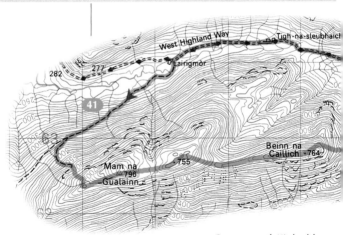

Start out of Kinlochleven along the **B863** towards the north side of Loch Leven and Fort William. At the village edge, fork

West Highland Way passes through Lairig Mor

up right on the signposted footpath of the West Highland Way. It slants uphill, crossing the tarred lane of Mamore Lodge, to reach a high track along the 250m contour.

Turn left on this wide, smooth track, still the West Highland Way. It contours above Loch Leven then turns up the valley of **Allt Nathrach** (serpent stream). ▶

Across the stream you should spot the steep descending path of the return route.

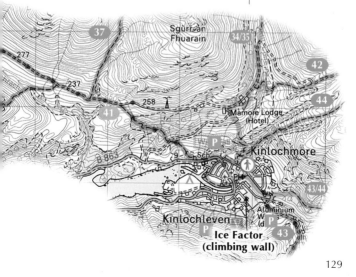

The path above Lairig Mor to Mam na Gualainn

Follow the wide track through a pass and past the 'dangerous building' of **Tigh-na-sleubhaich**. After another 400 metres, cross a footbridge beside the track's ford. After another 1km, beside stone sheep-handling pens, turn off left onto a path with a wobbly signpost for Loch Leven Side. The path fords the stream (**Allt na Lairige Moire**) – or cross just upstream at a rocky narrows. The path slants uphill, southwest. Just below the top of the heather, at a small cairn (NN 108 630), fork up left on a smaller path. Once out of the heather and on grass, you can head up anywhere to the ridge crest. Join the fence running uphill, east, along the crest, crossing it to reach **Mam na Gualainn** cylinder trig point which lies south of the fence.

Head down east, across a wide damp col, and then drop slightly right, on a small path still east, to a lower col and the narrow ridge up to **Beinn na Caillich**.

Direct descent ahead is very steep. So, from the final cairn, backtrack 20 metres or so, and slant down northeast to a small shelf with a pool at the foot of the steeper slope. Here meet a good path that heads to the right and zigzags down steeply, to join Beinn na Caillich's east ridge below its steep section.

At the 450m contour the ridge steepens again; here the path heads briefly down onto the right (Loch Leven) side, then crosses the crest and heads down northeast. It is quite steep and eroded down to a footbridge over **Allt Nathrach**. It continues up to a kissing gate, and continues as a peaty trod to join the West Highland Way track above.

Turn right and retrace the outward route along this track. You can return along the West Highland Way path of the outward route. If the sun is setting along Loch Leven, you may prefer to stay high. So continue along the track, past a radio mast. At **Mamore Lodge** turn downhill. At the first bend below the hotel a path forks down left. It crosses the Allt Coire na Ba at a footbridge, then descends gently for 150 metres to a waymarked junction. Turn downhill on a steep zigzag path to the Grey Mare's Tail **waterfall**, then return for 100 metres to cross a footbridge with the **car park** just beyond.

ROUTE 42
Kinlochleven's Pipeline Path

Start/Finish	Grey Mare's car park, Kinlochleven (NN 187 622)
Distance	11km/7 miles
Total ascent	450m/1500ft
Time	4hr
Terrain	Paths, sometimes small and steep, and track
Max altitude	High track 400m

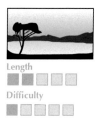

Length
Difficulty

With the closure of Kinlochleven's aluminium works, funding came for a network of waymarked walks by woodland and riverside and on the lower slopes of the mountains. Where those mountains are the Mamores, even the low slopes are rather high. This walk takes you to a waterfall that'll be just as good whether it's swollen with rain or a mass of winter icicles. Above, you'll wander the 300m contour with a view past the Pap of Glencoe along one of Scotland's loveliest sea lochs.

Start along the smooth path at the back of the car park, turning up left signed for Grey Mare's waterfall. The main path soon drops

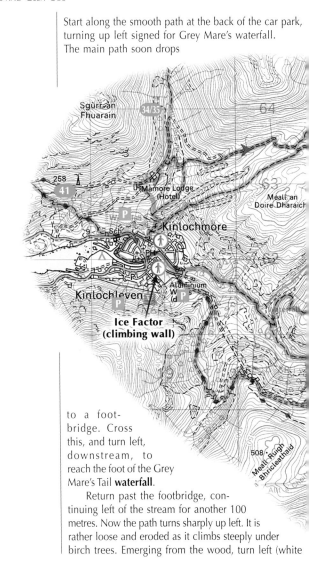

Ice Factor (climbing wall)

to a foot-
bridge. Cross
this, and turn left,
downstream, to
reach the foot of the Grey
Mare's Tail **waterfall**.

Return past the footbridge, continuing left of the stream for another 100
metres. Now the path turns sharply up left. It is
rather loose and eroded as it climbs steeply under
birch trees. Emerging from the wood, turn left (white

arrow) on a path under two sets of electric wires. The path rises gently to a wooden footbridge above a waterfall, then zigzags up towards a white house with dormers. The slope eases under larch and rhododendron to a tarred track. Turn right, uphill for 50 metres past **Mamore Lodge** (former hotel).

Turn right at a track T-junction just above. When this leads to the Stalkers' Cottage, a footpath sign marks a way round to right of the buildings, rejoining the track beyond. After another 150 metres, short cut the track's dogleg up Coire na

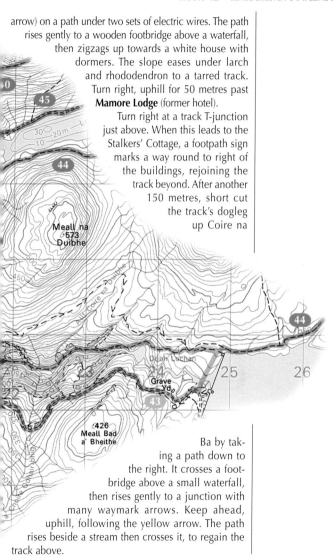

Ba by taking a path down to the right. It crosses a footbridge above a small waterfall, then rises gently to a junction with many waymark arrows. Keep ahead, uphill, following the yellow arrow. The path rises beside a stream then crosses it, to regain the track above.

*Grey Mare's
Tail waterfall*

Turn right. After 1km, a path down right (NN 208 635) would take you back to Kinlochleven but is rather steep and eroded. In another 100 metres, the track reaches a pass with a view ahead to Loch Eilde Mor.

Keep on down the track for another 400 metres, when a cairn marks a path on the right. It crosses stepping stones, then forks right (the smaller left fork just leads to the loch shore). The path bends round to right of a knoll, to the dam across the loch's outflow.

Cross the dam, and turn right on a narrow muddy track that runs above a concrete waterpipe. After 1.8km

Na Gruagaichean, Binnein Mor, and Sgor Eilde Mor, from Loch Eilde Mor dam

the track crosses the pipe to run below it; 200 metres later, look out for the cairn where the path turns steeply down to the right.

The path zigzags down into birchwood, becoming rather rough. At the slope foot, turn right on a much gentler path. This runs above the **River Leven**, with a long wooden footbridge across a side stream with a waterfall.

Just outside Kinlochleven bear left on the main path to a junction of tracks. Keep ahead following a West Highland Way marker along Wades Road. ▶ In 50 metres bear left on a path under larches beside the river, soon to join the tarred path of the West Highland Way. Keep ahead under the road bridge of the B863, to a tarred path continuing along the right bank of the River Leven.

Ahead now would lead back to the car park.

The path bends right, past black garages, to an earth path that follows Kinlochleven's other river, Allt Coire na Ba, upstream. It runs under hazels to join a street. Turn left to cross the main B863 road into Wades Road, which leads back to the **car park**.

ROUTE 43
Blackwater Dam

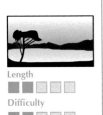

Length

■ ■ □ □ □

Difficulty

■ ■ □ □ □

Start/Finish	Behind Ice Factor, Kinlochleven (NN 189 619)
Distance	16.5km/10 miles
Total ascent	400m/1300ft
Time	4½hr
Terrain	Path and track
Max altitude	Blackwater Dam 340m
Parking	Parking alongside River Leven past the Ice Factor (ice-climbing wall), or a formal car park behind the Visitor Centre library (NN 187 618)

In an area where low-level walks are rare, this is, quite simply, the good one. It leads through beautiful woodlands into rugged country, with an easy return along a high track.

See map in Route 42.

◀ Start along the track to right of River Leven, past the old aluminium works, to turn left across the river on a track bridge. Opposite the end of a track into Kinlochleven (Wades Road) turn right up a small path.

Keep ahead on this path. After 1.2km it crosses the footbridge of **Allt na h-Eilde**, then climbs. ◀ Keep ahead, following the river valley, with a waterfall high on the other side, whose flow depends on water being released at the top of the hydro pipe.

At its high point, a path from above left joins, the Pipeline Path (Route 42).

The path descends gently to a riverside meadow, passing concrete pillars and foundations of prisoner-of-war huts from World War II. The path continues in woods above the river, and is very beautiful. It dips into a little gorge, with a fallen bridge, but an easy crossing anyway unless in spate. Then it climbs onto moorland, where it passes above the two **Dubh Lochans** to join the high pipeline from Loch Eilde. After 500 metres, you arrive at the corner of **Blackwater Reservoir**.

The walkway across the dam has low but pad-locked gates. Many walkers cross anyway (and the Scottish access law includes a presumption in favour of dam tops). One alternative is to head down concrete and bare rock along the dam foot; otherwise retreat 15 metres along the approach path and turn left onto a small path along the down-valley edge of scattered birch below the dam.

At the wide swathe of bare rock that's the valley's occasional waterway, the small path is lost. Cross into scattered birch on crushed rock. Below the centre of the dam is a fenced hut. From this a faint track runs to the right, soon joining a clearer one, which in turn joins the main track running up to the southern end of the dam.

Follow this track, and its culvert, down-valley. After a stream crossing, a knoll on the right has the low concrete gravestones of some of the navvies who built the dam. ▶

The track follows the conduit; you can walk on either. At the hydro pipe top, the West Highland Way's broad path joins from up on the left. The track ahead winds downhill through woods, with some short-cut paths at zigzags. It passes below a small, high dam, then rejoins the pipeline, and crosses it just above the old aluminium works. Keep ahead on the track to River Leven and the **Ice Factor**.

One of the gravestones is labelled as 'unknown'. The men were buried as they died in their mud-stained work clothing, their cheeks unshaven.

ROUTE 44

The Back of the Blackwater

Start/Finish	Behind Ice Factor, Kinlochleven (NN 189 619)
Distance	26.5km/16½ miles
Total ascent	1150m/3800ft
Time	9½hr
Terrain	Paths, rough grassy hillsides
Max altitude	Glas Bheinn 792m

Length

Difficulty

Away from the main mountain areas, this is a taste of the wild moorland. The ground is pathless, the solitude complete. You'll grab a Corbett, 2597ft Glas Bheinn, and even one from the next lower category of hill heights, a Graham, 2120ft Beinn na Cloiche. This long ramble into the back country can be made into an easy two-dayer using the bothy at Loch Chiarain.

See also map in Route 42.

◀ Start by following Route 43 to the north end of Blackwater Dam.

Cross the culvert arriving from the left, and follow sketchy paths above the shore of **Blackwater Reservoir**. A better path soon forms, about 200 metres in from the reservoir. It bends left alongside the small river Allt an Inbhir. After 500 metres there's a Celtic cross monument visible on the opposite side. As the river turns north, the path crosses it and keeps its previous direction, northeast,

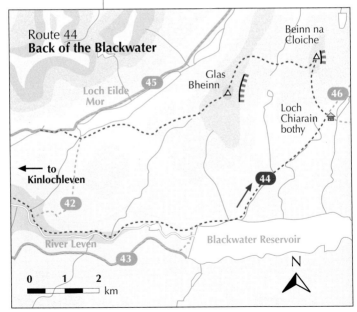

Glas Bheinn above Loch Eilde Mor

over a spur. Still northeast it drops slightly to join a new stream; follow it briefly, then contour to the bothy at the foot of **Loch Chiarain** (13km; 4½hr). ▸

The bothy has working fireplaces, so it's worth carrying in some fuel.

Go straight up the grassy slope behind the bothy, northwest at first, with the uphill direction bending imperceptibly right (north) to the summit of **Beinn na Cloiche**. This has outcrops, pools, and a small cairn.

Head down southwest for 400 metres/5mins, then turn down right, west, to cross the valley floor 500 metres to right of Lochan Tom Ailein. This lets you take the slope opposite to right of its steepest part. After a stiff climb, reach the smoothly rounded northern ridge of **Glas Bheinn** and proceed pleasantly and gently up it to the well-built summit cairn.

Descend gentle slopes southwest. These get rough and heathery below 550m, so aim to join the stalkers' path at its closest point. Turn right along it; the path is washed out in places. After crossing the southern slopes of Meall Beag (Point 561m), it drops to contour pleasantly above **Loch Eilde Mor** to its southwest corner. ▸

For a longer but beautiful continuation, divert now to Route 42, the Pipeline Path.

Cross the dam at the beginning of the pipeline to Blackwater. The path bends round right and back left to join a track. Turn up left for 600 metres through a broad col, then turn off left on clear well-built path that climbs slightly onto a ridgeline. The path then descends rather steeply and eroded, eventually in woods.

After a gate through a deer fence, a path to the right leads to the Grey Mare's Tail **waterfall**. Otherwise keep ahead, to join a wide path that in a few steps reaches the Grey Mare's car park in **Kinlochleven**. Turn left along Wade's Road to a track bridge over River Leven, with the walk start just downstream.

ROUTE 45
Loch Eilde Mor to Lairig Leacach

Start	Grey Mare's car park, Kinlochleven (NN 187 622)
Finish	Spean Bridge (NN 222 817)
Distance	30km/18½ miles
Total ascent	650m/2200ft
Time	2 short days (9hr walking time)
Terrain	Tracks and path
Max altitude	Meall Mor col 600m
Transport	Citylink coach Spean Bridge to Fort William, then local bus to Kinlochleven

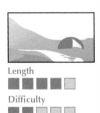

Length

■ ■ ■ ■ □

Difficulty

■ ■ □ □ □

The one problem with this route is the river crossing at Luibeilt, difficult after rain and impossible after heavy rain. Otherwise it's the easiest through route in the area, nearly all on smooth tracks. While it passes through seriously remote country, it does have two bothies for shelter. A good choice for a first-ever backpack trip – just so long as the river isn't in spate.

A worthy pre-amble would be to cross from Kings House to Kinlochleven by the Devil's Staircase of the West Highland Way. This is equal to the main walk in easiness and scenery, and gives a short first day to shops and shelter. It's also convenient, as Kings House and Spean Bridge are served by one Citylink coach.

See overview map Ben Nevis & Glen Coe north.

◀ Start from Grey Mare's car park, and follow paths of Route 33 up to the high track below Na Gruagaichean. Turn right, after 2km passing through a col. The track then passes to left of **Loch Eilde Mor** and **Loch Eilde Beag**, before ending at the ruined house at **Luibeilt** (11.5km, 4hr).

Just upstream from the house is the crossing point of the Abhainn Rath, on jagged red boulders. If the river is too full, the first option is to head 6km downstream past Staoineag bothy to the bridge at **Creaguaineach Lodge**; then take either Route 5 to **Corrour station** or Route 24 to **Spean Bridge**. The second option is to head upstream, crossing further up or switching into Route 5 out to **Glen Nevis** (22km, 5½hr, Luibeilt to Fort William). All of these are fine walks.

Having successfully crossed Abhainn Rath, the bothy at **Meanach** is over on the right. But the path of this route turns left upstream briefly, then heads up, north, beside **Allt nam Fang**. The path is old but still fairly firm and dry, and the stream alongside has waterfalls. As the stream dwindles and then turns away north, the path keeps ahead, northeast, through a wide flat col. It crosses Allt Feith nan Sac and other streams, as it slants down around the flank of Stob Ban to reach **Lairig Leacach bothy** (17.5km, 6hr).

A track runs north through the steep-sided **Lairig Leacach** pass, and down through a plantation. Back in the open, it descends grassland to **Coirechoille** and the end of a tarred lane below. Thus runs alongside River Spean for 3km to **Spean Bridge**. ▸

For a slightly longer finish through woodland see Route 24.

Meanach bothy, intersection of many long paths. Aonach Beag above

ROUTE 46

Gleann Iolairean or Leum Uilleim to Corrour

Start	Behind Ice Factor, Kinlochleven (NN 189 619)
Finish	Corrour station (NN 355 664)
Distance	24km/15 miles via Treig; 22.5km/14 miles via Uilleim
Total ascent	600m/2000ft via Treig; 1050m/3500ft via Uilleim
Time	1 day or 2 short ones (7½hr via Treig; 8½hr via Uilleim)
Terrain	Rough paths and grassy hillsides
Max altitude	Leum Uilleim 902m

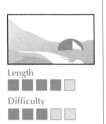

Length
■ ■ ■ ■ □

Difficulty
■ ■ ■ □ □

This is rougher backpacking than Route 45 (Loch Eilde Mor), with a path that vanishes here and there. After a green beginning to the Blackwater Dam, it passes through bleak and unpeopled country and a bothy that really is at the back of beyond. Consult the overview map to see how this can also be a trail to Glen Nevis or Spean Bridge.

Leum Uilleim is a grassy hump with great views. With the cloud down, you'd probably prefer the dramatic little valley to Loch Treig.

See overview map Ben Nevis & Glen Coe north.

◀ Start by following Route 43 to the north end of Blackwater Dam.

Cross the end of the culvert arriving from the left, and turn right on sketchy paths along or just above the shore of **Blackwater Reservoir**. A better path soon forms – a lapsed stalkers' path – about 200 metres away from the reservoir. It bends left alongside the small river Allt an Inbhir. As the river turns north, the path crosses it and keeps its previous direction, northeast, over a spur. Still northeast it drops slightly to join a new stream, follows it briefly, then contours to the bothy at the foot of **Loch Chiarain** (13km, 4½hr). ◀

The bothy has a fireplace, so it's worth carrying in fuel.

142

To Corrour by Loch Treig

In bad weather, or if your destination is not Corrour but Fort William or Spean Bridge, then continue above the bothy on a path that at once drops to the side of Loch Chiarain. Along the valley that follows, the path sometimes disappears as it crosses the firm stony grass of a stream run-off. Keep along the foot of the left-hand slope and the path should reappear.

As the slope on the left steepens across the foot of **Meall a' Bhainne**, the path rises about 10–20m above the valley floor. It is mostly firm and quite comfortable. Once through the pass, the path (now boggy) runs down to left of a new stream, and joins the track by **Loch Treig** at a SRWS green signpost towards you saying 'Kinlochleven' (19km from Kinlochleven; 6hr walking time).

Here you would turn left for Fort William (Route 5, 28.5km, 7½hr to Fort William) or for Spean Bridge (Route 24, 19.5km, 5½hr). For Corrour, turn right across a bridge. After a second bridge the track turns uphill away from the reservoir. After 2km it turns left, passing under the railway by a bridge which also has a stream passing under it.

For Corrour station: don't pass under the railway, but keep ahead over the stream, and take a green track that keeps to right of the railway. The track fades to a rough, soggy path; then joins a nice firm one for the last 500m to **Corrour station**.

The lonely setting of Creaguanich Lodge, at the head of Loch Treig

For Loch Ossian youth hostel: stay on the track as it passes under the railway alongside the stream, then reappears across the stream running southeast around the flank of Beinn na Lap. After 2km you can fork right onto a rough old track, or keep ahead on the smooth new one. Either way, you join a big track at the head of **Loch Ossian**, with the **youth hostel** just ahead and Corrour station 1km up to the right.

To Corrour by Leum Uilleim

From **Loch Chiarain** it's almost as easy to get to Corrour over the Corbett Leum Uilleim (less distance, more climb). Or if you're overnighting in the bothy, you can make an afternoon up-and-down of this undemanding hill.

Cross stepping-stones below the bothy at the foot of Loch Chiarain. Even if the stones are underwater, this wide sandy bit of river is the best wading point. Above the stepping-stones there's a small path, which is most welcome as it gets you up into the zone of shorter grass. Moderate grassy slopes lead up to the preliminary top **Beinn a' Bhric**. Its final ridge has small outcrops of orange rock (dykes of porphyry).

From the small cairn on Beinn a' Bhric you may need to take a compass bearing to avoid being carried down slopes southwards. Make a way east down a short, quite steep slope to reach a wide col. Head east up the slope opposite to summit **Leum Uilleim** with its fair-sized cairn with small shelter arms.

Retrace your steps westwards into the wide col. Contour round right, eventually north, below the northeast ridge of Beinn a' Bhric, finding quad-bike wheelmarks. The quad-bike trail climbs very slightly, to reach the crest of the northeast ridge, and goes straight down it. The faint track over short grass and moss is a very pleasant stroll. The wheelmarks lead to a small cairn at the ridge tip (**An Diollaid**), then bear down to the right. Across the moorland below the going becomes peaty and swampy; then abruptly a well-surfaced path starts. It takes you across the **Allt Coire a' Bhric Beag**, and reaches the railway and **Corrour station**.

6 GLEN COE

Glen Coe runs in between craggy walls of Aonach Eagach (left) and Bidean nam Bian

Glen Coe, Glen Coe – it's the place to go. Nowhere else in Britain has such a concentration of top mountains. Having been up Bidean nam Bian for this book four more times, I'll say there's no other hill with such richness of interest. The summit summary for Bidean nam Bian is in Part 7.

But then there's Beinn a' Bheithir, the Thunderbolt, a classic high ridge-line. There's Buachaille Etive Mor, the mountain for climbers of rock and ice, but still supplying another lovely ridgeline behind its classic pointed pyramid. There's Buachaille Beag, with the same atmosphere but on a smaller and more approachable scale. And looking at them all from across the glen is the thrilling ridge of the Aonach Eagach, the hillwalkers' mountaineering bit.

What the glen doesn't have is attractive low-level walks. Routes 49 and 50 (Signal Rock and the Hospital Loch) are short and rather tame. Route 58 (Lost Valley) is short, but is at least adventurous. Route 56 (the Two Passes) is, if you catch it in the week when the bogs dry out, a long and satisfying plod. All these are ways of resting the legs before the next fierce, fantastic, big hill.

ROUTE 47
The Thunderbolt: Beinn a' Bheithir

Length
■ ■ ■ □ □

Difficulty
■ ■ ■ ■ □

Start/Finish	Ballachulish (NN 083 584)
Distance	15.5km/9½ miles
Total ascent	1300m/4400ft
Time	7–7½hr
Terrain	Ridge paths, but a rough descent
Max altitude	Sgorr Dhearg 1024m

Beinn a' Bheithir means Hill of the Thunderbolt – and it's certainly a cracker. This is classic ridgewalking, pleasantly narrow in parts, but without scrambling. (If you want scrambling, Sgorr Bhan's northeast ridge is Grade 1.) There's an easy descent from between the two Munro summits, but this route completes the horseshoe beyond Sgorr Dhonuill, with a steep descent into Coire Dearg.

Beinn a' Bheithir, the Hill of the Thunderbolt. The Munros are Sgorr Dhearg (back left) and Sgorr Dhonuill (right)

Start at the information centre and car park at the east end of Ballachulish village (East Laroch) below a slate quarry face.

Leave the car park by its entrance, and take the village street opposite (southwest) past a useful Co-op shop. After 500 metres the street crosses **River Laroch**, with a footbridge alongside. Turn left, following an SRWS

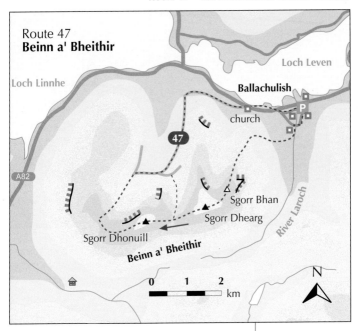

Route 47
Beinn a' Bheithir

Loch Linnhe

Loch Leven

Ballachulish

church

47

A82

Sgorr Bhan

Sgorr Dhearg

Sgorr Dhonuill

Beinn a' Bheithir

River Laroch

0   1   2
km

N

signpost with its writing on the back, to pass a primary school. Just after it, a gate on the right leads onto open hill.

Go straight up quite steep grass, to a low fence crossing at 250m. Not far above (depending on where you crossed the fence) a small path runs across to the right, onto the northern spur of Sgorr Bhan. The path turns left up this. It is fairly eroded, often down to bare rock (grey schist).

After the levelling of Beinn Bhan, the ridge steepens, with one path taking to the right flank – but following the crest is good. The rock changes to quartzite, whence 'Sgorr Bhan' (white peak). A sharp elegant ridge leads to **Sgorr Bhan**, and then to the first Munro, **Sgorr Dhearg**.

In mist you might be tempted onto a sharp, pathed, ridge running north – but the correct path turns left,

Sgorr Dhonuill from the slopes of Sgorr Dhearg

Here a popular descent route runs down north into the forest.

southwest, down a broader slope to the 757m col. ◄ The ridge path continues ahead, quite steeply at first. After a knoll at 950m, where the side ridge to Point 782m (the Dragon's Tooth) branches off, a narrower and slightly rocky ridge leads up to **Sgorr Dhonuill**.

Descend a wide ridge west, with drops on the right and views of islands ahead (Lismore, Mull, Jura). At the ridge base (NN 031 554), a gully down right has a cairn at its head. Easier is to continue 100 metres over the next slight rise to the next dip. Turn right to confront the drop into Coire Dearg (NN 030 555), then slant down left, passing along the base of a small crag, to the top of a wide scree slope. Directly below is a gully cleft. Pass straight down the scree to just above the cleft (NN 0310 5573 – a lone Sitka spruce grows in the scree). Now slant down left, still on scree, for 100 metres to a clump of Sitka spruce. Descend directly to the grassy corrie floor. Keep directly downhill, through fence remains, and pick up a rebuilt path that starts at a boulder (NN 0327 5609). It runs into forest to left of a stream, and follows it to the corner of a forest road.

Turn right (blue marker arrow), and follow the main track gently downhill. Above South Ballachulish keep ahead with a waymark for St John's Church. From **St John's Church**, follow the pavement of the A82 to the edge of **Ballachulish village**. Move right, onto the old main road running parallel. Before the junction on the outward route (near the Co-op), turn left into a street that bends right then offers a short path between trees into the car park.

ROUTE 48
Meall Lighiche and Sgor na h-Ulaidh

Start/Finish	Parking 200 metres east of Gleann Leac na Muidhe track end (NN 120 563)
Distance	14.5km/9 miles
Total ascent	1100m/3700ft
Time	6½hr
Terrain	Grassy ridges, a steep, broken hillside, path and track
Max altitude	Sgor na h-Ulaidh 994m

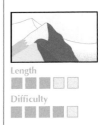

Length
■ ■ ■ □ □

Difficulty
■ ■ ■ ■ □

Gleann Leac na Muidhe is green and fertile, as the name 'Slab of the Milk-churn' suggests. Here was the home of the MacDonalds' chieftain in the days before the Massacre. At its head lies Sgor na h-Ulaidh, one of the less-visited Munros. Its 'standard' route, a straight up-and-down from the upper glen, is used here for the descent – the little path beside the stream is a delight. Fiercer is the first half of the day, with extra effort added by the Corbett Meall Lighiche, followed by a steep ascent to the main mountain.

Start up the smooth track into **Gleann Leac na Muidhe** (private road, no parking). The track crosses a bridge to houses. Keep on the track, past a farm, to its end at a gate below a plantation corner (NN 106 545; the route can be cycled to this point).

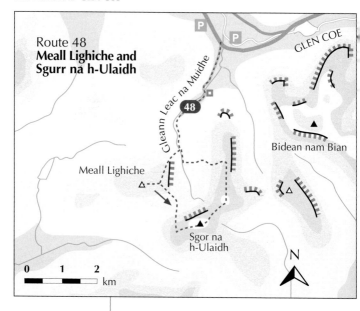

A rough path continues ahead. Where it approaches the stream after 200 metres, cross at an island – the footbridge on old maps has been swept away. Head up onto the spur of Creag Bhan. Turn left along the crest, with the first knoll offering scrambling (bypassed down right if necessary). Grassy wide ridgeline leads up to the top of Creag Bhan, where the ridge levels and bends right (west). Now a small path and old metal fence stakes lead over a preliminary knoll to the small cairn at the summit of **Meall Lighiche**.

Return along the old fence to the end of the level section, then follow the fence down right, quite steeply, to a broad col. Here the fence has a former gateway (NN 104 524). Above, the fence runs up to crags, so stop following it and head away slightly to the right, south. Slant up steep ground, to right of a small stream to start with. At 750m head straight uphill, southeast, on steep grass. As a slight re-entrant forms, keep to its right-hand side (west)

to reach the ridge-end knoll **Corr na Beinne** (NN 1055 5164). Follow the easy ridge eastwards, level at first, soon joined from below by the fence remnant, to the summit of **Sgor na h-Ulaidh**.

Sgurr na h-Ulaidh and Meal Lighiche seen from Beinn a' Bheithir

Head east for 100 metres, then turn northeast down a fairly well defined ridgeline. As it steepens, take a path down the left flank (northeast, not east-northeast down the crest) to reach the col below. The ridgeline opposite leads on up onto Stob an Fhuarain.

Head down north, on ridgeline not clearly defined but with path traces, to the col at the start of Aonach Dubh a' Ghlinne. Here turn left (west) to head straight down grassy slopes and join the stream below. A charming small path follows the right bank of the stream back to the gate at the plantation corner.

IN REVERSE

When descending northwest from Ulaidh people have got into difficulties among crags. If attempting this, follow the west ridge right out to Corr na Beinne; even from there, it's tricky.

151

ROUTE 49
Signal Rock

Length

Difficulty

Start/Finish	An Torr car park (NN 127 564)
Distance	2.5km/1½ miles
Total ascent	150m/500ft
Time	1hr
Terrain	Paths
Max altitude	An Torr 100m

The Signal Rock was used to gather Clan MacDonald in the centuries before the Massacre. It is an atmospheric spot, even if the views would benefit from some clear-felling. So short a walk scarcely needs the pub break after the first mile – but it could be a summer evening stroll after a Clachaig pub meal.

Start at An Torr car park where the Glencoe Visitor Centre once stood (considered intrusive, it has been resited 2km down the valley). A tarred path runs to a footbridge over the **River Coe**. Across it, turn back up left, through a gate in a deer fence. The wide path runs into woods, after 100 metres forking, with ahead marked with blue/black topped posts (right, with black/yellow markers, is for Clachaig Inn).

Take the path ahead, over a ridge and down to a path junction. The wide main path to the right is signed 'Signal Rock'. At a fork, bear left (blue post). The path crosses a glacier-scratched rock (the glacier's direction was 8 o'clock to 2 o'clock relative to today's path). Then it passes out through a gate in a deer fence, across a faint track, and up to **Signal Rock**. Scramble the front, or take a path around the knoll to steps at the back. ◀

Return through the deer fence and over the glaciated rock to the path junction. Turn down left (black marker) – ignore a gate ahead but turn down right across a stream. Where the path is faint under trees, keep uphill to the top of An Torr.

Turn down left – schist underfoot is thinly covered with earth. ◀ The path soon meets a wider crossing path.

We are 1km outside the Glencoe ring-fault, on the grey schist 'country rock'.

A boulder on the left is not squiggly schist: the unmossed underside shows dark andesite, brought down-valley by the glacier.

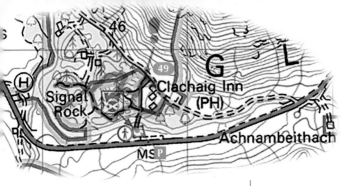

Turn left, through a gate in a deer fence, to reach the road through a kissing gate.

map scale 1:25,000

Turn right past **Clachaig Inn**, to a road sign (clearway) just after its car park. Here turn off right on a smooth path beside a stream to the footbridge across River Coe and back to the **car park**.

ROUTE 50

Glencoe Lochan

Start/Finish	Glencoe Lochan car park (NN 1045 93)
Distance	2.5km/1½ miles
Total ascent	100m/300ft
Time	1hr
Terrain	Smooth paths
Max altitude	110m
Parking	At the east edge of Glencoe village, the main street crosses the River Coe. At once, a tarred driveway on the left is marked with a forest walks signboard. Drive up it, and where it bends left to Glencoe House keep ahead on a forest road signed for the car park.

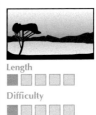

Length
■ ☐ ☐ ☐ ☐

Difficulty
■ ☐ ☐ ☐ ☐

153

A short walk on pre-laid paths through woodland designed in imitation of the great forests of America. It also involves a wooded lochan, and great views of Loch Leven and Beinn a' Bheithir. Glencoe Lochan was formerly 'Hospital Lochan'.

Start at the trail signboard. The simple path around the main lochan is waymarked with 'Red Indian' feathers, because of a story (which you can read on the signboard) about Lord Strathcona and his quarter-native-American homesick wife. But head out of the car park uphill, following the blue-top posts of the Mountain Path, immediately turning right and climbing. After quite a stiff ascent the path contours left to a viewpoint with a picnic table. Past this it drops to the side of **Glencoe Lochan**.

Turn right around the lochan, following the red waymarks. Pass across the end of the lochan and down its northwest side to its west corner. The car park is ahead around the lochan,

Glencoe Lochan, with Beinn a' Bheithir

but turn right, now following yellow-top posts. The path wanders through woods, gradually bending left. On the right a short side-path branches off to a viewpoint bench – the view is to Beinn a' Bheithir. The path bends left away from the sea view, through woods, clear and waymarked. Ignore a smaller side-path down right. The path

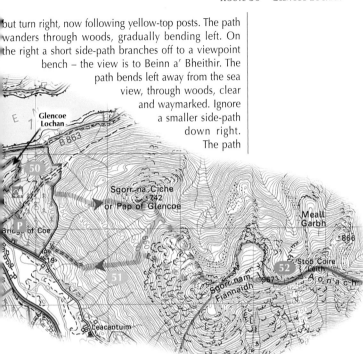

descends to a cross-track (left to the lochan, right to Glencoe House). Cross it to pass a rhododendron-and-lily pool, and regain the **car park**.

ROUTE 51
Pap of Glencoe

Length
■ ■ ☐ ☐ ☐

Difficulty
■ ■ ■ ■ ☐

Start/Finish	Glencoe Lochan car park (NN 104 593)
Distance	6.5km/4 miles
Total ascent	750m/2500ft
Time	3½hr
Terrain	Steep rough hillsides and paths
Max altitude	Pap of Glencoe 742m
Parking	See Route 50

It's not just the name that's provocative; this is the area's outstanding small hill, with rocks at the top making some scrambling likely. You could include Sgorr nam Fiannaidh for a walk of 9km with 1100m climb (5½ miles, 3600ft, 5hr), then get the second of Aonach Eagach's Munros, with hardly any Aonach Eagach scrambling, by Route 53.

See map in Route 50.

◄ Start back towards the public road for 300 metres. Just before the bend right to the public road, a clear small path heads up left, to right of a stream, passing through a narrow gateway in old fencing. At a forest road the continuing path is now to left of the stream. It climbs steeply, crosses another forest road then runs along a clearing under low-voltage power lines. At the high point of the wires (NN 111 596) a small, soggy path turns up right, under trees. It reaches the forest top at a fence bend without a stile (NN 1124 5954).

Turn right on a small path above the trees, then head uphill to a levelling. A dry stream on the right has paths alongside. At the stream top the path contours southwest towards the Pap-back col, but head left up the rough hillside. At the foot of the final outcrops, you may find the old path giving one easy way through to the rocky summit of **Pap of Glencoe**.

A slightly trodden direct descent southeast involves some easy scrambling. Easier is to descend northeast towards Loch Leven for 50 metres, when the path turns back right along the foot of the outcrops. (The two routes rejoin at NN 1255 5932.) Various paths zigzag stonily down to the wide Pap-back col. ▸

A path of stones and peat runs down to the right, crossing a small stream then slanting down and left (south). At the 430m contour it turns back right and improves, to run down to left of a ravine. At the ravine foot, take the path contouring right to a smooth track, and descend this to the road near a plantation edge.

Turn right, and after 400 metres fork left onto a riverside path to the **car park** turn-off.

The Pap of Glencoe, with Sgorr nam Fiannaidh

To bag Sgorr nam Fiannaidh now, head straight up the pathless ridge opposite, then east along gentle ridge. Descend using Route 52.

ROUTE 52
Aonach Eagach

Length
■ ■ ■ □ □

Difficulty
■ ■ ■ ■ ■

(scramble Grade 2)

Start	Allt-na-reigh (NN 173 567)
Finish	Old road near Glencoe village (NN 111 585)
Distance	8.5km/5½ miles (plus 7km/4½ miles valley floor back to start)
Total ascent	1200m/4000ft
Time	6–7hr (+ 1½hr valley floor)
Terrain	Exposed scrambling (Grade 2) on good rock
Max altitude	Sgorr nam Fiannaidh 967m

The Aonach Eagach, or Notched Ridge, links the two Munro hills on the north side of Glen Coe – so much so that the names of the actual hills, Sgorr nam Fiannaidh and Meall Dearg, are almost unknown.

Glen Coe's many excellent scrambling routes are well described in Cicerone's *Scrambles in Lochaber* (see Appendix D) and so are not covered here. However, as one of the most popular and best ridges in Scotland, the Aonach Eagach has to be included.

While it is not technically difficult, the hardest section has truly terrifying drops on both sides. *Scrambles in Lochaber* gives it a Grade 2 – implying that a rope would not normally be used in dry summer conditions – and I agree. Other authors have given it Grade 3, considering its exposure rather than actual difficulty. One even attaches Grade 3S, equivalent to a rock-climbing grade of Mod or Diff and certainly requiring the protection of a rope; that author must have taken the difficult option at the end of the Crazy Pinnacles.

While many hundreds of people cross the ridge every year, one or two do come to grief. Most rescues involve walkers cragfast and unable to continue or retreat, or else benighted on the final descent from the ridge. Between 2003 and 2006 just two walkers fell from the ridge, one of them losing his life.

If the party includes the inexperienced or nervous, a short length of rope could be carried by a member who understands its use – 10m is enough to protect the end of the Crazy Pinnacles and the chimney pitch. That rope could be kept concealed in the rucksack so as not to cause premature alarm.

There is **no safe descent** off the ridge between Am Bodach and Stob Coire Leith, apart from the ridge of Meall Dearg running unhelpfully north towards Loch Leven. More helpfully, though: on a westbound crossing, up as far as the Crazy Pinnacles, the difficulties are all in descent. So if you do turn back, retreating eastwards from the Crazy Pinnacles will be easier than it was getting there.

Start up the rough path slanting right. After 20 metres is the start of path repairs (not from the car park itself, as that might encourage casual walkers). The path is rebuilt or on bare rock to 450m altitude.

Alternatively a **Grade 2 scramble**, from the Study straight up onto A' Chailleach, is described in *Scrambles in Lochaber*. Good when dry, but its mossy central section is slimy when wet.

Now the ridge steepens, with an outcrop just above. Here the path bends back left (a small path ahead is a

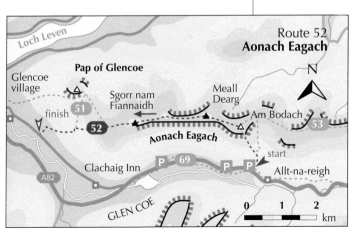

variant by Allt Ruigh's green valley). It zigzags northwest up the steep spur, with short sections over bare rock giving easy scrambling, finally becoming grassier and less steep to the first cairn on **Am Bodach**. Continue for 100 metres to a second cairn, at the true summit.

The ridge bends left (northwest) and narrows. Soon it steepens. Easy scrambling down the crest leads to a levelling. Here the well-trodden path descends on the right, by short rock steps and exposed ledges, then a gangway slants down left to a notch in the crest above a steep tower. Go through this notch, and down two moves of blocky scrambling, onto slabs to left (south) of the crest.

Scramblers enjoying the rock moves on Aonach Eagach

Take a ledge slanting down left to the slab's edge, then another ledge back right, to an old fence post at the base of the steep tower.

The path runs on along level ridge for a few steps, then descends bare rock on the left. There are various well-worn lines here, but the easiest one descends towards Glen Coe (south) straight down the ridge side, to a path running to the right. Descend a short slab step to regain the ridge crest at another fence post below the difficulties.

The path crosses a col northwest, and rises gently to a preliminary top (approx 920m, cairn). Here turn right, and descend a steep eroded slope to a col. Climb steep grass paths on the north flank, onto a grass ridge where old fence posts lead to the summit of **Meall Dearg**.

From here to Stob Coire Leith the ridge is narrow and almost continuously interesting. The way is well used and clear. Significant features are a narrow gully/chimney rising from a col; a gully descending to the right, with big holds on the rocks to its left; and a rock tower climbed on the left over a worn slab (look for a high handhold on the right for the awkward step onto the slab). A narrow arête leads to a sudden drop: just before this scramble down left, steep but with many handholds. Another narrow arête across a col is balanced along or avoided just down on the left.

After all this, the ridge narrows spectacularly to the so-called Crazy Pinnacles. A well-worn route passes to right of each of the pinnacles, to the col before a final 5m wall. The well-used direct ascent of this is a rock-climbing move of at least Moderate standard in an exposed situation. However, passing to the right will reveal an easier way on the north side, where some dampness of the rock is offset by largeness of handholds. ▸

There is an exposed path on loose dirt descending on the right (north) side, avoiding the Crazy Pinnacles; this looks less safe, and more difficult, than the rocky way described.

While the Crazy Pinnacles form the hardest section, three challenging moments remain along the ridge. A squarish rock tower is climbed by a shallow, open chimney on the left; as this steepens at its top, a fine final handhold is directly overhead. There's a long, slabby descent on outward-sloping ledges. At the lowest point of

Sgorr nam Fiannaidh, shot from Scotland's most scenic bus, the Citylink Skye to Glasgow

the ridge, a narrow col leads to a steep groove; after the first step, this becomes easy, and the dirty and exposed path avoiding it on the right again looks nastier.

The ridge path leads over quartzite rock of Stob Coire Leith (2–3hr from Am Bodach). It continues onto **Sgorr nam Fiannaidh**, where a stone trig pillar stands within a large shelter cairn.

The descent is where late or slow parties can get into difficulties. Continue west for 600 metres to a cairned col (NN 135 582).

STEEPEST DESCENT

The direct descent southwest, to right of Clachaig Gully to Clachaig Inn, is not recommended due to its steepness and looseness, and the risk of injuring oneself or others by falling stones. A way can be made down very steep slopes, southeast across the head of Alltan t-Sidhein and to the northern corner of Loch Achtriochtan.

The least uncomfortable descent is by a rough path roughly west (marked on Harveys map). From the cairned col, edge round to right of the final slight rise, to head directly towards Glencoe village, with the path gradually forming down stony quartzite slopes. At 480m (NN 124 586) turn left on a path descending from the **Pap of Glencoe**. This turns back right to descend beside a small gorge. Below the gorge, a path continuing downstream peters out in rough pastures, so take the path contouring right to join a track. This runs down to join the Old Glencoe Road at the end of plantations recently clear-felled.

There remains the 7km walk back to Allt-na-reigh. Two cars provide one solution, as does a strategically placed bicycle. However, the least disreputable-looking member of the party should be able to hitch-hike carrying the car keys, as most of the passing traffic is fellow walkers. Otherwise, the paths in Route 69 make fairly pleasant walking that avoids the busy A82.

ROUTE 53

Am Bodach and the End of the Aonach Eagach

Start/Finish	Altnafeadh (NN 220 563)
Distance	14km/8½ miles
Total ascent	1050m/3400ft
Time	6hr
Terrain	Gentle ridgewalking, with a steep descent. Excursion to Meall Dearg is scrambling Grade 2, fairly exposed
Max altitude	Am Bodach 943m

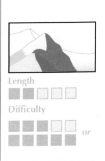

Length

Difficulty

or

Glen Coe abounds in high, demanding ridgewalks amidst spectacular surroundings. By contrast, A' Chailleach offers a ridgewalk over short, gentle vegetation and gravel, gently rising for 5km from the top of the Devil's Staircase. The surroundings, however, remain superb.

After Am Bodach, Meall Dearg could be reached by a first taster of the Aonach Eagach's scrambling.

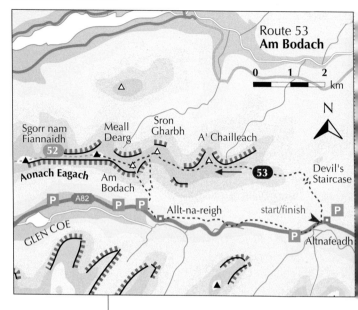

Start up the broad, smooth path of **Devil's Staircase**, usually companionable with West Highland Way walkers. It zigzags to a col. At the first of two cairns, turn left on a small rough path up gently onto **Stob Mhic Mhartuin**. Pleasant walking on smooth short grass and gravel, with occasional peat, leads to **Sron a' Choire Odhair-bhig**.

Rocky drops on the right add character to the still pleasant ridgeline onto A' Chailleach (**903m**, unnamed on most maps). ◄

This belongs to the obscure hill class called 'Metros', those that would be Munros if Munros started at 900m rather than 914.4m. Pinky-orange rhyolite boulders decorate its summit.

Grassy ridge continues to the col before **Sron Gharbh**. This summit could be bypassed left without difficulty. In the col beyond, a large cairn marks the possible descent path left to Allt Ruigh. For now take the well-used path, over stones or easy-angled bare rock, up to the main top of **Am Bodach**.

It is now possible to use Route 52 for an excursion to the Munro **Meall Dearg**. The descent from Am

164

Bodach is exposed, but with big holds and at a lower level of terror – and because it's downwards, retreat will always be less difficult than it was to get there. Allow 1½–2hr for the excursion and return to Am Bodach. Meall Dearg can also be reached without any scrambling but over rough ground, by its north ridge from the West Highland Way above Kinlochleven.

There are two descent routes from **Am Bodach** to the valley floor at Allt-na-reigh.

Allt Ruigh

Easier but less exciting. Return to the col before Sron Gharbh (NN 171 581). A cairn marks the top of a path down to the right.

This path is eroded for the first steep descent, then joins Allt Ruigh stream down grassy slopes. Paths now are on both sides of stream. Keep near the stream as the valley narrows, closed on the right by a small steep crag. At 500m altitude, the path contours out to the right across a steep slope towards this crag, zigzags down scree, then

On Am Bodach, looking along the Aonach Eagach

again contours to the right, along the crag's foot. Here it rises slightly, to join the spur path descending from the right.

Spur path

More rugged, this reverses Route 52. From **Am Bodach** summit, head south for 100 metres to a lower cairn. Now a clear path heads down the steep rocky spur, southeast. The path is well marked, weaving among outcrops and occasionally crossing bare rock. Below the lowest out-crop, at 500m altitude, bend right as the alternate path rejoins from the left.

The path on down is rebuilt with occasional stone steps, to the car park 200 metres west of Allt-na-reigh.

It is fairly easy for folk dressed for the hill to hitch-hike up the A82. However, it is also a reasonable walk of 5km back along the valley floor. Take a small path above the road to the cottage **Allt-na-reigh**, and cross below it on the road bridge. Take another small path on the left, to where the Old Glencoe Road (NN 180 564) forks up left. Follow this track past the viewpoint called the Study, rejoining the A82 about 1km later. Cross diagonally onto a path for 250 metres, then re-cross onto a wet grassy track that remains near the A82 for 2km, to a car park. The Old Road track continues to left of the road for another 200 metres. Use a small path down to right of the road for the last 400 metres to **Altnafeadh**.

ROUTE 54
Buachaille Etive Beag

Start/Finish	Near the Study (NN 188 562)
Distance	11km/7 miles
Total ascent	1100m/3700ft
Time	6hr
Terrain	Valley and ridge paths, and moderate grassy slopes
Max altitude	Stob Dubh 958m

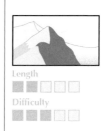

Length
■ ■ ☐ ☐ ☐

Difficulty
■ ■ ■ ☐ ☐

Buachaille Etive Beag means the 'Small Shepherd of Etive', but it's only small because of the company it keeps. Wedged between two of Glen Coe's giants, Bidean and Buachaille Mor, it can easily be passed over.

Better, however, to pass over it with your feet. It's a classic little ridge, technically undemanding but attractively sharp. In the original *Tables*, Buachaille Beag (being a single freestanding hill) was counted as a single Munro. But the second summit, Stob Coire Raineach, has 600ft (170m) of clear drop round it: considerably more than any other non-Munro. To the pedantic 20th century this seemed increasingly unsatisfactory, and from 1997 Buachaille Beag has been two Munros.

The standard way to get them is by a path out of Lairig Eilde to the Mam Buidhe col between; up left for Stob Coire Raineach; up right for Stob Dubh; and back down the path. But the proper way to do a ridgewalk is along the ridge, so this route heads up the long pass of Lairig Eilde, to complete the classic ridge end-to-end. This gives a very scenic ascent, with views along the fjord of Loch Etive. The northwestern facet holds long streaks of snow right through the winter, which can offer a fast and exhilarating descent. Indeed, the 'Wee Buachaille' is an excellent choice for a first winter Munro.

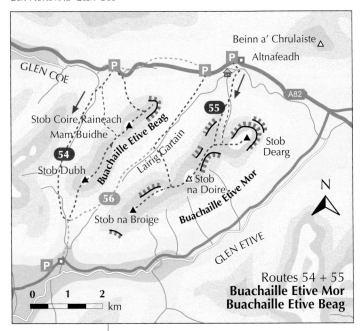

Routes 54 + 55
Buachaille Etive Mor
Buachaille Etive Beag

See also larger-scale mapping at Route 56.

The cairn doesn't commemorate the Massacre, nor the acquisition by the National Trust for Scotland, but marks the start of the coffin road through Lairig Eilde.

◄ Start from the car park at the large domed cairn, just east of where the A82 enters a ravine at the Meeting of Three Waters. ◄

A well-made signposted path climbs gently south-west. After 600 metres it dips right, towards the river 100 metres away. (At this point the 'standard route' continues ahead on a small side-path, after 400 metres turning up left between two streams to the Mam Buidhe col south-west of Stob Coire Raineach.)

The main path drops slightly to cross Allt Lairig Eilde on monster stepping-stones. After 1.5km it recrosses, and climbs gently to its high-point, which is 200 metres east of the actual Lairig Eilde col. The path descends south, to cross the new stream (also called Allt Lairig Eilde) and go down to right of it. At 300m (NN 1717 5239) cross the stream above its small gorge, onto

a small path slanting down across the grassy face above the stream, and contour round onto the grassy nose running up northwards.

A small but clear path runs straight up the ridge, which becomes a narrow grass crest. Its steepness demands pauses to look southwards along the gleaming length of Loch Etive. At the 600m contour a boulder has retained a small platform of level ground, ideal for a brief rest or longer lunchstop. ▶

Above this, the spur runs up into scree – tiresome in summer, better if snow-covered. A short section of stony ridge leads to **Stob Dubh** (Black Spike), which at 958m is the main summit of Buachaille Etive Beag.

The ridge runs down northeast, and after 200 metres it steepens. This north-facing slope gets less sun than the ground you've been on, and any snow may suddenly become harder at this point. This narrower ridge can carry a cornice, more commonly on the right-hand side. After this first descent, the ridge undulates gently. A long, gently angled, descent leads to the low col of **Mam Buidhe** ('mam bui', the yellow pass, unnamed on some maps at NN 187 544).

Looking along Glen Etive from Stob Dubh of Buachaille Beag

From this point the author has watched a herd of about 100 red deer cross the ridgeline below.

169

*Buachaille Etive
Beag (Stob Dubh)
with Lochan Urr,
Glen Etive*

From here, a rough path down left is the normal approach to the mountain; your **escape line** if avalanches are forecast on northwest-facing slopes (such as this route's descent line off Stob Coire Raineach).

From Mam Buidhe a steeper climb leads to the summit of **Stob Coire Raineach**. Descend gently northeast onto a rocky plateau at 800m altitude. From here the descent will be northwest: but first wander out to Stob nan Cabar, a rocky viewpoint.

From Stob nan Cabar return across the rocky plateau to the foot of Stob Coire Raineach (NN 195 552). From here descend northwest. If there is snow, simply seek out the longest streaks for a bit of fun downhill. Otherwise a comfortable way down is to follow the small spur immediately to right of the stream (Allt Coire Raineach). Once below the steep rocky ground, slant left to the path of the outward route, or head straight downhill to the closest point of the **A82** road.

ROUTE 55
The Big Buachaille

Start/Finish	Altnafeadh (NN 220 563)
Distance	13.5km/8½ miles
Total ascent	1200m/4000ft
Time	6½hr
Terrain	Easy scrambling (Grade 1) or rough grass; hill paths
Max altitude	Stob Dearg 1022m

Length

■ ■ ■ □ □

Difficulty

■ ■ ■ ■ ■

(scramble Grade 1)

Seen from Kings House, Buachaille Etive Mor is an iconic hill; a cone of bare rock composed of exciting rock climbs divided by gullies filled with last winter's ice. But at the back, like the tail on a tadpole, is a fine 4km ridge for walkers. In 1996 that ridge was unpathed, and I had to find my own way down the steep, steep slope of Stob Coire Altruim. The following year, Stob na Broige at the far end was elevated to Munro status; consequently, by 2006 the path down was so eroded that it was ready to receive its first helicopter loads of repair stones.

The hill is very steep on all sides, making the ridgewalk along the top very fine. By the same token, getting on and off the ridge is not such fun. The new-built path is the only pleasant way off (a descent southeast into Etive from the western knoll, NN 179 518, is possible but not nice). The standard way up, by Coire na Tulaich, is an atmospheric trudge with a nasty steep scree (often snow-covered and sometimes avalanche prone) to finish. The alternative here, a ridge just to the west, offers rough grass or an easy scramble.

You may occasionally see the hill and its neighbour named as 'Buachaille Eite'. This is correct Gaelic, but the English name for over a century has been, like the glen it guards, Etive. 'Buachaille' is a cattle herdsman.

▶ Start at Altnafeadh, where a track leads down to a footbridge over the River Coupall. Continue on well-made path, past **Lagangarbh** cottage and up towards Coire na Tulaich, the corrie that's the standard walkers' route onto the Buachaille. To right of the corrie is a broad spur.

See map in Route 54 and 56.

Buachaille Etive Mor from Devil's Staircase, looking into Coire na Tulaich

Creag a' Bhancair, out of sight from here, is noted for its extremely difficult rock climbs.

Over the bottom half of this, the left side (next to Coire na Tulaich) is a ridge of rocky humps that form a Grade 3 scramble (the northeast ridge of Creag na Tulaich). To right of this is a band of steepish grass, and to right again a line of broken rocks. These rocks will be the line of ascent: they form the top edge of Creag a' Bhancair, a steep crag facing northwest. ◄

The good path from Lagangarbh crosses the Allt Coire na Tulaich. After another 50 metres, strike off to the right, contouring below the foot of the Grade 3 scramble and across the grassy band onto the broken rocks. Go up gentle slabs, and then rocks above. At one point, a short drop on the left hinders escape and lends a smidgeon of commitment to the scramble; the steepish tower here is scrambled most easily from bottom left to top centre.

At 600m, opposite the top of the Grade 3 scramble, ease left onto the grassy centre of the spur to avoid a fairly steep slab. Above this, the grass band runs up to the base of a rock tower blocking the spur line. Pass up to right of this for 50 metres, then up left into a grassy bay. Directly above is a short but very steep rock wall;

however, up and to the right is a rake with a stream, easily ascended, before slanting up left to the level ground at the top of the tower (720m, a couple of tiny pools here). Continue up the ridge, on stones and small outcrops of clean rock, with drops on the left into Coire na Tulaich (where you can see walkers toiling up the steep scree of the standard route). At **Point 902m**, bend round left to the cairn (NN 2162 5413) at the top of Coire na Tulaich.

To **descend** Coire na Tulaich go down steep scree zigzags until you can contour left into a small subsidiary corrie. Here is the top of the built path.

Scree paths lead up the stony outcroppy slope above to the first top of Stob Dearg. Our altimeter gave this 1021.5m, which is good as it enforces the continuation for 150 metres along a narrow, stony ridge. ▶ This true 1022m summit of **Stob Dearg** is a splendid perch overlooking Rannoch Moor.

On this section take care with loose stones, as there are climbers below.

Return past the top of Coire na Tulaich. Skirt left of the minor rise Point 902 to find a ridge path ascending to **Stob na Doire**. ▶ A misleading path runs down the narrow ridge ahead, but this is actually the east spur running to crag tops. Instead turn sharp right at the summit on a pathed ridge that descends west, bending left to southwest. The path crosses a col, then rises to a slightly higher col: here the clear path down on the right will be the descent route. Keep ahead up the gentle short slope to Stob Coire Altruim, then along almost-level ridge to the final rise to **Stob na Broige**.

Calculations of drop and distance suggest that this may one day become the Buachaille's third Munro summit.

Return over Stob Coire Altruim to the first and slightly higher of the paired cols beyond (NN 2008 5291). The rebuilt path heads down, north, to left of the stream, to a crossing (currently without stepping-stones) of River Coupall (NN 198 541). Turn right on the well-used and somewhat boggy path down **Lairig Gartain** to a **car park** on the A82.

Turn right along the A82, with a small path down right of the road for the final 750 metres to the walk start.

ROUTE 56
Round Buachaille Beag: the Two Passes

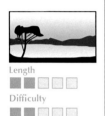

Length
■ ■ ☐ ☐ ☐

Difficulty
■ ■ ☐ ☐ ☐

Start/Finish	A82 at Lairig Gartain end (NN 213 559)
Distance	13km/8 miles
Total ascent	400m/1300ft
Time	4hr
Terrain	Paths rough or boggy in parts
Max altitude	Both pass tops are 490m
Parking	Parking area on the south side of the road, below the cone of Buachaille Beag. (Alternatively, the north end of Lairig Eilde NN 188 562.)

This route is Glencoe's only serious walk at lower levels. It links two passes that were used by cattle drovers, and so are long-established rights of way. It used to demonstrate the principle: 'In the Western Highlands, you walk high or you walk in a bog.' But with increasing use, the Munro approach paths forming much of the walk have been renovated by the National Trust. So that, after a dry spell at least, this can be enjoyed as walking as well as for the massive mountains all around.

After heavy rain, however, not only will the southern end of the walk be boggy, but the crossing of Allt Lairig Eilde (South) may be impossible in spate.

A SRWS signpost indicates the path start. The well-built path runs southwest to join the **River Coupall**, and goes up the long valley keeping to right of it.

After 2km, you pass the end of a path that turns back left to cross the river, heading for Stob na Broige, the southern Munro of Buachaille Mor. Keep to the main path to the right of the river; this path continues well renovated. Approaching the head of the pass, now on stony grassland, the path passes cairns, with a final

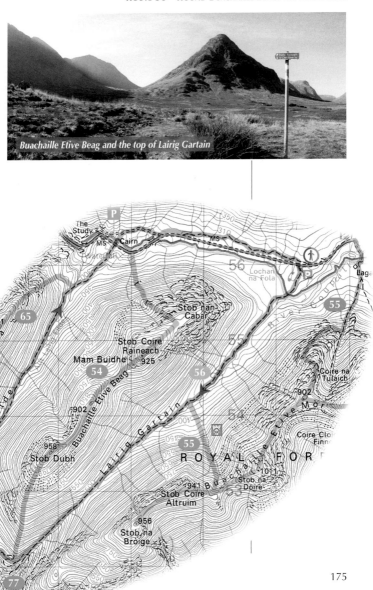

Buachaille Etive Beag and the top of Lairig Gartain

Stream crossing in Lairig Eilde

big one at the pass top **Lairig Gartain**. Ben Starav fills the slot, with Glen Etive unrolling in front of it.

Heading down towards Glen Etive, the path is at first unclear over wet grass, but as the new stream forms, the path becomes eroded to its right. At about 400m altitude, the path starts to slant out onto the right-hand hill face; the path is gently downhill but gradually getting higher above the stream. At 300m the path reaches the nose of **Stob Dubh**, with a regeneration fence (with a gate in it) 20 metres below (NN 174 521). Here leave the main path, which continues down through the gate to Dalness at the valley floor.

If the stream is too full to cross, your best chance is 400 metres upstream, where it runs more level either below or above a middle-sized waterfall.

A small path runs on around the base of Buachaille Beag above the deer fence to cross the **Allt Lairig Eilde** just above the fenceline (NN 172 521). ◄ A grassy path heads up to the right: a few metres further on, a better path runs parallel, this one having just come up through a gate in the regeneration fence.

The path runs uphill to left of the Allt Lairig Eilde stream. As ground eases towards the pass top, the path crosses the now small stream (NN 170 530) and heads north alongside an even smaller stream. The path crosses the **Lairig Eilde Pass** some 200 metres to the right of its lowest point.

The path is clear, down north to join the new stream, also called **Allt Lairig Eilde**. The path runs to right of it for 800 metres, then crosses. ▶ The path here has been reinforced over wet bits. After 1.5km it recrosses the Allt Lairig Eilde at huge stepping-stones, then rises up the moor for 200 metres, before running down to a car park on the A82 (NN 188 562).

If the stream's in spate then stay on the right bank, to avoid recrossing lower down.

Cross A82, then a stream, to the Old Glencoe Road on its stone embankment. Turn right along the pleasant track. In 500 metres it rejoins the A82. Follow a meagre trod left of the road for 300 metres. At the end of a car park, a wider path continues to left of the main road; it is soggy in places, and leads to the start car park.

ROUTE 57
Beinn a' Chrulaiste

Start/Finish	Kings House (NN 260 547)
Distance	12.5km/8 miles
Total ascent	700m/2300ft
Time	5hr
Terrain	Moderately rough slopes and gentle plateau
Max altitude	Beinn a' Chrulaiste 857m

Length

Difficulty

or

This one is for the views of Buachaille Mor, or else climbed just as a Corbett. After the mildly challenging start, it's possibly the book's least exciting hill – so take a friend for conversation.

Start west along the Old Glencoe Road. After 1.2km fork right onto the broad stony track of the West Highland Way. After 800 metres uphill, it runs slightly downhill for 400 metres to ford a stream with a small gorge above. Turn up to left of the gorge. As the slope steepens at 400m altitude, the stream above is in a small ravine.

Buachaille Etive Mor and Beinn a' Chrulaiste
from the track into Rannoch Moor

A quick descent takes steep slopes southeast then east to Allt a' Bhalaich, and follows it downstream to Kings House.

Head up the fairly steep spur to left of the ravine on a small deer path. (An alternative scrambling route goes up the ravine: see below.) On plateau above, turn right up gentle slopes to **Beinn a' Chrulaiste**'s trig point and cairn of rhyolite boulders. ◄

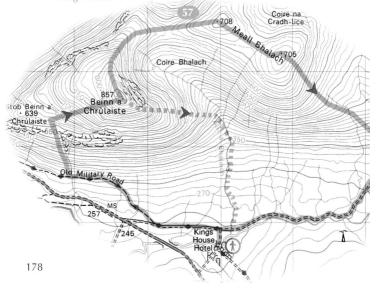

Head away west of north, a direction that's unexpected in mist, down a wide outcroppy spur bending right (northeast) to a wide col. Cross this eastwards, with a small path somewhere among the peat, then up to the small cairn on **Meall Bhalach**. Head southeast across plateau, past some glacier-dumped granite lumps, to the even smaller Meall Bhalach Southeast Top (705m).

Descend southeast, on soggy grass, which becomes heather at the slope foot. Join the small gorge of **Allt Chailleach**, with a track just below. Follow it to the right back to **Kings House**, with Allt Chailleach forming foreground for photos of Buachaille Etive Mor ahead.

Scramble up the ravine

An alternative route goes up the ravine, which is shallow and not too steep, with scrambling (Grade 1) mostly on vegetation. It will be awkward or impossible if the stream is full.

At half-height, the ravine has stream on left, stonefield on right, and a midway spur of rocks and heather rising to a triangular buttress. From the foot of the buttress, you can escape left out of the ravine; otherwise follow heather to right of the buttress top. Above, the ravine narrows, with a few very short rocky moves.

On Beinn a' Chrulaiste: a hill that's mostly for looking at Buachaille Etive Mor and Bidean nam Bian

ROUTE 58
The Lost Valley Visit

Start/Finish	A82 car park opposite Coire nan Lochan (NN 168 569)
Distance	4.5km/2¾ miles
Total ascent	250m/750ft
Time	2hr
Terrain	Rough path
Max altitude	Lost Valley 380m
Parking	Coming from Glencoe village, the car park is first on the right after Loch Achtriochtan, 2km after the loch. Coming down Glen Coe it's the second car park on the left after the passage between the little crags of Meeting of the Three Waters.

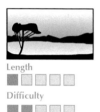

Length
■ ☐ ☐ ☐ ☐

Difficulty
■ ■ ☐ ☐ ☐

This walk is short but very rugged, with an exposed passage above a waterfall gorge, boulder-clambering, and an awkward stream crossing. For hillwalkers it makes an excellent pre-amble to a day on Bidean's ridges (see Route 63 and Route 64). For others it's a challenging and spectacular little outing in its own right. I start it at a car park that's not the closest, to make it a little less short and add some River Coe and Old Road.

Start downhill to the gravel track of the Old Glencoe Road. At a cairn, a path continues ahead across the track, heading for Coire nan Lochan (the gap between No 2 and No 3 of the Three Sisters). Before a footbridge over **River Coe**, turn left, upstream, on a small path. This passes some pools full of clear water and bottomed with pinky-grey and grey-blue boulders.

On the opposite bank, a fence to the riverbank is the start of a regeneration area, where the exclusion of deer has let heather and birch flourish. As you pass opposite this fence end, don't stray onto a sheep path that runs on a ledge along the gorge side. Keep a little higher on the left, along the gorge rim.

The path joins a much larger clearer one. Turn right for 20 metres to the ravine edge. The path descends a ladder, to a footbridge, then up out of the River Coe gorge on easy rock steps. ▶ It runs up through the birch and heather of the regeneration area to a gate. In another 80 metres the main path turns left, with a boulder perched on the path.

Easier route avoiding exposure
The path ahead is about to run along the side of a gorge, rather exposed. If you don't fancy this (there have been accidents, particularly when it's wet), then look for a path continuing uphill on the right, not obvious for its first few metres. This upper path runs along the top edge of the gorge, to pass a monster 15m boulder with a tiny rowan in it. Just after this it turns sharp

The safety cable is there because in winter the steps can be solid ice.

map scale 1:25,000

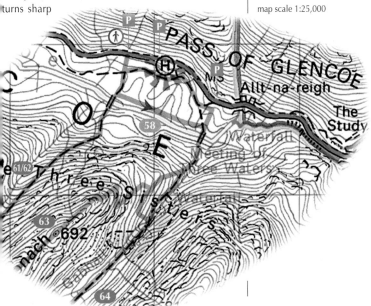

181

left, down into the gorge, and heads downstream for 50 metres or so to the crossing place.

The main path – and more exciting route – runs along the gorge side, above a waterfall, soon getting less exposed. The river rises to join the path, which clambers over big boulders to reach the crossing point.

On either path, the crossing point of the stream is a gravel beach below a hut-sized boulder. The stream here is wide and fairly shallow, so can be paddled if the stepping stones are under water or wobbly. On the opposite (east) side, the path continues to left of the stream as refurbished stone steps. There's a section up a rock groove, harder in descent and when wet. The path then crosses the boulderpile that blocks off the Lost Valley and descends onto the gravel plain. It arrives beside a notable boulder, with a much larger one back on the right.

From here you can wander up the gravel valley between its high walls of steep grass, little streams and big crags. Return the same way. If you came by the gorge wall, you could return by the upper path. After the stream crossing, that upper path turns left, upstream, for 50 metres before clambering up right, out of the gorge.

The path into the Lost Valley

7 BIDEAN NAM BIAN

The name has been interpreted as Bidean nam Beann – the hill of the hills – and that would be entirely right. Take four normal mountains and squash them together; the compression will also make for some unusually steep slopes all around.

The three rocky pillars you see from Glen Coe, known as the Three Sisters, are mere foothills. Three interestingly different ravines lead up between. Coire nam Beitheach is a steep 'V' between rock faces; Coire nan Lochan opens to the sky with its three little pools; and Coire Gabhail, the Lost Valley, is a gravel-floored sanctuary among the crags.

Above the ravines, high and misted and bearing the snows of previous winter, are the preliminary summits: Stob Coire nan Lochan, Stob Coire nam Beith and Stob Coire Sgreamhach. There are several miles of sharp ridges to link the various tops together; and round the other side a remote and shaggy back country.

It takes at least four visits before you begin to discern the big themes, and feel how it all hangs together. These 10 routes are just a start! Be on Bidean in winter, when the ridges are crisp white edges, and the black crags drop into corries filled with golden afternoon light, and a hundred mountains surround you except in the west, where the sea reaches its bronze finger in under the Ballachulish Bridge – and ignore it all as you worry about

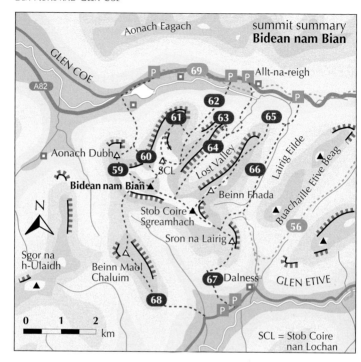

summit summary
Bidean nam Bian

your crampon technique, and how easy it's going to be getting down that headwall into the Lost Valley.

In summer too there's plenty to get anxious about. Noel Williams' *Scrambles in Lochaber* offers 10 more scrambling routes alongside the Zigzags described here. (Ben Nevis itself only gets nine.) For real rock-climbers there's enough up Bidean to wear out several sets of fingertips; and all of it on rough, chunky volcanics allied to the Lake District and Snowdonia, but all much higher.

The Wordsworths, Dorothy and William – probably the most observant observers ever of British hills – came up the glen in 1803. Dorothy was overwhelmed: 'I cannot attempt to describe the mountains. Those on our right were the grandest I have ever seen... more majestic in their own nakedness than our imaginations could have conceived them to be, had they been half hidden by clouds yet showing some of their highest pinnacles. They were such forms as Milton might be supposed to have had in his mind when he applied to Satan that sublime expression – His stature reached the sky.'

Whether Bidean with its satanic slopes is actually the UK's most majestic hill is arguable. Maybe it is; maybe it isn't quite so fine as An Teallach, or Sgurr nan Gillean, or Coire Mhic Fhearchair of Beinn Eighe. Undoubtedly, Bidean is the finest hill that could be seen from a wheeled vehicle in 1803.

Pretty it isn't. Pretty amazing it is.

SUMMIT SUMMARY: BIDEAN NAM BIAN

Routes 59–66 are from Glen Coe; the headwalls to the main ridge on this northern side carry steep snow into early summer. Routes 67 and 68 on the southern side are wild and untrodden. Route 69, around the mountain's base, allows you to link any of the others. All routes in summit summary are in uphill direction and to Bidean summit. Routes 59, 62, 64 and 66 are also described in descent.

BIDEAN NAM BIAN ROUTES
Route 59 Coire nam Beitheach to Stob Coire nam Beith
Route 60 East Coire nam Beitheach
Route 61 Aonach Dubh to Stob Coire nan Lochan
Route 62 Stob Coire nan Lochan Northeast Ridge
Route 63 Gearr Aonach by the Zigzags
Route 64 The Lost Valley
Route 65 Beinn Fhada
Route 66 Stob Coire Sgreamhach from Lairig Eilde
Route 67 Dalness Waterfall Way
Route 68 Beinn Maol Chaluim

ROUTE 59

Coire nam Beitheach to Stob Coire nam Beith

Start	Loch Achtriochtan (NN 146 571)
Distance	4.5km/3 miles
Total ascent	1100m/3700ft
Time	4hr up
Terrain	Rebuilt path, stony ridge
Parking	Lay-by on the north side of the A82, 400 metres up from Loch Achtriochtan. (There are also spaces at the track end of Achnambeithach house.)

Difficulty

▓ ▓ ▓ ☐ ☐

Despite its steepness and uncompromising surroundings, the well-built path makes this the least difficult route up Bidean. The corrie headwall can hold snow late into spring. In descent the turn-off from the ridge is fairly easy to find, making this the least tricky route for coming down.

See Bidean nam Bian summit summary map.

◄ From the lay-by, a path below the road runs alongside Loch Achtriochtan to the Achnambeithach track end. Rejoin the A82 and cross its bridge over the **River Coe**. Immediately after the bridge a well-made path sets off uphill. It soon climbs steeply, with a rocky passage next to a small stream, straightforward unless the stream has playfully coated the rocks with ice. The path zigzags, then enters the slot valley Coire nam Beitheach.

The path joins the stream bed, with scrambling above the water if the stream is full. Cross the stream just below a small waterfall with a rock block just above. The path continues to left of the stream for 50 metres, to where the stream divides at 500m altitude. ◄

Route 60 forks left here.

The main path crosses the left-hand branch and goes up between the two streams. Above is Stob Coire nam Beith's crag face. Below the bottom outcrop the rebuilt

On the northwest ridge of Stob Coire nam Beith

path turns to the right, then heads up into the upper corrie to right (northwest) of Stob Coire nam Beith. It passes up the left side of the corrie and up the steep headwall to a slight col (NN 1347 5468). This col, Bealach an t-Sron, is just south of a small summit with cairn that could be considered the summit of An t-Sron. ▶

The short ridge to it is good and it makes a scenic lunch-spot.

Turn left along a fairly narrow ridge, which bends left and steepens. The zigzag scree path ascends the edge of a stony slope, with crags dropping on the left into Coire nam Beitheach. At the slope top, the cairn of Stob Coire nam Beith stands on a promontory overlooking the corrie.

Turn right, as the gently undulating ridge continues southeast. After a couple of minor bumps, the ridge narrows pleasingly (path to right of the crest) to arrive at **Bidean's summit**.

Descent

The first essential is to find the correct ridge – the one running west from the summit of Bidean. After a narrow bit (with the path to left of the crest) it levels, descends again, and turns northeast over a hump to the summit of **Stob Coire nam Beith**, whose cairn is poised over the northern abyss.

Turn left, on scree zigzags down the edge of a stony slope, with the abyss to your right. The ridge narrows again, descending northwest to a col before the slight rise to a cairned minor summit. A few steps before the col **Bealach an t-Sron** there's a small cairn (NN 1347 5468) marking the top of the clear path running down to the right.

The path descends the right (east) side of the upper **Coire nam Beitheach**, then keeps to right of the stream to the stream junction at 500m altitude. Descend into the stream ravine, and go down it to left of the stream. The well built path leads rather steeply and with one scrambly passage down into Glen Coe.

ROUTE 60

East Coire nam Beitheach

Start	Loch Achtriochtan (NN 146 571)
Distance	4.5km/3 miles
Total ascent	1050m/3500ft
Time	4hr up
Terrain	Path, steep stony slope to col

Difficulty
■■■■□

The upper corrie under Bidean summit is crag-rimmed and romantic. The ascent out of it is good in crampons, but arduous and uncomfortable in summer.

See Bidean nam Bian summit summary map.

◀ Start by following Route 59 through the ravine of Coire nam Beitheach to the stream junction just above (NN 139 553).

The left-hand stream has a long waterslide. Head up to right of this, southeast, on a rough path. Above the waterslide the ground eases into the upper corrie. The small path stays to right of the stream, wandering over grass to a band of clean rock bounded by a waterfall. Cross this band to rejoin the stream and cross the right-hand branch of it. Scree zigzags lead up ahead to a hollow with a tiny pool (NN 1440 5465). Ahead is steep scree with outcrops, where snow can linger into early summer. Go straight up this, on a loose steep eroded path, to reach the col south of **Stob Coire nan Lochan**.

Turn right on a path just below the col crest, continuing up the ridge to **Bidean** summit as on Route 61.

The steep but rewarding path up Coire nam Beitheach

ROUTE 61

Aonach Dubh to Stob Coire nan Lochan

Start	A82 opposite Coire nan Lochan (NN 168 569)
Distance	4.5km/3 miles
Total ascent	1150m/3900ft
Time	4hr up
Terrain	Paths and stony ridges
Parking	The car park is on the downhill side of A82 (there's a twin car park 300 metres up-valley).

Difficulty
■■■□□

A beautiful route of ravine and ridge, and one that cleverly avoids steep climbs and late snowfields.

See Bidean nam Bian summit summary map.

◄ Start by heading downhill to cross the track of the Old Glencoe Road at a cairn, where a built path ahead runs down to a footbridge over the **River Coe**. If there are ladder steps down to it, it is the wrong footbridge, and you are 700m too far upstream.

A well-made path heads uphill, then contours to the right across a stream. It turns uphill again before slanting up to the right, eventually to join the stream in lower Coire nan Lochan. The path runs up to left of the stream to where it bends left at a slight easing of slope (630m) below a small crag with a scooped front (NN 155 553). ◄

Route 62 now bears left up the stream.

Bear right across the stream. Head up west, on a small path to left of two small streams. Small outcrops for scrambling are available. Above the streams is a gentler slope of grass and rock. Keep straight up northwest to the bare rock summit of **Aonach Dubh**. Visit its north edge for the view down into Glen Coe.

Descend bare rock south, to pass a small pool in a col. Head up the ridgeline opposite, along the pinnacled and turreted top edge of crags. The ridge of stones and rocks leads to the summit of **Stob Coire nan Lochan**.

Aonach Dubh from Clachaig Inn

Descend south, on a fairly wide stony ridge, with the path to right of the crest. After the col, the path leads up the steeper ridge; the crampon-scratched boulders of its crest can be taken direct, especially if the path on the left flank has old snow. **Bidean's summit** has an elegant conjunction of three ridges.

ROUTE 62
Stob Coire nan Lochan Northeast Ridge

Start	A82 opposite Coire nan Lochan (NN 168 569)
Distance	4.5km/3 miles
Total ascent	1150m/3800ft
Time	4hr up
Terrain	Paths, stony ridge, a little avoidable scrambling (Grade 1)

Difficulty

A fine ridge with a little easy scrambling.

On the ridge from Bidean nam Bian to Stob Coire nan Lochan

See Bidean nam
Bian summit
summary map.

◄ Follow Route 61 to the stream bend at 630m below the small crag with scooped front (NN 155 553). Here the path bends left, keeping to left of the stream, which is now a narrow ravine topped with a waterfall. As the path divides and becomes unclear, make a way up the slopes to left of the waterfall, and over the rim into the shallow upper Coire nan Lochan (the bit that actually has the lochans in it).

Head left (east) along the corrie rim and up the gentle slope onto the foot of Stob Coire nan Lochan's east ridge. Go up the grassy, rocky crest on a small path. At half-height is a rock tower with a little easy scrambling, or a scree path down left. Then comes a steeper scree ridge with a zigzag loose path. At the top take the final rocky steepening up its crest, on ledges, or contour out left on scree onto the south ridge.

From the summit of **Stob Coire nan Lochan** continue on Route 61 to **Bidean**.

Descent from Bidean

From Bidean summit take the well-defined pathed ridge down northwards. At 1080m the ridge crest appears to bend left, but this arrives at a buttress top. So at this bend either slant down the right flank on a path, or keep ahead northeast down the crampon-scratched boulders. From the col below, ascend onto **Stob Coire nan Lochan**.

The top of the northeast ridge is not obvious. Head down east, keeping to the crest of the first rocky step to find good ledges and footholds – or divert around to the right, north, on loose scree. Follow the ridge crest (over, or down right of, a rocky section) until it levels off at the beginning of the Gearr Aonach. Here head down left, without path, into the shallow Coire an Lochan.

Drop over the corrie edge to right (east) of the stream (NN 1540 5515 is okay), and slant down left to join the stream below the waterfall as the various possible paths converge. Stay to right of the stream to find the clear path that leads down the lower corrie to Glen Coe.

ROUTE 63
Gearr Aonach by the Zigzags

Start	500 metres down-valley from Allt-na-reigh cottage (NN 173 568)
Distance	4.5km/3 miles
Total ascent	1050m/3800ft
Time	4hr up
Terrain	Pathed ledges, scrambling (Grade 1)

Difficulty

(scramble Grade 1)

The Zigzags are a genuine scramble, so don't really belong in this book. But the scrambling is short, and the situations are spectacular, so in it goes anyway!

Gearr Aonach and Aonach Dubh

See Bidean nam
Bian summit
summary map.

◀ From the car park on the north side of the road, cross
and follow a wide path downhill to the **River Coe** (see
Route 58). Cross a footbridge hidden in the gorge, and
take the path up to the gate at the top of the regeneration
area. After 80 metres the path bends left into the gorge:
here fork up right onto the upper path and follow it along
above the gorge. The heather ledges of the Zigzags are
visible from here on the towering face of Gearr Aonach,
above on the right.

The path reaches a monster boulder with a tiny
rowan in it. Turn uphill, trending right then back left to
avoid black damp outcrops, to the base of the crag above.
Turn up left along the crag base to the start of the ledge
heading back right (NN 167 558). This is the most obvious of the ledges, with marks of path, and small over-
hangs immediately above.

Follow the broad ledge on grass and some bare rock
to just before the nose of Gearr Aonach (trees on skyline).
Here another rocky ramp heads back up left; but first,
continue ahead round the corner on a small path along
grass for 40 metres, for the view of the north face.

About 10 metres along this grass path a **Grade 3 scramble** heads straight up the face, the 'Easy Route' – its rock is good but steep and exposed, holds plentiful but not positive. The climbing gets less steep to a grassy terrace, then steepens again immediately above.

Return along the grass path, and head up the rocky ramp. This develops into a damp slab; avoid this by scrambling a metre or two up to its right, on big holds. The scrambling is soon over, but the situation remains spectacular. Continue on a small path between trees; after about 100 metres the ground above becomes broken, with paths heading up right. Take one of these, slanting around onto the nose of Gearr Aonach at its crag top. Turn left, up the nose, with more scrambling on small outcrops, to reach the almost level ridge above.

Follow the ridge southwest, on small path with big views, until the steeper northeast ridge of **Stob Coire nan Lochan** rises directly ahead. Go up it, now on Route 62, following the crest for a little more scrambling.

Descent from Gearr Aonach

The top of the Zigzags is not easy to find. The best way may be to descend the nose of Gearr Aonach to the top of the north face crags, then contour right on sketchy paths to find the top of the upper zigzag slanting back left below (NN 1663 5598).

ROUTE 64
The Lost Valley

Start	500 metres down-valley from Allt-na-reigh cottage (NN 173 568)
Distance	5.5km/3½ miles (including Stob Coire Sgreamhach)
Total ascent	1150m/3800ft
Time	4½hr up
Terrain	Paths, steep scree to col, stony ridge
Note	The headwall is steep and nasty, and can hold snow right into May.

Difficulty
■■■■□

The Lost Valley must be visited at some point in your Bidean career.

See Bidean nam Bian summit summary map.

◄ For a detailed version of the route start see Route 58 (Lost Valley Visit). Cross the road and follow a path downhill towards the towering face of Gearr Aonach, to cross the footbridge hidden in the gorge of the **River Coe**. Take the path up to a gate at the top of the regeneration area. After another 80 metres, the path bends left into the gorge, where it contours above a waterfall then reaches the stream. Head up the stream among boulders, to cross it at a gravel beach below a hut-sized boulder, with the remade path continuing opposite.

The path crosses the hill of rockfall debris and drops to the gravel floor of the **Lost Valley** (Coire Gabhail). Head up-valley; as the slope rises again at the end of the gravel area, a well-made path forms immediately to right (west) of the stream. It rises gradually across the steep slope above the stream's ravine. Finally it crosses the very top of the stream, to leave you at the foot of the final steep scree.

The apparent pathline up the scree centre is OK for descending by the sure-footed. Going up it's better to choose the chunkier, more stable scree or zigzag up rough ground on the left. Finally, a steep path leads up left towards the pass in a horrid, loose groove; it's better to take the un-eroded grass and sound rock forming the outer rim of this groove (to its left). Emerge at the pass (Bealach Dearg) just west of Stob Coire Sgreamhach (small cairn, NN 1510 5366).

If you want to bag **Stob Coire Sgreamhach**, the up and down on stony ridge path is soon accomplished. Then head west-northwest, on an undulating ridge with path. Drops on the right are steep crag, those on the left are gentler, and where a mild rock obstacle is met, it may be avoided on the left although the clearer path stays on the crest. Two small subsummits precede **Bidean's summit**, which has a large cairn and is the convergence of ridges from east, west and north.

Descent from Bidean

From Bidean summit take the ridge eastward, which dips and rises over a slightly lower summit. There are a couple

Skyline walkers on Bidean nam Bian's east ridge

If you find snow and lack the skills or the ice axe, then switch into the descent of Route 66 over Stob Coire Sgreamhach to Lairig Eilde.

more rises on the way down, with a slightly rocky section. The Bealach Dearg (NN 1510 5366) has a small cairn, and an obvious steep ascent on the ridge ahead. The path down to the left is also clear – unless it's under snow. ◀

Descend the right-hand rim, not the bottom, of the initial loose groove. Below, the steep scree path quite soon gets less steep. Head down to left of the ravine to the flat floor of the **Lost Valley**. A low boulder at its far right-hand corner marks the start of the continuing path down to **Glen Coe**.

ROUTE 65
Beinn Fhada

Start	Lairig Eilde car park (NN 188 562)
Distance	6km/3½ miles
Total ascent	1200m/4000ft
Time	4½hr up
Terrain	Steep grass, stony ridge, a short scramble (Grade 1)

Difficulty
■ ■ ■ ■ ■

Third Sister of Glen Coe is Beinn Fhada, pronounced 'Attow' and meaning long. Long it is but also rewarding, little trodden in its entirety because of the trouble getting onto its end. However, there is a way on steep pathless grass. In descent that gap between the crags would be hard to find, unless possibly with GPS.

See Bidean nam Bian summit summary map.

◀ Start by taking the Lairig Eilde path (signed for Glen Etive) for 1km until it dips and crosses the Allt Lairig Eilde on big stepping-stones. Leave the path and head west, gently uphill, for 300 metres, crossing a slight spur with a rocky knoll below, to reach a shallow grassy valley. Keep slanting up to the lowest point of the steep rocks (NN 1789 5578).

Now a grass rake slants southwest up the left flank, along the foot of broken crag. Head up this rake, using rock slabs sticking out of the grass for easier going, to a slight shoulder spur at its top (NN 1769 5560). The rake line continues gently rising along the left (east) flank of Beinn Fhada, now with only a low rock wall above. You could head up through this at various points, but the simplest line is to follow it until it levels off, then strike to

Scrambling on the ridge between Beinn Fhada and Stob Coire Sgreamhach

the right up a little runnel of stones at 600m altitude (NN 1760 5542). Slant up to the right (north) to gain the ridge crest at exactly the point where it becomes gently angled (NN 1755 5553, 670m).

Enjoy the ridge of grass and outcrops, over a minor top to a col with a cairn. Here most descending walkers strike off down the east flank or, with difficulty, down to the Lost Valley. Accordingly the ridgeline onwards has a clear path. Continue over 931m Beinn Fhada (Harvey map) or Beinn Fhada NE Top (*Munro's Tables*). After a col, climb to the rather rockier 952m summit of **Beinn Fhada**.

In the following col the ridge narrows, to the base of a rock buttress that looks from below to be a formidable small overhang. Pass to left of this along a ledge for 30 metres, then turn back up right in a well-trodden rocky groove with good holds – a moment of Grade 1 scrambling. A gangway continues up to the right onto the ridge crest above the steep crag. Turn up the crest, scrambling easily by ledges and low walls, until the ridge eases. Take the rocky crest or the path to its left to the summit of **Stob Coire Sgreamhach**.

Head west to find the top of pathed, stony ridgeline leading down to Bealach Dearg at the head of the Lost Valley. Continue up pathed stony ridge on Route 64 to the summit of **Bidean**.

ROUTE 66
Stob Coire Sgreamhach from Lairig Eilde

Start	Lairig Eilde car park (NN 188 562)
Distance	6.5km/4 miles
Total ascent	1050m/3800ft
Time	4hr up
Terrain	Path, steep pathless to col, stony ridge

Difficulty

■■■■□

A roundabout route that avoids the difficulties of Bidean, and may be safe when the northern corries are carrying hard or avalanche-prone snow.

▶ A signpost for Glen Etive indicates the path up the **Lairig Eilde**. Follow the path for 3.5km to the cairn at its high-point, and fork off right, dropping slightly to cross the high-point of the pass. Ahead is a fairly steep hillside that you will ascend to the col to right (northwest) of Point 778m. To the right of the ascent slope, a buttress rises to a higher high-point: the Sron na Lairig, a Grade 2 scramble and winter climb that leads to a short but very airy crestline.

Low down on the face below Point 778m is a rocky boss; to its right is an impressive little ravine. Go up to right of the ravine until the slope eases at the stream top. Ahead is a further steepening to the col; go up to right of screes. ▶

At the col (NN 164 528) below Point 778m turn up right, and follow a gentler stony slope, eventually with crags dropping on the right, to arrive at the top of **Sron na Lairig** (unnamed, NN 160 532). Turn left, and follow

See Bidean nam Bian summit summary map.

Route 67 joins here.

Bidean (left) and Stob Coire Sgreamhach, seen from Creise

drops on the right around the rim of Coir' Eilde to the top of **Stob Coire Sgreamhach**.

Head west down the pathed, stony ridge to the col Bealach Dearg at the head of the Lost Valley, and follow the ridgeline (Route 64) up west-northwest to **Bidean's summit**.

Descent from Bidean

From Bidean summit, descend as in Route 64 to Bealach Dearg, and ascend the stony ridge ahead to **Stob Coire Sgreamhach**. Descend south for about 50 metres to clear the top rocks, then work round left to find the tops of crags. Turn down to the right (southeast) along the tops of these drops, until a slight rise leads to the top of Sron na Lairig. Turn right to avoid falling over crags ahead, and descend with crags dropping on your left, then down open slopes, to the wide col (NN 164 528) before Point 778m.

Turn down left (northeast), and descend to left of screes to a grassy hollow. Descend from this to left of its stream, to the saddle at the head of **Lairig Eilde**. Cross the saddle point to find the clear path just beyond. Turn down left for **Glen Coe**, or down right for **Glen Etive**.

ROUTE 67

Dalness Waterfall Way

Start	Glen Etive, at Allt nan Easan (NN 165 509)
Distance	5.5km/3½ miles
Total ascent	1200m/4100ft
Time	4½hr up
Terrain	Steep grass, then gentler slopes and stony ridges

Difficulty

The back of Bidean lacks its craggy character, but has some fine waterfalls. This route starts up steep grass, then eases.

▶ Start at a parking area at the start of plantations, 300 metres down-valley from **Dalness**; or at another one, 100 metres further down, beside Allt nan Easan. Head up the left-hand bank of this stream, northwest between trees, to a deer fence. This is crossed by a primitive stile 10 metres in among the trees. Continue on grass beside the stream to the foot of the lowest waterfall. Here easy rock to left of the water is an alternative to the grass slope further left.

See Bidean nam Bian summit summary map.

Above the waterfall's top is a small steep crag with an overhanging top. The straightforward way is to pass up to left of this, next to the trees, to a derelict fence. The interesting way is to pass up to right of the crag – one awkward step – to find a mini-ridge of grass and rocky knobs rising across the front of the middle waterfall, to reach the same derelict fence.

Pass through a fallen section of the fence, and go straight up, steeply, to a flat-topped boulder perch with a face-on view of the upper waterfall. Directly above the boulder perch, a steep grassy bay leads up between small crags – slightly easier slopes are further left. Above the crags, you arrive on the small ridge that encloses the half-hidden upper valley above the waterfalls.

Head left up the small ridge for 50 metres, then contour right on a sheep path to cross the stream at its bend (NN 159 519). Go up steep grass, soon becoming gentler, to the small but scenery-surrounded Point 778m. Drop northwest into a wide col, where you join Route 66.

ROUTE 68
Beinn Maol Chaluim

Start	Glen Etive, bridge over Allt Fhaolain (NN 158 508)
Distance	6km/3½ miles
Total ascent	1300m/4400ft
Time	5hr up
Terrain	Pathless, with a very steep ascent
Warning	The slope onto Bidean is formidably steep; this is not advised as a descent route.

Difficulty

■ ■ ■ ■ ■

Bidean the back way is a different experience: less cragged, but more wild and remote. It also bags you a Corbett on the way.

See Bidean nam Bian summit summary map.

◄ A forest ride runs up west with a small path in it. At the top of the ride, the path ducks in under trees. Head uphill, on a faint path to left of a dry watercourse; dead lower branches have been cleared to ease passage. Then slant up left away from the watercourse, and into wet ground with low scrubby spruce and a fence just above. Turn left along the fence for 25 metres to a break in it at the high-point of forest (NN 1525 5092).

Directly above is broken ground with low wide outcrops. A way could probably be made straight up through. Easier is to slant up left, along the foot of the broken ground, to gain gentler slopes running up northwest. Above, the grassy ridge undulates to the summit of **Beinn Maol Chaluim**. It has two cairns, the larger standing on white quartzite and made of it, with a smaller but higher-up cairn on schist.

Descend north, down quite steep quartzite stones, then along a grassy ridge with some iron fence posts. An iron gateway, lacking gate, marks the col. Fence posts continue uphill, bending northeast to the foot of a steep

boulderfield. Slant up left for 200 metres, to a pair of seasonal streams. Go up beside (or between) these, very steeply, to pass through a band of broken ground. Above are boulders and grass, still steep but more comfortable as the boulders are rough and blocky.

The ground relents, and a stony slope leads up east to the Bidean ridgeline. Here is the small ridge path across, and sudden drops ahead. Turn right, up the ridge. As it narrows, the path keeps to right of the crest, to the **summit of Bidean**.

Beinn Maol Chaluim from River Etive

ROUTE 69
Old Glencoe Road

Length

Difficulty

Start	Kings House (NN 259 546)
Finish	Glencoe village (NN 098 587)
Distance	20.5km/13 miles
Total ascent	75m/250ft
Time	5hr
Terrain	Paths, minor road
Max altitude	Military Road 320m

This must have been a most magnificent walk in 1929. Today it is ruined by the road – and what of the hideous proposal from Fort William Chamber of Commerce to render the A82 dual carriageway, thus letting us arrive 20mins earlier at what would no longer be worth visiting?

If we can't escape the noise of the A82, we can at least escape its traffic. This route links the various start-points of Bidean, or the two ends of Aonach Eagach, without more than a few metres of smelly and dangerous verge.

West Highland Way opposite Meall a' Bhuiridh and Creise

Start at the Kings House, and cross a bridge behind the hotel onto a tarred section of the Old Glencoe Road. After 1km fork off right on the waymarked West Highland Way. The wide path wanders up the northern slope of the valley, then down again to the roadside at Altnafeadh.

Now you must walk a small path just down to left of the smelly verge, to a large car park. You'll find the old road again a few steps off the A82 opposite the car park.

The old road is a clear path, mostly grassy and in some places rather wet – what has happened to the firm surface my Grandpa drove along? After 2km, the path runs into the A82. Follow a rough trod to right of the road for 250 metres, when the Old Road bears off right as a clear, firm track. In 500 metres it passes the large domed cairn at the foot of **Lairig Eilde**.

Continue along the old road for 500 metres to a cairn at the sudden and stunning viewpoint the Study (Stiddy, anvil, Gaelic An t-Innean). The old road track wiggles downhill to run into the new road. Continue on a small path just to right of the main road. It joins the road again just above the first (dated 1930 in a 1930s typeface) of two bridges at **Allt-na-reigh**. Walk the verge past the cottage to cross a bigger bridge made of pink stone.

Step over the crash barrier on the left, onto a small path beside the road through gorse. After 50 metres fork off left, directly towards Gearr Aonach, down a small path to arrive at a larger one.

The more scenic way turns left towards the Lost Valley. Just before a birch/willow clump, and 20 metres before the gorge, turn right on a small path that follows the gorge edge. ▶ After 600 metres it approaches the footbridge below Coire an Lochan. Turn right, away from the river, and then turn left on the clear wide path of the old road.

The old road crosses a small bridge, then goes through a gate. Approaching Achtriochtan house, take a stile beside a second gate. The track ahead joins the road, so fork left on a made path below the road to join the access track of Achtriochtan house. As this in turn joins the road, again take a made path below the road. This path is noisy and littered, so after 300 metres, just after a culvert marked 1929, cross the main road onto a grass path opposite (the old road again).

For a smoother route turn right on a wide built path that merges into the track of the old road. It passes below two large roadside car parks, often equipped with bagpipers.

As an alternative a good path between the A82 and the river leads to An Torr car park, where you could divert around Route 49 to Signal Rock.

It slants away from the A82, passes above a tree clump, and slants back to rejoin the main road at a car park lay-by. Cross to a path below the road (the same path that you left earlier). It runs between road and loch, to join the access track end of Achnambeithach. Cross the main road (but not its bridge) into a tarred side road to **Clachaig Inn**. ◄

The road, or a path on its right, continues past the campsite and hostels. Finally you can take a riverside path on the left to the edge of **Glencoe village**.

8 GLEN ETIVE

*Ben Starav, Glas Bheinn Mhor, Stob Coir' an Albannaich
and Meall nan Eun from the south*

On a first visit you may miss out Glen Etive. To get there you have to drive down between Buachaille Etive and the Black Mount – and it's rather hard to drive right past such fine mountain guardians.

But on a second or subsequent visit, make sure you do turn left at Kings House, and follow the green gorge of the Etive river down its long, long glen to the sea. This is granite country – but granite rainwashed, to give long grassy valleys with waterfalls, and above them great slabs of bare rock, and ridges all lumpy with granite boulder. How much of it you do at once depends on day length and your legs: use the sketch maps, and permute Routes 73 to 76 accordingly. Across the loch is Beinn Trilleachan, whose granite slabs are celebrated by rock-climbers; but the bare granite across its top deserves the appreciation of walkers as well.

ROUTE 70
Beinn Sgulaird

Length

Difficulty

Start/Finish	Druimavuic (NN 008 450)
Distance	17.5km/11 miles
Total ascent	1200m/4000ft
Time	7½hr
Terrain	Tracks and open hill
Max altitude	Beinn Sgulaird 937m
Parking	There is a small parking pull-in at the north end of the floodable section of road, where the private road bypass rejoins.

Most folk visit the Appin Munros once each and never come back. A shame, as this one in particular is rugged and lovely, with great sea views. It's the only one of the three that's conveniently approached from the west, and was going to be the high-point of Part 11 of this book: Oban, Lismore, Glen Creran…but there wasn't space for Part 11.

Start along the road north for 800 metres, then a farm track on the right passes Taraphocain to join a larger one arriving over a wooden bridge from the left. Continue past large Loch Baile Mhic Chailein and a small artificial lochan on the right. The track continues across open hill, then through a plantation, to pass near **Glenure farm**.

The track runs along the floor of **Glen Ure** then climbs, covering up the previous path marked on maps. Follow it all the way up: the valley is dramatic, despite this newly bulldozed scar. At the top the track runs towards a bridge (NN 078 470) with Airigh nan Lochan ahead; but before this bridge, turn right up rough grassland with outcrops. Keep to left of the ridge crest at first to avoid craggy ground, then work up to the right onto the crest. It ascends in small undulations to the hummock of

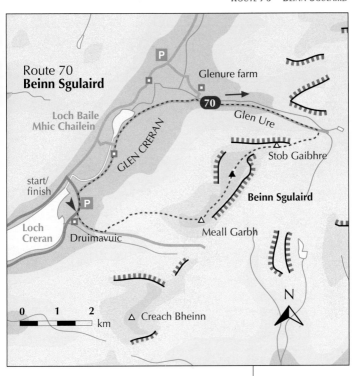

Stob Gaibhre. Above this is a small shallow corrie; go up the spur that forms its right (northern) wall. This spur is fairly steep with granite boulders and small outcrops. At the top, pass to right of a minor top and make a final short ascent to **Beinn Sgulaird** summit.

The ridge down southwards looks narrow on the map, but is mainly grass, with a small path. Descend into a col, cross the hummock of **Meall Garbh**, and drop to a second col. A final climb leads up to Point 863m. ▶

A grassy broad ridge runs down west, steepening to the gap before the hummock Point 488m. After a stiff little climb to the hummock, descend just south of west towards **Allt Buidhe**. A track, marked on Explorer 377

For a longer and even more rugged outing, you could continue over the Corbett, Creach Bheinn.

Beinn Sgulaird's high northeastern corrie

map, runs just north of the stream, to enter woodland at a gate (NN 010 448). It runs down through woods above **Druimavuic**, to the start-point.

ROUTE 71
Beinn Fhionnlaidh

Length

Difficulty

Start/Finish	River Charnan (NN 143 484)
Distance	13.5km/8½ miles
Total ascent	1100m/3600ft
Time	6hr
Terrain	Rough path, steep hillside, outcroppy ridge
Max altitude	Beinn Fhionnlaidh 959m
Parking	Parking is just up-valley from the bridge over Allt Charnan near Invercharnan.

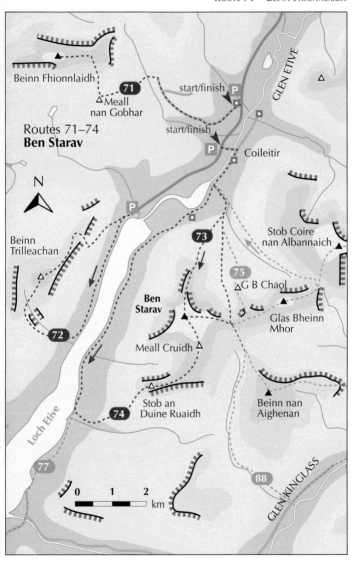

Beinn Fhionnlaidh

△ Meall
nan Gobhar

71

start/finish

P

GLEN ETIVE

△

Routes 71–74
Ben Starav

start/finish

P

Coileitir

N

Beinn
Trilleachan

P

73

Stob Coire
nan Albannaich

75

△ G B Chaol

**Ben
Starav**

72

Glas Bheinn
Mhor

Meall Cruidh △

Stob an
Duine Ruaidh

74

Beinn nan
Aighenan

Loch Etive

77

0   1   2
▬▬▬▬▬ km

88

GLEN KINGLASS

213

Solitary and steep among forests and bogs, Fhionnlaidh is most comfortably climbed by its 'standard' route, a straightforward up-and-down out of Glen Etive.

Start across the bridge and down the road another 200 metres, and turn through the gates towards **Invercharnan**. Pass the house onto a forest road with rhododendron for 3km. At a sharp bend right, keep ahead on rough track for 300 metres to the forest edge.

Ignore quad-bike wheelmarks ahead (a boggy back way to Sgor na h-Ulaidh!) but turn left beside the trees on a boggy path slightly downhill to a stream. This is crossed by a loose footbridge.

The path, boggy at first then firmer, runs up to left of the stream. As the spur of **Meall nan Gobhar** steepens, the path crosses the stream, which above this point becomes a fine little gorge. The path crosses slopes to right of the gorge to the col behind Meall nan Gobhar. ◀ The small path turns right, and zigzags up a steep slope, generally west of north, to a slight levelling at 680m, with a strip of quartzite stonefield above. Here the path peters out. Slant up and left, past occasional small cairns, to reach the main ridge.

If it's misty, note landmarks between here and the main ridge to help your way back down.

Turn left along a fence, with a path continuing as the fence turns down left. The final rise to the summit has two short, easy, scrambling steps that could be bypassed to the left. A short plateau leads to the summit of **Beinn Fhionnlaidh** with its concrete pillar trig.

In descent, from the fence corner follow the fence for 250 metres then slant down on a compass bearing (170° magnetic) for the col behind Meall nan Gobhar.

ROUTE 72
Beinn Trilleachan

Start/Finish	Loch Etive head (NN 108 449)
Distance	8km/5 miles
Total ascent	850m/2800ft
Time	5hr
Terrain	Steep grass, bare rock, and a path with some rock steps
Max altitude	Beinn Trilleachan 839m
Parking	At the end of the Glen Etive road is a turning place (no parking) and some pull-ins.

Length

Difficulty

This 'Hill of the Sandpipers' is interesting in quite a different way from the big ones all around. Instead of sharp ridges here are smooth, rounded slopes of bare granite. The normal route is an up-and-down of its northeast ridge. Here instead are the Etive lochside, the brink of a fine chasm, a grassy gully to descend, and a visit to the bottoms of the rock-climbs.

Start following a signpost for Bonawe, along **Loch Etive** shore path. There are boggy bits before the path enters a deer-fenced enclosure, and runs into woods with spring primroses. The path exits by a similar gate.

In further woods, the path is joined from above by a small bulldozed track. Ahead through the wood it's a green track, in spring adrip with bluebells. The path reverts to bulldozed dirt track on moorland, and passes above a small fenced enclosure, to the start of another wood. Above now is the ravine of Eas Doire Dhonncha.

The track enters the wood and starts to descend, but now leave it and strike up through the wood (less heather than the open hill but more bracken). At the top of the wood, cross the stream Eas Doire Dhonncha, and then cross a fence by a supported strainer post.

Primrose woods, west shore of Loch Etive

The ravine ahead is nicknamed the Chasm of Beinn Trilleachan. Go up rather steep grass with rocks in, to left of the ravine, with views into

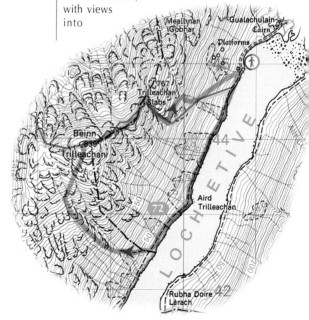

Beinn Trilleachan, with the Etive Slabs gleaming in low sun

its wooded depths. As the slope eases continue uphill along the ravine brim. Eventually the ravine terminates at a cave pitch. Above this, easily cross its stream, and head uphill over ground with much bare granite, to the neatly cairned summit of **Beinn Trilleachan**.

Head down northeast over grass and granite, with a small path forming at the first col. It runs slightly uphill to cross bare rock along the ridge of Point 729. Ahead rises the granitty **Point 767**. The standard route crosses that, and continues down the northeast ridge to the forest edge. Instead, from the col before Point 767, a grassy gully strikes down right, towards the loch. It is steep, but has a tiny path. Go down it.

As the rock walls either side get low again, an eroded stream runnel forms in the gully middle. Go down the last grass to left of this, then cross it onto heather slopes on its right. Keep downhill, with the edge of **Trilleachan Slabs** coming into sight on the left. With woods not far below, re-cross the gully runnel, now rock-floored, to the foot of the slabs.

A small path forms as you pass the feet of the climbs. The path contours on, still above all trees, then turns downhill. It is now clear, but rugged, sometimes on bare rock, with a couple of scrambling moves – one quite exposed move across a little stream, and then a steep step down alongside a larger stream. The path slants down towards the road end, becoming swampy, then arrives at the signpost at the walk start.

ROUTE 73
Ben Starav

Start/Finish	Track end, Coileitir (NN 136 468)
Distance	12km/7½ miles
Total ascent	1100m/3700ft
Time	6hr
Terrain	Pathed ridges, short rocky arête (avoidable)
Max altitude	Ben Starav 1078m
Parking	A parking pull-off (four cars) is just north of the Coileitir track end.

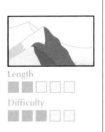

Length
■■□□□

Difficulty
■■■□□

The grandest of the Etive hills, Starav would be much more popular if not for the 15km drive down the glen. Its north ridge is a classic, reasonably gentle but with drops on the left and views along Loch Etive on the right. The descent offers a sharp granite arête, sadly short and also avoidable.

One Etive Munro may not be enough; the bagging continues by switching into the following Routes 75 and 76 for up to three more.

See map in Route 71.

◀ Start across the road to a bracken path down onto the track. It crosses a bridge over a deep pool of **River Etive** then bends right. Ignore a track off left, and approach **Coileitir** house. Turn up left, to bypass the house along a deer fence above it. At the deer fence corner, follow the soggy path down again, to join a path emerging behind the house.

Sleepers reinforce the path across boggy ground, as it bends right to run alongside River Etive. At the side-stream Allt nam Meirleach it turns left for 200 metres to a pair of footbridges.

Cross and turn upstream on a rough path. Attractive waterslide falls are on the left. The path steepens for 30 metres; then fork off it to the right, on a path that's unclear to start with, up the north-northeast ridge of Ben Starav. This path is rough and quite steep until the ridge itself gets less steep at 400m. Follow the ridge, with well-marked drops on the left, to the summit of **Ben Starav**. Just before the cairn, the base of a concrete cylinder trig point is still visible.

The summit area is a curved plateau with drops to the northeast corrie. Follow the corrie rim round to a minor top with a cairn, the former Stob Coire Dheirg (NN 1283 4249).

Escape route avoiding arête

If the sharp ridge ahead discourages you can avoid it altogether by now descending the south ridge to 930m, then turning sharp left down a vague spur-line. Slant

Ben Starav, arête to Stob Coire Dheirg

leftwards and gently downhill, to cross a small stream above its ravine at about NN 133 423. Slant onwards, northeast, with a sketchy path contouring into the 766m col, Bealach an Lochain Ghaineamhaich.

A steep and eroded little spur runs down northeast, soon becoming a narrow rocky arête. The scrambling here is avoidable down right. The ridge runs level, then up the stony pyramid of the current Stob Coire Dheirg (1068m). Here a tempting spur heads away north – ignore. Take the eroded path southeast, next to the brink. It runs down the stony ridge, then in grassy zigzags southeast to the major 766m col Bealach an Lochain Ghaineamhaich.

At the far end of the bealach, at the foot of the quite steep rise towards Meall nan Tri Tighearnan, a cairn stands in the final dip (NN 1394 4235). Here paths join, with the one we want slanting down back left, northwards.

> At this same point another, smaller, path bears right, contouring southwards, continuing through a lower col and up to **Beinn nan Aighenan**. Meanwhile the path ahead is for **Glas Bheinn Mhor** (Route 75).

The path down north reaches, then keeps to left of, the gorges of Allt nam Meirleach. It divides, with one branch staying close to the gorge. The path is fairly rough but scenic. At the valley foot it becomes the path of the outward route, taking you back to **Coileitir**.

ROUTE 74
The Back of Starav

Start/Finish	Track end, Coileitir (NN 136 468)
Distance	22km/13½ miles
Total ascent	1300m/4300ft
Time	9hr
Terrain	Rough paths and pathless hill, stony ridges
Max altitude	Ben Starav 1078m
Parking	A parking pull-off (four cars) is just north of the Coileitir track end.

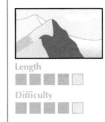

Length
■ ■ ■ ■ ☐

Difficulty
■ ■ ■ ■ ☐

Route 73 is the Starav standard, and very good at that. For something wilder and less visited, here is Ben Starav's back way. It offers Loch Etive's shoreline, a little granite slabwork, and a couple of untrodden tops.

▶ Start along the track to **Coileitir** house. Follow a deer fence above the house and down again onto a continuing path, which bears right to River Etive. At the side-stream Allt nam Meirleach you can ford the stream ahead, or follow the path upstream for 200 metres to a pair of foot-bridges, and back down.

Continue along **River Etive** for 600 metres. As the river bends right, the path continues along the foot of the left-hand slope, past Kinlochetive hut (locked up), to reach the shore of **Loch Etive**.

The small path follows the shoreline, crossing out-flow fans of streams from above. The third of them, Allt Coire na Larach, has spate boulders indicating there could be problems after much rain. ▶ In 6.5km from Kinlochetive hut, don't cross the next large stream, Allt Ghiusachan. Head up sheep paths to left of the stream, through ruined shieling enclosures, to get above the

See map in Route 71.

The ridge to Ben Starav above this point is possible, over rather steep heathery grass with stonefields at the top.

221

Above Loch Etive

bracken patches. Then head straight up a steepish grass spur with some bare slab near its right edge. Near the top, at 760m, a low crag crosses – bypass this on its left or scramble its good granite direct.

Above this crag the spur eases, with more bare granite slab to cross. Then it narrows to the slightly pathed ridge of rocks and grass to **Stob an Duine Ruaidh**, which was promoted to Munro Top in 1997. From its 918m summit, a stony ridge leads over a second Munro top, **Meall Cruidh**. Here bear down left (northeast) to find the col Stoineag. The stony spur above has a grass streak just left of its crest, with a small path, giving the easiest way to the Starav plateau. Level ground is reached at a small shallow pool. At the crag edge beyond, turn left on the path along the brink to **Ben Starav**'s elegantly poised summit cairn.

The distances and times at the top of this route are for joining Route 73, retracing your steps around the rim for the rocky arête to Stob Coire Dheirg, to descend from Bealach an Lochain Ghaineamhaich northwards along Allt nam Meirleach. Alternatively, you could continue straight ahead from the summit cairn down Starav's north ridge, reversing Route 73 – a small path, and drops on the right, guide you down the ridge.

ROUTE 75
Glas Bheinn Mhor

Start/Finish	Track end, Coileitir (NN 136 468)
Distance	13.5km/8½ miles
Total ascent	1050m/3500ft
Time	6hr
Terrain	Hill paths
Max altitude	Glas Bheinn Mhor 997m
Parking	Pull-off (four cars) just north of the Coileitir track end.

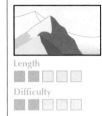

Length
Difficulty

Glas Bheinn Mhor is a simple east–west ridge, which taken on its own makes a pleasant and not demanding day. However, it's the Munro in the middle, and as the list of complicated combinations suggests, it really comes into its own as the easier peak in a walk starting over Ben Starav (Routes 73, 74) – or continuing over Albannaich ('Extension', below) – or both.

COMBINATION ROUTES

Ben Starav with Glas Bheinn Mhor: 15km/9½ miles with 1400m/4600ft; 7½hr

Glas Bheinn Mhor to Meall nan Eun: 20km/12½ miles with 1600m/5400ft; 9hr

Ben Starav to Meall nan Eun complete: 21.5km/13½miles with 2000m/6600ft; 10½hr

▶ Start across the road to a bracken path down onto the track. It crosses a bridge over a deep pool of **River Etive** then bends right to approach **Coileitir** house. Turn up left, to bypass the house along a deer fence above it. At the deer fence corner, follow the soggy path down again, to join a path emerging behind the house.

See map in Route 76.

Sleepers reinforce the path across boggy ground as it bends right to run alongside River Etive. At the side-stream Allt nam Meirleach it turns left for 200 metres to a pair of footbridges.

Cross and turn upstream on a rough path. Attractive waterslide falls are on the left. The path slants up right away from the stream, then eases left across the flank of the spur and rejoins Allt nam Meirleach.

From here you could reverse Route 73 to continue up the well-used path, to right of the stream's fine ravines, to the 762m pass Bealach an Lochain Ghaineamhaich. There turn left, up a ridge path. After a steepish rise, the ridgeline levels, before rising gently to **Meall nan Tri Tighearnan**.

Variant: Glas Bheinn Chaol

For an equally scenic, but tougher, ascent, where the path reaches Allt nam Meirleach (NN 138 450) cross the stream onto a smaller path that zigzags onto the end of the long narrow ridge **Glas Bheinn Chaol**. Easy walking follows the crest of this to level ground at its end. Now ascend a steep stony slope, with no path, southeast onto **Meall nan Tri Tighearnan**. ◀

Or, more easily, contour right to join the valley path up to the col to the west.

Ben Starav from Meall nan Tri Tighearnan of Glas Bheinn Mhor

Meall nan Tri Tighearnan is the Hump of Three Houses. The ridgeline continues east, dipping then rising gently to the summit of **Glas Bheinn Mhor**.

At the last minute the ridgeline bends so that you reach the summit (surprisingly) from the south: turn back sharp right (south of east) for the start of the descent ridge. At first it is gentle and grassy. It levels, then drops more steeply towards a 738m col. Just before reaching the col the path turns left, to cross the top of Allt Mheuran stream (NN 1630 4333). ▶

If continuing to Albannaich, you would now keep straight ahead up the opposing slope (see below).

The path descends alongside and to right of the stream. As the descent gets less steep at 200m, the path eases away above the stream; Eas nam Meirleach (Robbers' Waterfall) is in the ravine below. The path continues 50 metres to right of the stream, with a small soggy path down at the streamside for viewing waterslide falls. The main path joins the stream side for the lowest waterfalls.

At the bottom corner of a fenced birchwood, the main path bears away right. This direct route north to **Coileitir**, below the birchwood fence, is horribly soggy. Better to take a smaller path staying beside the stream down to the footbridge of the outward route (NN 136 460).

Extension: Stob Coir' an Albannaich and Meall nan Eun
If you don't fancy the 'Tarsuinn Slabs' ascent to Stob Coir' an Albannaich (Route 76), then this fine three-Munro outing is better eastwardly, as the rough Allt Ceitlein is more comfortable done downhill. ▶

For the extension without the main route, ie just Albannaich and Eun, start on Route 73 until the footbridge of Allt Mheuran; don't cross it, and take the rough path up that stream to the col east of Glas Bheinn Mhor.

At the 738m col below Glas Bheinn Mhor, cross the stream top 100 metres down left of the actual col, and ascend steeply on a small zigzag path. At the top of the first steep rise (NN 164 435) head north crossing stream tops, then up a long, sloping lawn to **Albannaich** summit. The small contemporary cairn stands on the flat top of a wide, circular, ancient one.

Descend east, along the top of drops on the left, down a ridge that's bare rock to start with. Soon it steepens, with a deeply worn path. After 350 metres (5mins or so) just before a very small rise, a sandy patch occupies a tiny col (NN 1731 4424). Here turn down sharp left, down a grassy gully with a small path in it. Overshoot this turn-off and in 200 metres, after descending some bare granite, another little grassy gully leads down left: this is the line of the boundary on OS maps and, while unpathed, is a comfortable way down.

The small, pathed gully reaches a wide flat col below (NN 1725 4462). Cross the col northeast, and head up **Meall Tarsuinn** (I like Meall Tarsuinn a lot) over grass, bare rock slabs and boulders. Cross the summit and follow an ill-defined rounded ridgeline down east: the descent briefly steepens at the tip. Once across the following col the ground becomes simple grassland. Slant up right, east, to the summit of **Meall nan Eun**.

Descend northwest, along the top of drops on the right, to the ridge end with a small knoll. Here ignore the natural ridgeline bending down north, but keep the previous direction, north–northwest, down to the 750m contour; then turn north. Even on this line there are outcrops to be avoided by zigzags left and right. On the 'natural' line, further to the right, on coming to any crag top bypass it to the left (west).

And so, probably after a little entanglement in some crag, reach the wide, slabby 633m col. Cross it, and turn left down the right-hand side of the main stream.

The descent is pathless, through longish grass. The easiest line is to right of the stream, moving away from it to a knoll at 375m (NN 177 464). Pass down to right of this, then slant right, along a line of low drumlins with slightly less vigorous plant life. At the foot of the drumlins, across an old fence, slant down to the right, over ground with a little bare rock showing, to join a stream. Go down to left of this, cross it, and head down to the stream junction below.

Now a rough path runs to right of the main Allt Ceitlein stream over cowpoked grassy meadows. After a gateway in a dead deer fence, a track forms. Follow it down to the valley's end, bending left to cross Allt Ceitlein. In another 1km the track rejoins the outward route.

ROUTE 76

Tarsuinn Slabs: Meall nan Eun and
Stob Coir' an Albannaich

Start/Finish	Road end Coileitir (NN 136 468)
Distance	17km (10½ miles)
Ascent	1350m (4500ft)
Time	8hr (approx)
Terrain	Rough paths, easy-angled granite slabs (or walk around them on grass)
Max altitude	Stob Coir' an Albannaich 1044m
Maps	Due to bad overlaps, Meall nan Eun is particularly difficult to navigate on Explorer maps; Harvey 'Glen Coe' or Landranger 50 suggested

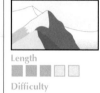

Length ▮▮▮□□

Difficulty ▮▮▮▮▮

On the west side of Loch Etive, the Etive Slabs offer a special sort of climbing: magnificently rough and grippy granite, but without any actual handholds. The same granite on Meall Tarsuinn is at a much, much gentler angle: bare rock, but sloped so you can simply walk up it, for almost 500m of height gain.

If you want it, some easy scrambling is available on the lower, streamside section. Alternatively, if the granite is unattractive – perhaps it's iced up – you can always walk on grass alongside it. The out-and-back to Meall nan Eun adds more slabby granite, this time horizontal, and grabs the outlying Munro. The descent from Albannaich needs care in mist.

Follow the track across River Etive and fork left in the birchwoods on a track towards Glenceitlin. Just before the house the track crosses **Allt Ceitlin**; now turn off upstream, to left of the river, on a much rougher track.

At ruined sheepfolds the track becomes a rough path, still to left of the main stream. It crosses a sidestream, to

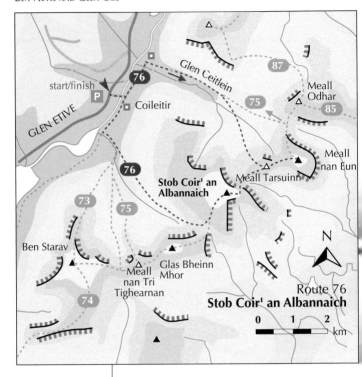

Route 76
Stob Coir' an Albannaich

0   1   2
km

pass below two ravines (Coire Glas and Coire Leacach) joining in a V. To left of the Coire Leacach ravine, the upper slope of Meall Tarsuinn is grass and granite slabs, and a small stream runs from this down a band of stream-washed granite slabs. Cross the main valley stream to the foot of this slabby stream.

Go up the slabs beside the stream, with occasional small scrambly bits (or the grass on either side if the stream is very full). At about 400m level the angle eases a little. The upper slope is a mix of easy-angled granite and grass. Head up on whichever surface you prefer to the rounded crest of **Meall Tarsuinn**, which you'll reach west of the summit. A small path runs up left, to the cairned top. ◄

Meall Tarsuinn means transverse hump.

228

The small path continues east, down into a col of granite slabs, though you'll probably lose it in the slabby ground beyond. Head up east then southeast, on grass then moss, to the flat summit of **Meall nan Eun** ('Hump of Birds').

Return northwest down the wide, grassy plateau for 500 metres, with a path trace, but in mist only the GPS or the watch will tell you when to swing down west for the slabby col. Follow the small path back over Meall Tarsuinn and down into a wide 754m col. Here you swing south towards the steep face of Stob Coir' an Albannaich.

Two small pools are at the col's low point. Pass to right of them to a stream just beyond (NN 1725 4462). This runs up slantwise across the face of Stob Coir' an Albannaich, south, in a grassy couloir. Follow this up, on a small path or the tiny spur to its left, to arrive suddenly on the upper ridge. Follow it up, on eroded path, to **Stob Coir' an Albannaich** summit.

From here it's not easy to hit off the slope top above the col for Glas Bheinn Mhor. There's no path and no distinct hill features, so in mist a careful compass bearing or GPS is needed. Head down a mossy slope southwest, across a shallow dip where streams run down south, and across a very slight stony ridge beyond. As the slope steepens down, you can see the steep nose of Glas Bheinn Mhor opposite.

As the slope becomes stony, a zigzag path leads down (to right of a harsh-looking stonefield) towards the

Slabs on north side Meall Tarsuinn, with Meall nan Eun

Stob Coir' an Albannaich from the east

Glas Bheinn Mhor makes a worthy bonus peak: see Extension below.

738m col east of Glas Bheinn Mhor. It reaches the head of the stream 100 metres down to right (west) of the true col (NN 1630 4333). ◄

A rough path leads down to the right, following the stream (Allt Mheuran). At the valley foot, don't bear right below a birchwood (very soggy) but follow the stream right down to **River Etive**, and turn right to **Coileitir** House. A path bypasses above the house to join its driveway out to the bridge over River Etive.

Extension over Glas Bheinn Mhor

The three-peak day comes at 20km/12½ miles with 1600m/5300ft of up – about 9hr.

On Explorer maps it's Bealachan Lochain Ghaineamhaich.

From the 738m col, a ridge path runs up to **Glas Bheinn Mhor**. Surprisingly, it arrives at the summit from the southeast: you must turn back sharp left, south, to depart. The ridge path rises again over the narrow hump **Meall nan Tri Tighearnan** then drops to the 766m col with an excessively long name. ◄

Paths cross here. Turn down right, on a stony, rough path that passes down to left of all the ravines of Allt nam Meirleach, to a double footbridge down in Glen Etive. Across it, the path turns left to River Etive, then upstream to **Coileitir** House. A path bypasses above the house to join its driveway out to the bridge over River Etive.

ROUTE 77
Loch Etive Linear

Start	Dalmally station (NN 160 272) or Taynuilt (NN 004 312)
Finish	Kings House (NN 259 546) or Kinlochleven (NN 187 620)
Distance	Dalmally to Kings House 50km/31½ miles; Dalmally to Kinlochleven 56km/35 miles; Taynuilt to Kings House 42.5km/26½ miles; Taynuilt to Kinlochleven 49km/30½ miles
Total ascent	Dalmally to Kings House 1100m/3700ft; Dalmally to Kinlochleven 1350m/4400ft; Taynuilt to Kings House 650m/2200ft; Taynuilt to Kinlochleven 900m/3000ft
Time	Dalmally to Kings House 2 days (15½hr going); Dalmally to Kinlochleven 2 long days (17½hr going); Taynuilt to Kings House 1½ days (12½hr going); Taynuilt to Kinlochleven 2 short days (14½hr going)
Terrain	Tracks, rough paths, and 3km of rough hillside (Dalmally only)
Max altitude	Lairig Dhoireann 612m (Dalmally start); Lairig Gartain 465m
Access	If arriving by train, start from Dalmally (as Lochawe involves an unpleasant verge walk). If by bus, alight at Stronmilchan road end (NN 132 283).

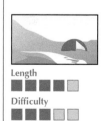

Length
■ ■ ■ ■ □

Difficulty
■ ■ ■ □ □

This is a long and varied through route – especially from the Dalmally start – with high passes, an empty valley, and the side of salt-water Loch Etive.

The Taynuilt start is easier, but could give you more Etive lochside (20km) than you actually want. The 7km of tarmac up Glen Etive can be avoided by pleasant paths east of River Etive before the impressive and well-trodden Lairig Gartain brings you through to Glen Coe.

See overview map Ben Nevis & Glen Coe south.

◄ **Starting from Taynuilt**

The Taynuilt start is described under Route 89 (Glen Kinglass) to Glennoe over the euphonious River Liver, and down to cross the fine track bridge near Ardmaddy, at the exit of **Glen Kinglass** (12.5km/8 miles and 200m/700ft so far).

Route 98 (Eunuch and Cockle) gives extra detail of the first part of this walk.

◄ Starting from **Dalmally station**, follow B8077 to a bridge over **River Strae**. Immediately north of this, turn onto a track up Glen Strae. In 600 metres fork left past a long pool, then keep ahead on a wider track for 1km. Just before a bridge, turn left on quad-bike marks following the map's old stalking path, to left of the stream, up to the **Lairig Dhoireann** pass.

An old and almost vanished zigzag path leads down the first steep descent into the upper valley of Allt Dhoireann. As the slope eases (400m level) there's a path to right of the main stream. Recross the stream at the

Long, low-level paths between the mountains give this area some of Britain's best backpacking. Upper Loch Etive, with view to Beinn Trilleachan (Route 72)

Loch Etive at dawn

300m contour, just below a couple of waterfalls, to find a small, wet path down to left of the Allt Dhoireann to **River Kinglass**. ▸ Head downstream on traces of path to a sturdy footbridge near **Acharn** (NN 123 356).

Turn left along the track, keeping to the older track alongside the river for the first mile towards **Narrachan**. The hut has in the past 10 years been available for unofficial bothy use. After another 3.5km the valley emerges to the side of Loch Etive (20km/12½ miles and 600m/2000ft so far).

Take the northward track past **Ardmaddy**. The track becomes a small path along the high-tide mark keeping to left of a fenced enclosure. This path is hard to find at first, then clearer. It has some boggy bits but is mostly pretty good, if always small. (At extreme high tide parts of it vanish, and small streams become awkward tidal inlets to bypass inland.)

Cross **Allt Ghiusachan** – awkward in spate, judging by the wide swathe of spate-carried boulders. The path now gets clearer and better. Opposite, Beinn Trilleachan displays its sweep of granite slabs. After another 6km of

An adventurous short cut here turns upstream for 1km to a footbridge, and follows descents of Routes 88 and 73 to reach Glen Etive by the high pass east of Ben Starav.

rough but beautiful walking, the path arrives at the head of Loch Etive. It continues along the foot of the right-hand slope to the hut at **Kinlochetive**, which was a bothy at one time but is now locked.

Beyond the hut a wider, but initially very soggy, path continues along the right-hand edge of the valley floor, then alongside **River Etive**. It turns upstream alongside Allt Mheuran (in dry seasons you can just ford the stream) to a footbridge, then returns downstream to the River Etive. In 800 metres it reaches **Coileitir** house. Bypass above this to join its entrance track. Once in the woods, this reaches a junction.

The main track would take you down left to cross the River Etive at a deep pool, and reach the Glen Etive road (from Taynuilt: 25.5km/16 miles and 200m/600ft; from Dalmally 33km/20½ miles and 600m/2000ft), but there is no shop, hostel or bus stop. A very rough path does lead west from the loch head into Glen Ure; or one could turn down the west shore of Loch Etive on a path that starts nicely but becomes a wide timber track and eventually, at Bonawe, a road. However, the comfortable

Glen Etive track under Stob Dubh of Beinn Ceitlein (Route 87)

234

continuation is northwards through Lairig Gartain to Kings House or Kinlochleven.

At the junction in the woods near Coileitir, turn up right on the smaller track. This runs to **Glenceitlin**. A still smaller track continues above the house for another 1km.

At the track end a muddy trod turns up to the right, soon joining the line of an old, small path contouring up-valley. The path is little used but clear. It rises to pass above a river bend opposite Lochan Urr, crossing a fairly steep slope and then slanting down to the flat valley floor. The path passes along the right-hand edge of the flat ground to join River Etive, and runs alongside it below another steep bank. Keep ahead to a small footbridge over a stream from Beinn Ceitlein, and rejoin River Etive above **Dalness** house for a sturdy bridge.

Across River Etive, follow the path round to the left and through a gate. Ignore another footbridge ahead leading to Dalness house; turn right, with wall to your right, to the road bridge over Allt Gartain. Climb onto the bridge, or pass under the bridge to gain the road from the other side. Turn left a few steps, to the SRWS signpost at the foot of the Lairigs Eilde and Gartain.

Turn up the signed path, through a gate in a deer fence. The well-made path heads straight up the wood (planted in 2000 and coming on nicely) up the southern end of Buachaille Etive Beag. Where the path forks, ahead would be the path for Lairig Eilde. ▶ So turn right, contouring to cross Allt Lairig Eilde.

The path heads up to a deer fence gate high above. The path is good at first then faint, wet and peaty. Above the deer fence gate the path slants up right, climbing gradually across the steep hill face to join the **Allt Gartain**. After a short but rather nasty steep section, you reach **Lairig Gartain** pass top. A good path to left of the **River Coupall** runs out through the pass to a car park on the A82.

A rough path to right of the A82 is less nasty than the road verge to **Altnafeadh** (from the foot of Glen Etive, 13.5km/8½ miles and 450m/1600ft).

Take this path, joining Route 56, for the Old Glencoe Road to Glencoe Village (Route 69); also if the stream just ahead is uncrossable.

Dalness and Lairig Gartain from the path east of River Etive

The wide, waymarked path of the West Highland Way now heads straight up the hillside on the left for **Kinlochleven** – a tempting continuation (10km/6 miles, 250m/800ft). For Kings House, follow the West Highland Way the other way, beside and to left of the road, then slanting left up the hillside for 2km. It then descends to join the Old Glencoe Road to **Kings House** (3.5km/2 miles).

9 BLACK MOUNT

Coire Ba and the Black Mount from Rannoch Moor

The rock is Buachaille Etive Mor: the soft place is peaty Rannoch Moor. Between the rock and the soft place – where you look at both the Mor, and the moor – is the Black Mount.

The Black Mount ridge between Kings House and the Inveroran is the best pub-to-pub in all Scotland. It's gentle grass, and stony plateau, and at the plateau's edge a great rocky corrie half-full of cloud. The morning sun gleams on the hundred lochans of Rannoch, and early light turns the peatlands a delicious chocolate brown. At noon the hollows of the hill are as warm as a Spanish beach but considerably more private. Just the summit of Ben Nevis peers in disapprovingly over the jagged wall of the Buachaille.

Stroll a few more miles, while behind Ben Cruachan the evening sun gleams on the sea, and suddenly you're at ridge's end. Beneath your toes they've just switched on the lights in the Climbers' Bar at the Kings House. You could almost spring energetically off Sron na Creise and splash down into your first glass of beer.

Better not believe it. There's scrambling on the slope below, and heathery scree, and you'll be wading through the Etive by torchlight and into the bar just after the last bar meal. So stay up instead, and pitch a tent in Bealach Fuar-chathaidh. Chathaidh is cats and Fuar is cold – it is indeed a place for cool cats as the darkness gathers in the long glens between the ridge and the River Etive.

Once you've bagged the four Munros, and walked the long ridge between, those long glens are the next place. Down there are dark slits of river between bushy banks, bright waterfalls, deer, and fine old stalkers' paths with dangling footbridges. There, too, are a couple of Corbetts: 2500-footers to tick off as an extra excuse for coming to the Black Mount the back way. Beinn Ceitlein wouldn't fit on the map, so is a separate Route 87.

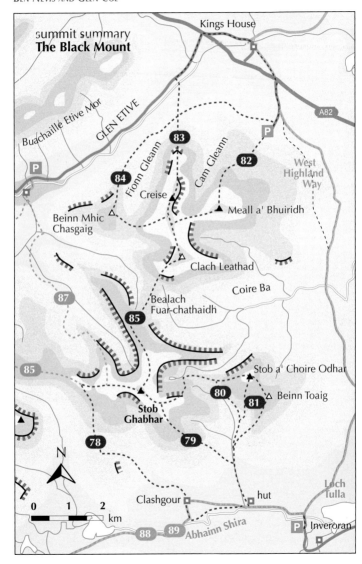

summit summary
The Black Mount

Kings House

A82

West Highland Way

Buachaille Etive Mor

GLEN ETIVE

Fionn Gleann

Cam Gleann

83

82

84

Creise

Meall a' Bhuiridh

Beinn Mhic Chasgaig

Clach Leathad

Coire Ba

87

Bealach Fuar-chathaidh

85

85

Stob a' Choire Odhar

80

81

Beinn Toaig

Stob Ghabhar

78

79

N

0 1 2 km

Clashgour

hut

Loch Tulla

Abhainn Shira

88 89

Inveroran

And when you've done all that, come again in winter for some crampon work in the Northeast Corrie of Stob Ghabhar, or the ancient ice-climb in the Upper Couloir. The Black Mount – or perhaps the 'you'll-be-backmount'.

SUMMIT SUMMARY: BLACK MOUNT

Routes 78–81 are from Inveroran, Routes 82–84 from Kings House or White Corries. Routes 85 and 86 are the main ridgeline taken northwards and south-wards; note how the West Highland Way lets you get back to your starting point (or there's the Citylink coach from Kings House to Bridge of Orchy, followed by 4km/3 miles northwards along the West Highland Way). A route to Stob Ghabhar from lower Glen Etive wouldn't fit in, and is the separate Route 87.

BLACK MOUNT ROUTES	
Route 78	Stob Ghabhar by Mam nan Sac
Route 79	Stob Ghabhar South Ridge
Route 80	Coirein Lochain of Stob Ghabhar
Route 81	Stob a' Choire Odhair to Stob Ghabhar
Route 82	Meall a' Bhuiridh to Creise
Route 83	Sron na Creise
Route 84	Beinn Mhic Chasgaig
Route 85	The Black Mount Traverse: Northbound
Route 86	The Black Mount Traverse: Southbound
Route 87	Beinn Ceitlein to Black Mount

Aonach Eagach of Stob Ghabhar

ROUTE 78
Stob Ghabhar by Mam nan Sac

Start	Victoria Bridge car park (NN 270 418)
Distance	10.5km/6½ miles (to Ghabhar)
Total ascent	950m/3200ft
Time	5hr up
Terrain	Path, moderate slope, gentle ridge

Difficulty
▪▪▪☐☐

A way to savour some of Stob Ghabhar's western ridge, and a safe descent.

See Black Mount summit summary map.

Inveroran Hotel with Stob Ghabhar

◀ Take the road over Victoria Bridge, and turn left on the track signed for Loch Etive. It runs beside **Abhainn Shira** to the green Clashgour Hut. After another 200 metres, the track bears right into trees, but it's nicer to fork left outside the deer fence along the riverside. A fairly good path reaches the sidestream Allt Ghabhar. Just before this, head right, on a track (if the gate here is locked, divert left around the fence end). The track leads up to **Clashgour**. Just below the buildings, turn left on a small track.

240

This old stalkers' path leads up into the wide col of Mam nan Sac. It can be followed further northwest until it peters out, then head up grassy slopes to Bealach Coire Laoghan (NN 213 457). Follow the main ridge gently up eastwards over Sron a' Ghearrain. Old fence posts guide along narrower ridge and up the stony summit knoll of **Stob Ghabhar**. ▶

On older maps this is shown as 'Stob Gabhar', pronounced Gower, meaning 'goat peak'.

Descent

From **Ghabhar summit** head down northwest, following the iron posts of the old fence. The ridge curves to the west and levels. After 400 metres of narrow, level ridge, the fencing posts swing down to the left, and you could follow them down the western rim of Coire Ghabhar; however, this runs down to crags. So it's best to keep following the wide gentle ridge northwest across Sron a' Ghearrain for 300 metres until it bends north. Here turn down left, south-west, apparently off the ridgeline but in fact down gentle slopes to the Bealach Coire Laoghan (NN 213 457). From here head down east of south to the wide Mam nan Sac.

From the col follow old iron posts left, to find the descent track which runs down-valley to left of the stream.

ROUTE 79
Stob Ghabhar South Ridge

Start	Victoria Bridge car park (NN 270 418)
Distance	6.5km/4 miles
Total ascent	900m/3000ft
Time	4hr up
Terrain	Path

Difficulty
■ ■ ■ □ □

The standard baggers' route is a trudge with a fine finish; also the most straightforward descent route.

See Black
Mount summit
summary map.

◄ Take the road on over Victoria Bridge, and take the track on the left as far as the green **Clashgour Hut**. Just beyond it a good path heads uphill to the right of the Allt Toaig. At a small cairn at 300m, fork off left and cross the nearby stream, on a sketchy path to the right of a side-stream and its waterfalls; then bear up west to a shoulder at 920m. Head up steeper slopes to the level top section of **Aonach Eagach** ridge. Turn left, and follow the corrie rim to the summit of **Stob Ghabhar**.

Descent

Follow old iron fence posts down southeast, with the huge drop to Coirein Lochain on your left, to the narrow col that's the top end of the **Aonach Eagach**. Now the fencing slants away southeast – in mist, follow it down. Otherwise continue along the crest for 100 metres, past a small cairn but before the narrow and more awkward section of the Aonach Eagach ridge, then turn down to the right, to rejoin the old fence posts and reach the 920m shoulder.

Head down southeast to join Allt Toaig and its path.

ROUTE 80

*Coirein Lochain of
Stob Ghabhar*

Start	Victoria Bridge car park (NN 270 418)
Distance	7.5km/5 miles (to Ghabhar)
Total ascent	900m/3000ft
Time	4hr up
Terrain	Path, steep broken hillside and stony ridge
Note	Check snow and avalanche conditions, pack crampons. Not recommended for summer unless you switch to Route 81.

Difficulty
■ ■ ■ ■ ☐

Coirein Lochain harbours a classic winter climb – the Upper Couloir. This route admires the icy crags from a snowslope on the left.

Stob Ghabhar from the head of Coire Toaig

▸ Start as Route 79 to continue up the path beside Allt Toaig to the col at the valley head. Turn left up the ridgeline for 400 metres, then contour out right into Stob Ghabhar's northeast corrie, **Coirein Lochain**. (Route 81 keeps on up this ridge.)

From the southernmost point of its lochan, head up southwest on a steepening snowslope without interrupting crag. It deposits you at the tiny col at the top end of the **Aonach Eagach** ridge. Turn right, up the rim of the corrie, to the summit of **Stob Ghabhar**.

See Black Mount summit summary map.

ROUTE 81
Stob a' Choire Odhair to Stob Ghabhar

Start	Victoria Bridge car park (NN 270 418)
Distance	9.5km/6 miles
Total ascent	1200m/4000ft
Time	5½hr up
Terrain	Path, then rough steep slope and stony ridge

Difficulty

■ ■ ■ ■ ☐

The standard baggers' route for the Munro pair, but a demanding way onto Stob Ghabhar.

See Black
Mount summit
summary map.

*Aonach Eagach of
Stob Ghabhar*

◄ Follow Route 79 to the green hut and up the path alongside Allt Toaig. At 450m it crosses a stream; at once fork right up an eroded path on the spur to left of the stream. Higher up, it zigzags up the steep southwest spur of **Stob a' Choire Odhair**.

From the summit, follow the ridgeline down west to the col at the head of Allt Toaig. The continuing ridgeline

rises gently and bends left, to run into the steep northern wall of Aonach Eagach. An eroded path zigzags straight up this to the crest. Turn right, along the **Aonach Eagach**, which offers a little very easy scrambling. ▶ At the ridge's end, follow the rim of Coirein Lochain up to the summit of **Stob Ghabhar**.

This isn't the famous and fearsome Aonach Eagach of Glen Coe (Route 52).

In descent

After the scrambly bit of the Aonach Eagach ridge, note where it kinks from just north of east to just south of east (cairn, NN 2369 4540). Here you must turn off left down the steep northern slope. Then head out right, east, to the col at the head of Allt Toaig and climb **Stob a' Choire Odhair**. From there, you can descend south then south-east to take in Beinn Toaig. Just before the first col, watch out for a small crag; it can be bypassed on the left. After the short climb to **Beinn Toaig**, the heathery southwest ridge is fun to descend, but less amusing uphill.

ROUTE 82

Meall a' Bhuiridh to Creise

Start	White Corries car park (NN 266 525)
Distance	5km/3 miles (to Creise)
Total ascent	950m/3100ft
Time	4hr up
Terrain	Pathed stony ridges

Difficulty

You may detest the ski paraphernalia, or quite like the way it lifts you to the 650m contour. Either way, the following ridgewalk is a fine one.

▶ Head up a fairly nasty path under the ski lift – there is a waterfall which drowns the sound of the clattering cables. From the top station a mud track leads to the 'Plateau Chateau' café. Head up to right of all the

See Black Mount summary map.

Meall a' Bhuiridh from Creise

ski runs, following the black-and-yellow 'edge of ski area' poles. Quite suddenly the ski zone drops out of sight behind and the summit cairn of **Meall a' Bhuiridh** appears 50 metres ahead.

Head down west, on a sharp stony ridge. Once across the narrow col, there's a steep climb through rocks. You'll use a handhold here and there, but the way is well trodden and clear. At the plateau, turn right along the cliff rim. There's a slight drop, and then a short, gentle climb to a cairn at 1100m (NN 238 506). This, unmarked on older maps, is the summit of **Creise**.

In descent

The drop-off for the east ridge is crucial, and not obvious in mist. Keep to the brink of the drop on the left, watching out for where it curves slightly to the left. A well-placed cairn (NN 2390 4999) marks the top of the descent spur.

ROUTE 83
Sron na Creise

Start	Glen Etive (NN 238 536) or White Corries car park (NN 266 525)
Distance	6km/4 miles (to Creise)
Total ascent	800m/2600ft
Time	4hr up
Terrain	Very steep, weaving among crags, with at least a little scrambling (Grade 1)

Difficulty

This is a serious route, up steep ground with big crags: spectacular, with scrambling possibilities. It follows the line of an excellent (Grade 3) scramble, but avoids the scrambling (apart from a little easy Grade 1). The route is on grass among small crags. If a path should be starting to form, encourage it into zigzags to reduce erosion.

The line is best inspected from Glen Etive. The key is a gully of pink boulders, rising to the skyline on the right (northwest) flank of the nose. The gentle rock ridge to left (north) of this gully is the key to the ascent. The start is from Glen Etive, or White Corries (convenient for a finish down Route 82).

▶ From Glen Etive road

In normal water conditions the River Etive has wide, shallow sections between its small gorges, and you can cross it on stones at NN 236 534, opposite the culvert where a stream off Buachaille passes under the road. Head straight towards the north-pointing steep spur. A low but wide outcrop crosses it low down, with a grassy gap to right of centre. Go up to the base of this gap (NN 2393 5272), ascend for a couple of metres then slant up left, on rock holds projecting from grass, to the top of this first small rise (NN 240 527).

From White Corries

Return down the access road to Blackrock Cottage and turn off past the cottages. A path is forming from here,

See Black Mount summit summary map.

247

and may be followed under some power lines, and then tending further to the left to look for drier ground around the base of Creag Dhubh.

Work round to cross the foot of **Cam Ghleann** (the Crooked Glen), then contour on around the base of Stob a' Ghlais Choire's northeast ridge. You can now slant off up steep grass, to join the steep northern spur above its first small rise (NN 240 527).

From the rise head directly uphill (south) on a vague ridgeline of grass with some rock, to the foot of the first scrambling crag (NN 2400 5254). Pass up to right of it, on grass, to the foot of a tiny waterfall (NN 2400 5250). Scramble up to left of this on gentle rock with many holds for 15 metres to the top of the crag.

Slant up left, on grass, to some shed-sized boulders visible on the skyline from below (NN 2409 5242). Directly above them swells the upper scramble crag. Pass up to right of it, on grass, then on loose stones to the foot of the gully of pink rocks (NN 2403 5226). This is the gully mentioned in the preamble, and has a small pinnacle above on the right. Contour left onto the crest of

Meall a' Bhuiridh and Creise, with the Sron na Creise forming the right skyline. The photo excludes Buachaille Mor, just to the right, which normally distracts the viewer from appreciating Creise

a ridge of gentle, easy, rock. Go up this ridge, or broken ground to its left, to the top of the pink-rock gully.

Head uphill across the top of the gully, to the foot of a final scrambling wall (NN 2401 5216). After 3m of genuine Grade 1 this eases for another 10m of scrambling: or avoid it by grass on the left. Head on up a well-defined ridge; those who avoided the scramble pitch can regain the ridge by a steep little grassy groove, or stay on grass to join the ridgeline further up. It leads by rocks and grass to the levelling Sron na Creise at 900m.

Go up stony ground, south, to Stob a' Ghlais Choire. After a short descent, a narrow ridge with a small path leads south to a preliminary cairn, and then after 400 metres almost level, to **Creise summit**.

DESCENT OF SRON NA CREISE

Given care – and spare energy for returning uphill where necessary – this intimidating line goes surprisingly well in descent. Crucial, but fairly straightforward, is to find the way through the upper crags. Below that it's possible to improvise.

From **Creise** follow the ridge northwards on a small path, to the rocky rise of **Stob a' Ghlais Choire**. Continue to the lower top, Sron na Creise. Descend stony ground north, on undefined ridge becoming clearer, and then becoming a well-marked and somewhat rocky edge.

Keep to the crest, on a small path, descending more steeply to the top of a 20m scrambling pitch (the top is NN 2399 5214). If you scramble this (Grade 1), you'll find it steepest at the bottom; a groove slightly right (east) of the crest is easiest. Or avoid it by a steep little grass groove down to right; or else backtrack up the ridge for easier access to the grass on the right.

From the foot of the scramble continue south down the ridgeline, to pass across the top of the pink-stone gully falling to the left. Go down the gently angled rock ridge to right (east) of the gully, or the easy groove to right of the rock ridge. Return to the ridge crest opposite the foot of the pink-stone gully and contour into the gully (NN 2403 5226).

A simpler description of the route down: descend northwest, avoiding crags as you come to them, to the valley floor. For a more precisely described route: go down the gully's right edge until you can slant down to the right on grass, still following the base of the rocks. From the crag toe descend grass to a clump of shed-sized boulders (NN 2409 5242). Slant down and leftwards to the top of the next scrambling crag. Head down the left edge of this, on grass with rock handholds, for 10m, to the foot of a tiny waterfall (NN 2400 5250). Head down between the stream (left) and the scrambling crag (right), and below the crag's foot reach an easing of the slope.

Here you can slant down right on steepish grass for the moorland trudge to the White Corries, or head down the ridgeline, north, on grass with occasional bare rock, to arrive above a wide, low rock band. Slant left on easy-angled rock, hands hardly needed, to reach the foot of a heathery gap in the crag (NN 2393 5272).Head straight across the moor, to cross the **River Etive** at NN 236 534, opposite where a stream off Buachaille passes under the road.

ROUTE 84
Beinn Mhic Chasgaig

Start	White Corries car park (NN 266 525)
Distance	9.5km/6 miles (to Creise)
Total ascent	950m/3200ft
Time	5hr up
Terrain	Pathless ridges and open grassy slopes

Difficulty
▪▪▪▪☐

A Corbett on the way to Creise gives one of the wild ways up.

See Black Mount summit summary map.

◀ Again, this route could be started by crossing the **River Etive** at NN 224 523 if water levels permit. Follow Route 83, and contour on around the base of Sron na Creise. Allt Fionn Ghlinne has slabby waterfalls. Cross it at around 330m, to gain the toe of **Beinn Mhic Chasgaig**'s northeast ridge. This is steep to start, but soon eases into a gentle uphill stroll.

From the summit, descend southeast across a col, and take the well-defined west ridge of Creise. It deposits you on the plateau 600 metres south of the summit. Turn left, with drops on the right, on a small path, slightly downhill at first, and then up to the summit of **Creise**.

In descent

In really bad conditions, with white-out and cornices on the east-facing crag top, it may be impossible to locate the spur to the west ridge; this is the safest descent route. Count paces carefully for 600 metres to a very slight rise (NN 2375 5013), then descend southeast, and east to the col at the head of the **Fionn Ghleann**.

ROUTE 85
The Black Mount Traverse: Northbound

Start	Lairig Dhochard (NN 187 460)
Finish	Creise summit (NN 238 506)
Distance	10.5km/6½ miles
Total ascent	950m/3200ft
Time	5hr end-to-end
Terrain	Wide ridgelines, steep grass slopes, mostly pathless

Difficulty
■■■■□

For Scotland's best high-level pub-to-pub this is the more difficult direction; but the intimidating descent of Sron na Creise will dry the mouth nicely in preparation for the Kings House beer. It is described from the Lairig Dhochard, north of Meall nan Eun, so as to link into Routes 73–76. That full ridge, from Ben Starav, is an over-the-top experience in both senses. For a more moderate exercise in high-timing it, start from Stob Ghabhar (Routes 78–81).

▶ Unless arriving along the Etive ridge, start from Coleitir road end (NN 137 468) and use Route 76; but keep on up Glen Ceitlein to gain the slabby 633m col **Lairig Dhochard**. Turn left, northwest. A broken wall

See Route 76 map, then Black Mount summit summary map.

crosses the col to end against the foot of the intimidating upslope (NN 1883 4608). From there, go straight up a knoll of grass and rock to a slight easing of the slope. Directly above is broken outcroppy ground. Slant up to the left along the foot of this, and follow a small stream up through a grassy gap. ◄ Now the slope is slightly less steep; slant up slightly right to reach the slope top (NN 1900 4633) and **Meall Odhar**.

> The top of the stream gap is NN 1888 4622.

A broad grassy ridge runs east, down into Bealach Odhar, then gently over **Stob a' Bruaich Leith**. From its 990m summit old fence posts lead east along the ridge. This narrows enjoyably, then rises to the stony pyramid of **Stob Ghabhar** summit.

Head down north-northwest, ignoring a small spur running north to crag tops, but then following the top edge of Coirein Lochain (the Northeast Corrie) on the right. As the broad ridgeline levels, the small path switches to its left-hand side, to follow drops on the left (Coire a' Chaolain) side. The path runs northwards, skirting to left of the 976m **Sron nan Giubhas** top.

The **Aonach Mor** ridge requires care or GPS in mist. Follow the spur down north, to a col with tiny pool, then uphill for 100 metres to a toplet with an even smaller pool. The ridge continues down northwest for 100 metres to another col, then up to another slight rise. After 200 metres of level ridge comes a gradual dip to a notch crossing the ridge (829m). Head up to the next flat-topped rock knoll, currently with a cairn on it (NN 2240 4748). ◄

> Find this cairn in mist, without GPS, and be rightly pleased with yourself.

Now head northeast down steepish grass, to reach either the beginning of the continuing ridge (NN 2255 4773) or else the marked flattening at 730m which lies just northwest of the ridgeline (a cosy campsite). Follow the ridgeline northeast, over the rocky hummock Creag a' Bhealaich. The defined ridge is followed north to a slight drop, then northeast along grass ridge to the base of the slope out of **Bealach Fuar-chathaidh** (NN 2296 4849) – the Pass of the Cold Cats.

Head uphill, slanting slightly right to the grass-topped ridgeline above. Turn right, up the broad ridge that becomes stony with drops on the left. It bends left to the cairn at the summit of **Clach Leathad** (Clachlet). The large cairn, perhaps reflecting Clachlet's former Munro status, has a big drop immediately behind it.

With drops on your right, descend initially north-west, but after 100 metres find the clear ridgeline with path heading north. After a shallow col, the path rises alongside drops on the right, to a plateau with a cairn at its corner (NN 2390 4999), marking the top of the spur to Meall a' Bhuiridh. The plateau edge bends slightly left, then back right, dips a little, then rises to the summit cairn of **Creise**. Route 83 (Sron na Criese) or Route 82 (M a' Bhuiridh) both have descent-direction notes.

It's cold for cats: in Bealach Fuar-chathaidh heading north to Clach Leathad

ROUTE 86

The Black Mount Traverse:
Southbound

Start	Creise summit (NN 238 506)
Finish	Stob Ghabhar summit (NN 230 455)
Distance	6km/4 miles
Total ascent	450m/1500ft
Time	2½hr end-to-end
Terrain	Gentle ridges and one steep drop, mostly pathless

Difficulty

The classic pub-to-pub ridgewalk in the easier direction.

Rannoch Moor and Meall a' Choire
Odhair from Stob Ghabhar

▶ Southward from **Creise** the ridge dips then after 600 metres rises very slightly. It dips again, then has a 60m ascent to **Clach Leathad** – pronounced (and sometimes spelled) 'Clachlet'. ▶

The descent to the next col – Bealach Fuar-chathaidh – needs care, as a direct compass bearing leads onto steep ground with outcrops. Go down the ridge to the 1000m contour, where it turns right, and continue down the ridge in its new, westward, direction for 400 metres (about 5mins). Here the ridge bends slightly right, eases its angle, and changes from stones and moss to grass (NN 2339 4895). Now steep grassy slopes on the left lead down southwest to the col (NN 2296 4849).

Cross the **Bealach Fuar-chathaidh** col, and ascend steeply onto **Aonach Mor** (the Great Ridge). The crest of this is a green ridge-wander, with small pools, and deep corries running out on either side. At the ridge's end the ground rises and becomes stony. In mist, simplest is to keep uphill onto the top of Sron nan Giubhas; then follow the drops on the left round to the summit of **Stob Ghabhar**.

See Black Mount summit summary map.

Until 1974 Clach Leathad was marked as higher than Creise and so was the Munro.

ROUTE 87

*Beinn Ceitlein to
Black Mount*

Start/Finish	Alltchaorunn, Glen Etive (NN 197 513)
Distance	22km/13½ miles
Total ascent	1700m/5700ft
Time	10hr
Terrain	Grassy slopes and ridges, mostly pathless
Max altitude	Stob Ghabhar 1090m
Parking	There's a small pull-off opposite the road end of Alltchaorunn.

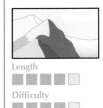

Length
■ ■ ■ ■ □

Difficulty
■ ■ ■ ■ □

This is Black Mount from the back. Behind the River Etive are long, little visited valleys with waterfalls and old stalkers' paths. The Corbett Stob Dubh gives motivation to the morning; 600m of drop into one of the little-visited valleys will occupy the noontide; arrive at Stob Ghabhar after the Munro-baggers have gone away. Through the long walk out, waters roar in black gorges, froth down slabs of pink rock, and gather in pools that reflect the orange sunset slopes.

Before the Access Law the gate was sometimes obstructed; there is a possible crossing of the Etive 200 metres upstream.

On Beinn Ceitlein, approaching its main summit, Stob Dubh

Start across the farm's bridgeCarraigh. ◄ Take the track towards **Alltchaorunn**. Where it bends away from the river through a gate, keep along the riverbank. Cross the Allt a' Chaorainn where it flows into the River Etive. If this is impossible there is a footbridge just above Alltchaorunn farm, but it leaves you inside a deer-fenced enclosure.

Cross a wet field diagonally, and go uphill alongside a broken wall and deer fence to the top of the fence. Cross the broken wall and slant uphill on quite steep grass to left of crags. Above, ease back right, still on grass, into the intriguing notch at 450m, shaped as though the Ghabhar goat had taken a great bite out of the Ceitlein

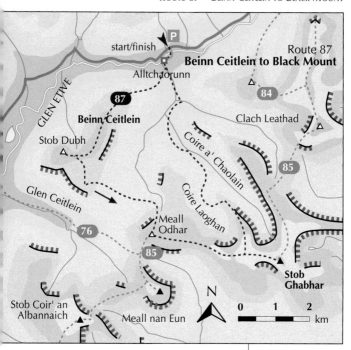

cabbage. Its faultline leaps across Glen Etive to become one of the gullies in the Buachaille opposite.

The rise out of the notch is slightly rocky, so contour out left for 10 metres then head uphill. Just above, the slope eases, to the gentler climb southwest up the long ridge of **Beinn Ceitlein**. The ground at the top is knolly, with the summit of Beinn Ceitlein being just the highest knoll. The rocky pyramid of Stob Dubh, the higher summit and Corbett, makes itself obvious ahead and to the right.

Continue from Beinn Ceitlein summit southwest over another slight rise, then dip into a col and go straight up the steepish ridge (surprisingly composed of quartzite) to the summit of **Stob Dubh**. The view down into Glen Etive is spectacular.

Return through the col, and continue ahead (south-east) around the right-hand flank to drop into a slightly lower col. Here head down to the left, into Coire Dubh-mor. The stream in this steep re-entrant has waterfalls and small gorges: keep to open slopes to left of the stream. At the foot of Coire Dubh-mor cross the stream and then the wide tussocky valley of Allt a' Chaorainn ahead. Gain the long gentle spur directly opposite (NN 186 482) that forms the right-hand rim of Coire na Cloiche. Keep to the crest to see the fine falls in the stream on the left. The spur rises to a very minor summit, where you cross a grassy col and head quite steeply onto **Meall Odhar**.

After all this tough ground, it's a treat to head east along the broad grassy ridge, down into Bealach Odhar, then gently up over Stob a' Bruaich Leith to Sron a' Ghearrain. From its right-hand (990m) summit, old fence posts lead along the ridge. This narrows enjoyably, then rises to the stony pyramid of **Stob Ghabhar**.

The descent starts by retracing steps. Head down northwest, curving to west, following the iron posts of the

Down Sron a' Ghearrain. The ridge of Buachaille Mor is ahead across Glen Etive; Ben Nevis is at the back

old fence. After 400 metres of level ridge, where the fencing swings down to the left, head northwest, along the wide and almost level ridge. After 300 metres it bends north, heading straight down the wide, gentle Sron a' Ghearrain.

The descent is easy to the 650m contour. Below there it steepens, so turn down left on steepish grass into **Coire Laoghan**. The stream at this point is a small gorge, so slant round to the right above it, dropping to join it below the gorge section. A small path on the opposite side leads downstream, and after 500 metres becomes a rather better stalkers' path.

This path runs above and to left of the lovely stream Allt Coire Laoghan. It drops in a zigzag, then contours across the steep slope of Meall Ghiubhas. Then it drops to cross **Allt Coire a' Chaolain** at a footbridge (NN 203 486). The clear path continues around the base of **Aonach Mor**, through a gate, then drops to a narrow footbridge across the gorge of Allt Coire Ghiubhasan (NN 200 500).

A carved rock ramp leads out of the gorge. The path beyond loses itself for a moment, but will be found again alongside the stream. It passes through a gate into a regeneration enclosure, then through another gate to **Alltchaorunn**.

ROUTE 88
Beinn nan Aighenan

Start/Finish	Inveroran, Victoria Bridge car park (NN 270 418)
Distance	37.5km/23½ miles
Total ascent	1300m/4400ft
Time	12½hr
Terrain	Tracks, paths, grassy hill
Max altitude	Beinn nan Aighenan 957m

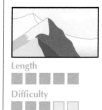

Length
■ ■ ■ ■ ■

Difficulty
■ ■ ■ □ □

Beinn nan Aighenan is usually bagged as a slightly tiresome out-and-back on the way down Ben Starav (Route 73). Make it into a proper mountain, no longer tiresome but instead very tiring, by approaching it along the glen it lives in. In theory we all celebrate the long walk in. In practice one way to shorten it is to take a tent in as far as Loch Dochard, or overnight in the slightly sordid shed there. The track in could be cycled; it is challengingly rough. The track from Taynuilt (Route 89) is smooth and graded, but 21km each way.

Start on rough path out of the car park, rejoining the road to cross Victoria Bridge. Turn left, to left of two lodges, on the track up Abhainn Shira. In 2km keep ahead on

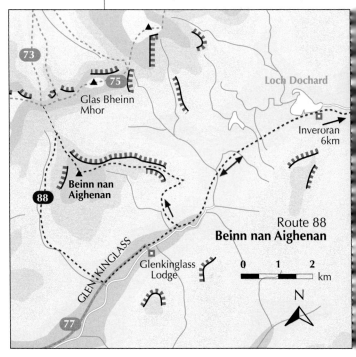

Route 88
Beinn nan Aighenan

the riverside path, swampy in parts (cyclists divert via Clashgour).

Ford Allt Ghabhar and turn right on a peaty path through the edge of forest. ▸ It crosses swamp to a footbridge and rejoins the track. Turn right, past **Loch Dochard** and down to River Kinglass. The bridge on maps is a disused suspension bridge; the new bridge is 400 metres downstream. In another 1km the track joins the river; 300 metres later, look out for wheelmarks on the right up the line of an old path.

It runs above the ravine of Eas a' Bhinnein into Coire a' Bhinnein. Turn east, up gentle slopes, onto the corrie rim. A wide ridge of grass and rocky slabs runs north, then northwest, over a 744m top to **Beinn nan Aighenan**.

Descend north, on a gritty path over ledges and rocks, to a well-defined col at 618m. The path ahead continues to the 766m col east of Ben Starav, but turn down left into the valley of Allt Hallater. Slant down grassy slopes to join the stream, with a small path to its left. It runs down through a ravine into **Glen Kinglass**.

Turn left along the wide, smooth track. Opposite **Glenkinglass Lodge** keep ahead on an older track paved with rocks, after 1km rejoining the outward route.

The former footbridge was permanently removed in 2009; there is an alternative bridge above Clashgour, up 800 metres of very rough riverside.

ROUTE 89
Glen Kinglass

Start	Taynuilt (NN 004 312)
Finish	Bridge of Orchy (NN 297 396)
Distance	40km/25 miles
Total ascent	750m/2500ft
Time	2 days (12hr going)
Terrain	Tracks, short soggy path
Max altitude	Kinglass Pass 290m; West Highland Way 330m

Length
■ ■ ■ ■ □

Difficulty
■ ■ □ □ □

A relatively easy route through some very tough country. With woodland regeneration Glen Kinglass should gradually get even prettier, but the pass at its head will always be bleak.

See overview map Ben Nevis & Glen Coe south.

◄ From Taynuilt station, start north through the village. Across River Nant, the road bends right, but a track ahead becomes path then rejoins the road. At once turn right beside the RC Church of the Visitation, and follow a street through **Brochroy**. It becomes a track, forking left to pass alongside the Bonawe Ironworks. At the entrance gate to Bonawe House move across right onto the other track. Follow it through shady woods, and then between high shady hedges. After 800 metres it bends right; here take a kissing gate on the left, down to the **River Awe**.

Cross an impressive suspension bridge and the field beyond to a small gate beside brown huts. Pass between the huts, and up to the corner of the car park for **Inverawe Country Park**.

In Glen Kinglass, below Meall Garbh

Turn left through the car park and right on the road beyond. After 800 metres turn left, up a forest track

tarmacked for its first rise, then gravel. After 500 metres, in a clear-felled valley, ignore a track right; 150 metres later ignore a fork left signed for Tigh na Ba. The main track ahead enters broadleaf woodland and passes a vehicle barrier and a disabled truck, then slants down to the side of Loch Etive beside a fish farm. After running out of the woodland, it passes two new-built houses then crosses River Noe. Keep on upstream to pass **Glennoe** farm.

The track runs across open moorland above Loch Etive, crossing first **River Liver**, and then the bridge near **Ardmaddy** (NN 079 374; 12.5km/8 miles and 200m/700ft so far).

Turn right on a smooth track to left of River Kinglass, using an older track on the right if you spot it. **Narrachan** hut has been available for informal bothy use. At **Glenkinglass Lodge** keep ahead on an older track paved with rocks. After 2.5km fork right to a sturdy bridge (NN 185 399). Cross, and turn left up the riverbank to a disused footbridge (which is the bridge still marked on maps). Just beyond, pick up a very rough track. Follow it northeast, as it improves. At **Loch Dochard**, a former stable is an open but uncomfortable shelter.

Loch Dochard. A camp here breaks the trek Route 89, or takes several hours off the long walk in to Beinn nan Aighenan (Route 88)

Long paths and tracks lead in among the mountains. The track towards Loch Etive and Glen Kinglass (Route 77) gives easy but rewarding walking

The former footbridge was permanently removed in 2009; alternative bridge above Clashgour, up 800 metres of very rough riverside.

In another 2km, turn left over a footbridge and cross peat swamp to a ladder stile and rough path between trees. Ford Allt Ghabhar. ◄ Now a pretty good riverside path is ahead, or a track via Clashgour if you prefer drier feet. The two rejoin to reach **Forest Lodge**.

Turn right past **Inveroran Hotel**, where the way-marked **West Highland Way** crosses the shoulder of Mam Carraigh then descends gradually to **Bridge of Orchy**.

10 BEN CRUACHAN AND OBAN

Oban from the Mull ferry

Oban is full of sailors and shoppers and people waiting for a ferry to the islands of the West. It's as busy as Fort William, but seems more of a real town – perhaps simply because of the smell of fish. And the circuit of Kerrera island is an offshore adventure that's a world away from the stony path up Ben Nevis.

But look back from Kerrera across the harbour, and high above the houses and the fanciful Coliseum rise the pointed summits of Ben Cruachan.

SUMMIT SUMMARY: BEN CRUACHAN

Cruachan is a hill of granite grandeur. Leaflets from the Forestry Commission list it as the highest in Argyll, and this usurping of Bidean nam Bian is not altogether presumptuous. (It is the highest in the Argyll and Bute district, but not in the old county of Argyll.) The super-steep northern slopes define its three triangular summits: Taynuilt Peak (Stob Dearg, 1104m); Cruachan summit; and Stob Daimh. These give its name – which means Hill of Stacks – and also its outline, so distinctive in views from Glen Coe and Ben Nevis.

Cruachan has two Munros, and a granite ridge between that offers a moment of scrambling. The best circuit is clockwise, with the awkward ascent by Bealach an Lochain in the easier uphill direction; the same for scrambling the 'Granny-stopper'; and so that, at the final col, you can decide whether there's time to include the bonus peak of Beinn a' Bhuiridh. That circuit is Route 90; the final diversion over the bonus Corbett Beinn a' Bhuiridh is Route 92.

If that's a Munro classic, the lesser classic is the Dalmally Horseshoe. This approaches from the east, taking only the second Munro but adding the Corbett, so that it lacks scrambling as well as the main summit of Cruachan. Instead it offers sharp but grassy ridges and a delightful descent.

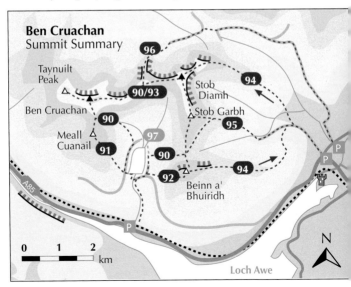

For romantics, Route 96 is a back way in under that impressive northern side, offering a little extra scrambling and a small arête to Drochaid Ghlas. For the even more romantic, *Scrambles in Lochaber* (see Appendix D) offers two wild but easy scrambles, the North Ridge of Taynuilt Peak and the East Ridge of Stob Garbh, both Grade 1.

BEN CRUACHAN ROUTES

Route 90	Cruachan Horseshoe
Route 91	Meall Cuanail
Route 92	Beinn a' Bhuiridh add-on
Route 92A	Descent North from Beinn a' Bhuiridh
Route 93	Cruachan Ridge in Reverse
Route 94	Dalmally Horseshoe
Route 95	Stob Garbh Southeast Ridge
Route 96	Drochaid Ghlas Northeast Ridge
Route 97	Cruachan Reservoir

On the ridge from Drochaid Ghlas towards Ben Cruachan

267

ROUTE 90
Cruachan Horseshoe

Start/Finish	Cruachan Power Station (NN 079 267)
Distance	13km/8 miles
Total ascent	1400m/4600ft
Time	7hr (including Taynuilt Peak)
Terrain	Steep paths, bouldery and rocky ridges with a short scramble (Grade 1)
Parking	Parking at the Power Station Visitor Centre isn't for walkers. Informal parking is 800 metres west, on the north side of the A85 below the station.

Length

Difficulty

The Cruachan horseshoe is one of the classic hill circuits of Scotland.

See Ben Cruachan summit summary map.

◀ Start up the steps towards the station platform, but keep ahead under the rails in a narrow tunnel. (The alternative path, to the west of the Falls of Cruachan, has been blocked off.) Half way up some concrete steps, the path heads off left towards the stream. It continues uphill, with steep zigzags through the wood, to a steep and awkward ladder stile (even humans may prefer the dog slot just to the right). With the stream on your left, continue to a track below the **Cruachan dam**. Turn left up the base of the dam, until steep steps lead up onto its top.

Turn left to the dam end, and up to a track just above. Turn right, and follow the track above the reservoir. At the reservoir end, look out for a cairn where a path turns off left; the path is initially undefined across wet ground. It becomes clear, first to left of a stream, then crossing it to run up on its right. As the path runs up the steep back

wall of **Coire Dearg** it is steep and eroded, but the craggy surroundings are compensation.

The path arrives at the small pass Bealach an Lochain, with a small pool and the posts and stile of a former fence. Turn up right, on a path that's still steep and eroded, and then up a boulderfield to **Cruachan summit**. The trig point, a concrete cylinder, has been broken off.

The 'Granny-stopper' scrambling moment on Cruachan's main ridge

The **out-and-back to Taynuilt Peak** gives an extra bit of scrambly ridge and a superb view. Taynuilt Peak (Stob Dearg) is only a Munro Top, not a fully independent Munro. The ridge path leads down gently, avoiding some slabby crest by keeping left. After a short rise, the ridge steepens downwards; here is a well-scrambled groove-line down the crest, with exposure on the right. The groove can be avoided by dropping left then contouring across, on mossy rocks that aren't much easier than the crest line.

The ridge continues gently downwards, then up Taynuilt Peak, a fairly steep cone of stones, boulders and grass. Return the same way to Cruachan summit.

Many grannies will find it nothing but fun; on the other hand, in wind, wet or flying snow, even the youngest and most vigorous may pause here.

The bouldery ridgeline descends gently east – this section could be avoided by a path a few metres down on the right (south). After a steeper descent, a col (NN 072 304) is below the scrambling obstacle, nicknamed (by guidebook writer Ralph Storer) as the Granny-stopper. ◄ There are three ways at it.

The direct line

The direct line up the crest is easy, on good rock, but is exposed, with big drops nearby on the left. From the col, a steep move to right of a 2m pinnacle leads onto slabs. Continue straight up. The lower section of slabs has good handholds; the upper part has less holds, but is easier angled.

The traverse

Alternatively, if you like delicacy rather than strain, contour out right from the col along a line of sloping footholds. The final steps, which lack handholds, are protected by a sort of rock trench just below. From the end of the traverse, a rocky groove leads up for 20 metres to the ridge crest above the obstacle.

Avoding the obstacle

The obstacle can be avoided altogether on steep grass, though in winter or spring this may be snow-covered. From the col, a steep and rather nasty path descends to the right (south). After 50 metres it descends more gently to the left, and soon crosses a narrow run of stones, often with a trickle of water. Although the path continues beyond, turn left up the stony strip, soon to enter a steep grass gully between low rock walls. It leads up to the ridge crest above the obstacle.

Continue along the ridge, which is narrow and bouldery, with a path. It turns northwest and rises gradually towards the midpoint summit Drochaid Ghlas. At a tiny col (NN 0834 3070) the right fork is the continuing ridgeline towards Stob Daimh, but first you could take the left fork for a few metres to the small cairn on

Ben Cruachan main ridge, looking down to the reservoir

Drochaid Ghlas (the 'grey bridge') between the two Munros. ▶

Return to the continuing ridgeline path. The ridge descends southeast. Avoid the left-hand path, which descends to left of some slabby rocks on stony slopes immediately above the northern drops. Go down to right of the slabs, on bouldery ground. The ridge levels delightfully, narrow but grassy, then climbs to the second Munro, **Stob Daimh**.

Leaving the summit, the path is initially unclear. Head down south; 50 metres from the cairn a path appears, running down a shapely ridge that dips then climbs to **Stob Garbh**.

It is a true bridge, as water gathered from Glen Noe passes below it into Cruachan Reservoir.

About 100 metres after this summit, in mist you might be drawn round left onto the top of its east ridge, but as this narrows to an unpathed mossy arête you realise your mistake. Instead keep south, to a wide grassy col with two small pools 200 metres from the summit. Beyond is a slight rise to 947m. ◀ The ridgeline bends right here; so leave the small top southwest, until a broad ridge descends gently south to Lairig Torran col below Beinn a' Bhuiridh.

The Southeast Ridge (Route 95) descends left from here.

> Now decide whether to include **Beinn a' Bhuiridh** (Route 92). It's not much extra ascent, and its evening views are quite magical as the sun sinks at the end of Loch Awe (in winter) or (in summer) considerably further round to the north.

From Lairig Torran, descend to right of the small gorge towards **Cruachan Reservoir**. At 550m as the ground steepens, a path forms at the top of a slight spur 50 metres to right of the ravine. The path drops to cross the stream at the foot of the ravine at the 450m contour, and runs around the slope down to a track end near the **Cruachan dam**.

Follow the track past the dam end, to a junction; here turn right towards the stream. Turn down onto the path used for the ascent, to arrive at **Falls of Cruachan station**.

ROUTE 91
Meall Cuanail

Start/Finish	Cruachan Power Station (NN 079 267)
Distance	12.5km/8 miles (full horseshoe)
Total ascent	1200m/4000ft
Time	6hr (full circuit)
Terrain	Pathless slope of grass and stones

Difficulty

This route avoids the eroded steep path in Coire Dearg, exchanging its craggy enclosure for more open views. It adds 100m of ascent, and a minor Munro Top.

▶ Start as Route 90 up to **Cruachan Dam**. From the dam's left end head up to a track just above and follow it to the left for 50 metres. Head straight up (left of outcrops) onto **Meall Cuanail**. A decaying fence along the south ridgeline leads up (with long Loch Awe views) to the summit, which is a Munro Top by 4m.

See Ben Cruachan summit summary map.

The fence line leads onward, down quite steeply into the Bealach an Lochain col, where continue as Route 90 on the steep path ahead to **Cruachan summit** and onwards (Route 90 perhaps with Route 92) to complete the horseshoe.

ROUTE 92
Beinn a' Bhuiridh add-on

Start/Finish	Cruachan Power Station (NN 079 267)
Distance	13.5km/8½ miles (full horseshoe)
Total ascent	1300m/4300ft
Time	6½hr (without Taynuilt Peak)
Terrain	Steep slopes with small outcrops

Difficulty

Extend the classic Cruachan circuit by adding its Corbett and the very best Loch Awe views.

▶ Follow Route 90 (or 91) over both Cruachan Munros and down to the Lairig Torran pass below Beinn a' Bhuiridh.

See Ben Cruachan summit summary map.

From Lairig Torran the slope of Beinn a' Bhuiridh ahead is rather steep, with stonefields at the bottom and outcrops above, then a fringe of broken crag along the top edge. Starting from the right-hand end of the pass, a slight spur gives a break in the initial stonefields. Then head up, zigzagging among the outcrops. If no clear way shows through the final crag, slant to the right below it for 300 metres. You can now round the end of the crag to arrive at once at a summit cairn. **Beinn a' Bhuiridh** has three summit cairns in a 50-metre triangle: you have arrived at the northwest one (NN 0939 2833), but the south one has the really Awe-some views.

From that south cairn head south, descending steeply for 100m to a flatter platform. Here turn right, directly towards the Cruachan dam, and descend steepish grass; a line of crag is above on the right, flanking the west spur of Beinn a' Bhuiridh (that spur itself would make an unattractive descent as it becomes steep and cragged at the bottom). The ridge has a final hump where you can continue ahead to the dam end or drop left to join the track just below.

Follow the track down left to its junction below the dam and turn right for 50 metres. Just before the stream, take the path down left to **Falls of Cruachan station** and the road just below.

ROUTE 92A
Descent North from Beinn a' Bhuiridh

Difficulty
■ ■ ■ ■ □

Start	Beinn a' Bhuiridh

If you want to do the Cruachan Ridge westbound (Route 93), you first have to get up Stob Daimh. Ascents from the east will be Routes 94 and 95, but the simplest is to reverse Route 90, or else Route 92. The difficulty there is to descend north from Beinn a' Bhuiridh to Lairig Torran – tricky, especially in mist.

▶ The best descent is not quite the same as the ascent line described in Route 92. Instead, from the three summit cairns, head east along the plateau for 300 metres to a small pool (NN 0962 2845). Follow its trickle to the steep northern slope top, and slant down to the right (northeast) to near drops on the right. Then double back left onto open ground above the Lairig Torran.

Now the slope below is steep but without large crags. Heading straight down should take you to right of the lower stonefields.

See Ben Cruachan summit summary map

ROUTE 93
Cruachan Ridge in Reverse

Start	Stob Daimh (NN 094 308)
Distance	13km/8 miles (circuit from Cruachan Power Station)
Total ascent	1400m/4600ft
Time	7hr (full circuit, with Taynuilt Peak)
Terrain	Steep paths, bouldery and rocky ridges with a short down-scramble (Grade 1)

Difficulty
■ ■ ■ ■ ■

Various route combinations may have you crossing the main ridge westbound (rather than the easier eastbound direction of Route 90). This direction does have even finer views, featuring the sea.

From **Stob Daimh** the well-defined ridge path runs down west, with drops on the right (north). After a grassy level section and steep stony rise, and 2km from Stob Daimh, a small diversion back sharp right leads to the precipice-poised summit **Drochaid Ghlas**.

The most striking section of ridge follows, with drops on the right sometimes vertical. The ridgeline runs down southwest, then turns just north of west and ascends gently to a sharp drop. This is the so-called 'Granny-stopper' (NN 072 304). A metre-long arête passes above a grass gully down left. At this point there are three onward routes.

Classic crest route

For the classic crest, continue up a slight rise, and take slabs down alongside a fierce drop on the right. The slabs are gentle but holdless, then slightly steeper but with holds. A steep step down alongside a small detached pinnacle leads to the col below the Granny-stopper.

Easier route

Alternatively, if your climbing is subtle rather than strenuous, from the one-metre arête descend left for 20 metres in a rocky groove. Then turn right and contour across slabs, with trodden footholds. The first steps are without handholds and you must simply step confidently on the sloping footholds; a rock trench below provides security. Continue with a similar move without the rock trench below, then across easier slabs with handholds, to the col below the Granny-stopper.

Avoiding the rocks

In windy weather, you may prefer to avoid the rocks altogether, although this grass option may be snow-covered in winter or spring. From the one-metre arête, descend left, but instead of taking the rock groove, fork slightly further left into a grass gully between low rock walls. After 50 metres, with the rock walls opened out, a small path crosses. Turn right up this, slanting uphill then straight up a rather eroded path to the col below the Granny-stopper.

For out-and-back to Taynuilt Peak see Route 90.

The ridge ahead is stony, then develops into a bouldery crest with a path a few metres down left if you prefer. Either way soon leads to **Cruachan summit**. ◄

Descent southwards is tricky in mist, as the boulderfield below the summit does not show the path, so keep the compass handy. After the first drop the path becomes clear, and indeed rather eroded, with the spur line defined by a steep drop on the left. After a steep descent, the col Bealach an Lochain is marked by a small pool and the posts of a dead fence. Here turn left to descend Route 90 – the easiest continuation with its clear, if steep and eroded, path.

ROUTE 94
Dalmally Horseshoe

Start/Finish	Stronmilchan road end, where B8077 meets A85 (NN 132 283)
Distance	14km/8½ miles
Total ascent	1300m/4200ft
Time	7hr
Terrain	Grassy ridges
Parking	Parking is 100 metres along the A85 east from its junction with the B8077.

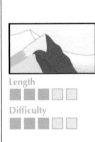

Length
■ ■ ■ □ □

Difficulty
■ ■ ■ □ □

The easier but still satisfying circuit that misses out Cruachan's main summit.

▶ Start along a track that leaves the B8077 at the road junction. After 1km, stop at a gate to survey the ridge ahead. In another 200 metres, the main track bends left uphill, with a fainter track contouring ahead; here turn off right, aiming for the bridge at NN 126 297 – the bridge is out of sight, but the eroded ground on the further bank can be seen.

Cross the wide bridge, and head up to the base of Sron an Isean. The steep ridge rises in bracken, with a worn path up the ill-defined crest. At 250m the slope eases slightly: here the path contours left for 20 metres before continuing straight up through more bracken.

See Ben Cruachan summit summary map.

The north ridge to Stob Garbh is part of both the Cruachan Horseshoe and the Dalmally Horseshoe

Above the bracken, slant up right, to the foot of outcrops. A grassy gap runs up and right; or head further right to bypass the outcrops, then back left to reach the grassy crest above. The slope is now less steep, with a small path along the crest. Ever pleasanter grassy ridge-walking leads to the summit of **Sron an Isean**.

The ridge now narrows, with boulders and grass, running southwest above Coire Lochain (a remote hollow that must reward its very infrequent visitors). **Stob Daimh** top is stony with a cairn.

Leaving the summit requires some care as the path is initially unclear. Head down south. By 50 metres from

Stob Garbh from Stob Diamh

the cairn a path has formed running down a definite ridge that rises to **Stob Garbh**.

Keep south, to a wide grassy col with two small pools 200 metres from the summit. Beyond is a slight rise; the path bears right to bypass this. ▶

The ridge now broadens and swings south, down to the broad pass Lairig Torran below Beinn a' Bhuiridh. The slope of Beinn a' Bhuiridh ahead is rather steep, with stonefields at the bottom and outcrops above, and a fringe of broken crag along the top edge. Starting from the right-hand end of the pass, a slight spur gives a break in the initial stonefields. Above them, zigzag up among the outcrops. If no clear way shows through the final crag, slant to the right below it for 300 metres. You can now round the end of the crag to arrive at once at a summit cairn. **Beinn a' Bhuiridh** has three summit cairns in a 50-metre triangle: you have arrived at the northwest one (NN 0939 2833), but the south one has the really Awesome views.

The descent of Beinn a' Bhuiridh is gentle pleasure. Head east past the rock knoll of Beinn a' Bhuiridh's east top, and down a broad gentle ridge with drops on the

A useful escape here is to descend Route 95, the southeast ridge, from the top of the 947m knoll.

left. The ridge rises slightly to the flat plateau of Monadh Driseig, a visit to the trig point, out right, is worthwhile for more views. The ridge down east is decorated with granite erratics, poised in textbook style on outcrops of schist.

At 450m the ridge turns northeast and steepens down to a col at 350m. From here a direct descent down right is steep and bracken-infested, so instead turn down left (north) on gentler slopes. After passing to left of a rocky outcrop, head directly down to Allt Coire Ghlais. Just above the stream you'll meet the upper part of the track of the upward route.

ROUTE 95
Stob Garbh Southeast Ridge

Start	Stronmilchan road end (NN 132 283)
Distance	11.5km/7 miles including descent over Meall a' Bhuiridh
Total ascent	900m/3000ft
Time	5½hr
Terrain	Grassy ridge
Parking	Parking on the A85, 100 metres east of the Stronmilchan road end.

Difficulty

The most comfortable way onto the Cruachan Ridge, with no steepness, scrambling, bog or shaggy vegetation. Combine it with the end of Route 94 for a half-day over the Corbett Beinn a' Bhuiridh. For those undertaking the full Route 94 (Dalmally Horseshoe) this route taken in descent makes a useful half-way escape.

See Ben Cruachan summit summary map.

◀ Start at the road end, where a track heads north, under power lines and below disused quarries. Fork right, to a bridge over Allt Coire Ghlais (NN 120 295). Turn left, on a path above and alongside the stream, for 400 metres to a small ruin. Here turn up right onto the ridgeline towards Stob Garbh.

The ridge ascends grassily and gently. Sometimes there is a small path. A small col at 450m has a pool. Two-thirds of the way up you'll keep ahead for Stob Garbh and Stob Daimh, or else aim off left for Beinn a' Bhuiridh.

Stob Garbh summit

For Stob Daimh the ascent is uncomplicated. Keep up the ridge, which steepens with drops on the right, and becomes a featureless steep slope to a knoll at 947m with a cairn. Turn right, northwest, on the ridge path to **Stob Garbh**. Keep ahead (north) for **Stob Daimh**; or turn back south (Route 94) for the short horseshoe over Beinn a' Bhuiridh.

Beinn a' Bhuiridh (bypassing Stob Garbh)

If you are aiming for Lairig Torran and Beinn a' Bhuiridh, ascend the ridge to the 700m contour only. In mist, try to find a marking boulder, with a W-shape excised from its left corner (NN 1029 2969). From here a grassy shelf runs to the left, with steeper ground above and below. In mist, contouring along this shelf needs concentration. Finally climb slightly to avoid slabby ground ahead, and reach the rise (750m) immediately north of Lairig Torran. ▶ Continue over **Beinn a' Bhuiridh** as on Route 94.

The rise has a boulder shaped like the smile on a crocodile, a striking-off point for those reversing this line in mist.

Descent of southeast ridge from Stob Daimh

Keep south for 200 metres, to a wide grassy col with two small pools. Beyond is a slight rise to 947m; the main path heads up onto its top (NN 0972 2997 – in mist beware a cairn 50 metres southwest, which isn't a good place to find the ridgeline from). Descend south-southeast, down steep grass, with even steeper grass on the left. There is a trace of path, but compass is the best way down here in mist. At 750m the slope eases and the ridgeline becomes apparent.

ROUTE 96
Drochaid Ghlas Northeast Ridge

Start	Castles farm track (NN 136 288)
Distance	10km/6 miles (to Cruachan summit)
Total ascent	1200m/4000ft
Time	5½hr up
Terrain	Pathless ridge, short scramble Grade 1
Parking	There are two small parking pull-offs at the bridge over Allt Mhoille. There is another pull-off 500 metres east (NN 141 290), and on the A85 just east of its junction with the B8077.

Difficulty
■ ■ ■ ■ ■

The romantic back way onto Ben Cruachan.

See map for
Route 98.

◄ There are two entrances to the track system towards Castles farm. At the eastern one (by a brown bungalow) enter and turn left on the track for 150 metres, then turn right. At the western entrance (marked Castles Estate) enter across a cattle grid, and keep ahead.

Follow the main track ahead to a junction near **Castles farm**. Turn left through a gate, onto the track, with traces of tarmac, climbing up across the flank of **Beinn Eunaich**. ◄

At NN 1297 3064, 270m, a small cairn and path on the right are the 'standard' route up Beinn Eunaich.

The track crosses **Allt Lairig Ianachain** and passes a side-track on the right – the side-track is where Route 98 descends from Beinn a' Chochuill – then it runs almost level to pass below a locked hut. Just before the next stream crossing, six tall marker poles mark the way up to **Lairig Noe**. The apparent track on Explorer maps here is actually a tunnel. (From the pass, steep grass slopes give access to Sron an Isean and Beinn a' Chochuill on either side.)

Two more tall posts guide through the pass and more are on the descent to the isolated track stretch across the head of **Glen Noe**. Turn left to go past a water-tunnel entry, and follow the track, green and little used, to its end at the foot of a slabby stream. Crossing the stream is usually easy as the water is gathered just above and taken away under the mountain!

Head up to right of the slabby stream until the slope eases into a shallow corrie at 550m. Bear up right onto the ridgeline, and go up it with drops on the right. The ridge bends from southwest to south and steepens; then at the 900m contour steepens even more into a rocky tower. This is overcome by a gritty narrow gully slanting right, with a scrambling moment. ▶ Regain the crest above, for a little easy scrambling over boulders and easy slabs, until the ridge levels to a charming arête with small path. A tiny gendarme (obstacle) is teetered past on the left. The ridge rises slightly to the small cairn on **Drochaid Ghlas**.

For descenders with GPS, the top of this gully is at NN 0843 3109.

ROUTE 97
Cruachan Reservoir

Start/Finish	Falls of Cruachan Station (NN 079 267)
Distance	7km/4½ miles
Total ascent	400m/1300ft
Time	3hr
Terrain	Steep rough paths
Max altitude	450m
Parking	Parking at the Power Station Visitor Centre is not intended for walkers and is locked at the end of the afternoon. Park opposite its entrance on the north side of the road; there are also small pull-ins further east, and a larger space 800 metres west below the station.

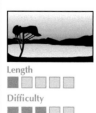

Length

Difficulty

This is a tough little walk, so allow more time than the distance and height gain alone would suggest. The views all the way up are fine, and the reservoir at the top is most attractive unless it's been emptied to power the UK's electric toasters and kettles (it provides quick power for surges like the ones in breaks of popular TV programmes). Afterwards, you can view the same terrain from underneath, on a tour of the power station inside Cruachan mountain. The walk is also the start of routes onto Cruachan's granite ridge, high above the reservoir.

This was a better walk when there were paths both sides of the Cruachan Falls stream (OS maps still mark only the closed-off one to west of it). For a gentler and much longer approach, there's the tarmac track to the dam from Lochawe village.

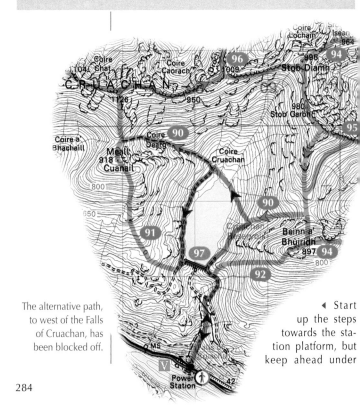

The alternative path, to west of the Falls of Cruachan, has been blocked off.

◀ Start up the steps towards the station platform, but keep ahead under the rails in a narrow tunnel. Half way up some concrete steps, the path heads off left towards the stream. It continues uphill, with steep zigzags through the wood.

Higher up, a branch path on the right takes a line through bracken rather than brushwood. The two rejoin at a steep and awkward ladder stile (even humans may prefer the dog slot just to the right). With the stream on your left, continue to a '7.5 tonne' bridge, on a track below the **Cruachan dam**.

Turn left, up to the base of the dam. Steps on the left lead up below the dam, until steep iron steps lead to its top.

Turn right, across the dam. ▸ Turn left to a tunnel outlet, and continue on a well-used path that slants gradually uphill above the reservoir. It reaches and crosses a stream just below its small ravine (NN 085 286, 450m). Now the path turns uphill, but keep ahead, gradually slanting down pathless grass to the head of the reservoir, crossing several small streams.

The big stream flowing into the reservoir head is often impassable, but don't worry: head upstream to find that it, too, flows out of a tunnel. Pass across the top of the outlet to a track starting beyond. Follow this along the western shore of the reservoir and back to the **dam**, which is crossed for the second time back to its eastern end.

Turn right down a track for 300 metres to a junction. Turn right, then down left onto the path used at the start of the walk, for the steep and rough descent to **Falls of Cruachan station**.

At the track at its eastern end, you could turn right for an immediate descent.

Beinn a' Bhuiridh from Cruachan Reservoir

ROUTE 98
Eunuch and Cockle

Start	Stronmilchan road end (NN 133 283)
Finish	Taynuilt (NN 004 312) or Stronmilchan
Distance	24km/15 miles
Total ascent	1500m/5000ft
Time	10hr
Terrain	Paths, grassy ridges, tracks
Max altitude	Beinn Eunaich 989m
Transport	Rail or Citylink coach Taynuilt–Dalmally (three of each daily)
Note	For a circular walk start/finish at Bridge of River Strae (NN 145 294)

Length
■ ■ ■ ■ □

Difficulty
■ ■ ■ □ □

Beinn Eunaich and Beinn a' Chochuill are usually considered as just two more to bag at the back of Ben Cruachan. Up the track behind Castles farm to a small cairn (NN 1297 3064); up Eunuch; then use the route below and its opt-out descent back to Castles farm.

But the ridge linking the two extends above 600m for 8km. Instead of doing just the little bit in the middle between the two Munros, how much better to do it all. East of Beinn Eunaich is narrow green ridgewalking of the best sort, and almost pathless. A descent westwards to Loch Etive gives a long linear outing with return by bus or train; or there is a less 'ridge-it' option to descend back to a car in Glen Orchy.

The Citylink bus will let you off near the Stronmilchan road end; from Lochawe station there's an extra 1km of verge to walk. For the non-linear walk, there's a small pull-in on the north side of the Stronmilchan road (NN 141 290), or at the start of the Glen Strae track.

Start northeast along B8077. Just north of a bridge over the **River Strae**, a track signed for Duiletter turns off up-valley over a cattle grid. After 500 metres, the track forks. Right

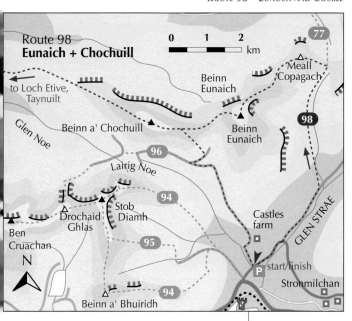

Route 98
Eunaich + Chochuill

0   1   2
km

to Loch Etive,
Taynuilt

Glen Noe

Beinn a' Chochuill

Lairig Noe

96

Beinn
Eunaich

Meall
Copagach

77

98

94

Drochaid
Ghlas

Stob
Diamh

Ben
Cruachan

N

95

Castles
farm

GLEN STRAE

start/finish

P

Stronmilchan

94

Beinn a' Bhuiridh

is signed for Duiletter, but take the track left past a build-ing. A pool is on the right, then the track passes through a deer fence to a junction. Keep ahead on the main track which has returned from Duiletter bridge. After 1km, the track reaches a bridge over the **Allt Dhoirrean**.

Before the bridge, turn left up through a field gate, on faint quad-bike tracks. The wheelmark track is faint, but if you lose it the going is over rough grassland, although comfortable enough. This track replaces an older stalk-ers' path.

The faint quad track heads up to left of the stream to a gate with stile just before the crossing of the side-stream Allt Raineach. From here, a few cairns mark the old path line into the col **Lairig Dhoireann** (620m), with a pair of cairns to pass between at the high point. ▷

Turn left, with rocky outcrops to thread among, then a stony slope to the summit of **Meall Copagach**. Now a

Route 77 to Glen
Etive uses this as
a true pass and
continues ahead here.

lovely ridge with a very faint path leads west over two minor humps to **Beinn Eunaich**.

> 'Eunaich' means birdish, with 'Eunuch' a **nick-name** bestowed by mountaineer Ivan Waller. He thought 'Cockle' was another nickname, but in fact 'Cochuill' already means a seashell.

Here is a 1.2m-long haggis-shaped boulder which marks the turn-off point if you later want to descend to Strath of Orchy.

Here make a sharp right turn, to descend northwest, soon finding a trodden baggers' path. It leads down across a col (Lairig Ianachain) then up a quite sharp ridge, to a very minor top at 896m. Behind this is a slight drop to a col where the ridge turns slightly to the right. ◄

Keep ahead, along a pleasingly narrow level ridge, then a short steeper climb to the summit of **Beinn a' Chochuill**. From here both tops of Cruachan appear pointy and the main one positively Matterhorned.

Return to Strath of Orchy
Retrace steps to the haggis-shaped boulder (NN 1181 3252). Bear right, southeast, to find within a few steps a path leading down a forming spur. The path fades, but

follow the spur down until a track crosses it. This track should be downhill to the right (if it's slightly downhill left, you've come down west of the track junction, and need to turn *left*). Turn right, the downhill direction, to a junction, then left on a more-used track with traces of tarmac. It leads around the flank of Beinn Eunaich, to turn right near **Castles farm** and reach B8077.

To continue to Taynuilt from Beinn a' Chochuill, head northwest down a ridge defined by the drop on the right. After 1.5km comes a sharp dip across the ridgeline just before Aonach Breac (Point 730m). The faultline groove down to the left harbours the beginning of the guiding stream Allt nan Gillean. Cross the dip to go down the spur to right of Allt nan Gillean, marked with some old iron fence posts. At 400m the spur levels to wet grassland. Here slant down its left edge to the bend in Allt nan Gillean where it leaves the faultline. To right of the stream (NN 073 340) find quad-bike wheelmarks, which run down westwards.

The wheelmarks lead onto grassland pasture below **Creag an Fhithich**, with green humps of old lazybed cultivation. Head down to the waterfalls marked on maps, with the top end of the track at a quarry nearby.

Follow the track out past Glennoe farm to join a bigger track running alongside Loch Etive. Turn left, on a smooth track that after 400 metres crosses the **River Noe**, and then reaches the side of **Loch Etive**. It runs into pleasant woodland, and (4km from Glennoe) arrives at the lane, the Old Military Road, near Inverawe house.

Turn right, signed for **Inverawe Country Park**. After 400 metres turn left to the far corner of the country park's car park. Beside the shop, a sign marks a path for the Riverside Walk. Follow it down, between a couple of brown huts, to a riverside field. Cross to a large imposing footbridge over the **River Awe**.

Head up the field beyond to a kissing gate, to turn right along a tree-lined track to Bonawe Furnace. The track and street beyond lead into the north edge of Taynuilt. At the Catholic church cross into a path that rejoins the street below. Follow this ahead, over the River Nant, to **Taynuilt station**.

ROUTE 99
Kerrera Island

Start/Finish	Kerrera ferry pier (NM 830 286)
Distance	18km/12½ miles (or shorter)
Total ascent	300m/1000ft
Time	Up to 6hr
Terrain	Tracks, fairly comfortable pathless grassland
Max altitude	50m
Maps	Landranger 49 (Oban) or Explorers 376 and 359
Transport	First ferry 8.45am; technically next 10.30am but timetable flexible; alternative crossing from Oban to Oban Marina at the north end of the walk

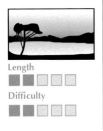

Length
■ ■ ☐ ☐ ☐

Difficulty
■ ■ ☐ ☐ ☐

Kerrera is a low-lying basalt island of great character. It has an impressive castle, a tea garden, and no real roads. The island's standard route, referred to below as the 'Classic Track', is a circuit by Barnabuck and Ardmore to Gylen Castle and along the east coast back to the ferry. It's an easy and rather busy walk of 11km. The present route extends that by diverting to the island's northern end, and then forking off for a walk along the west coast along raised beach and clifftops. This is rather rougher and much quieter than the standard track, but even so not very rough. Castle and tea garden do still get in on the act, and the time given includes proper attention to both.

The northern part, to the busy yacht harbour and the stone column overlooking Oban, could be bypassed. That shortened start is at the end of the description.

Kerrera Ferry at Gallanach

▶ From the slipway start through a field gate on the right, and turn uphill a few metres past a rusty diamond post (marking an underwater telegraph line). Just above it, the old path runs to the right under bracken, becoming clearer. Follow it along the shoreline, sometimes hidden under bracken but mostly good. Cross a damp shoreline meadow to find, 1km from the jetty, the start of a track. This slants left away from the shore below an overhead phone line (not the power line further left), then drops to a field gate near Ardantrive (NM 837 298). The track runs down a field, to meet a clearer one at the field foot – that track will be the return journey. Continue ahead to pass through **Ardantrive** farmyard with its five species of domestic fowl (including peacock and guinea).

From the ferry you can spot the old path running along the shoreline.

The track continues to the busy yacht harbour. Either pass through the harbour or take a track just behind the buildings. The green track beyond heads towards the tall stone monument. Turn up left through a wooden kissing gate to the **monument** to Mr Hutcheson, who greatly improved steam transport among the islands in the 1850s, as manager of what later became CalMac Ferries.

Gylen Castle, and former sea stacks on the raised beach

Return through **Ardantrive** farmyard, and bend right on the main track. It runs below basalt outcrops, and along the northern shore-line, to a

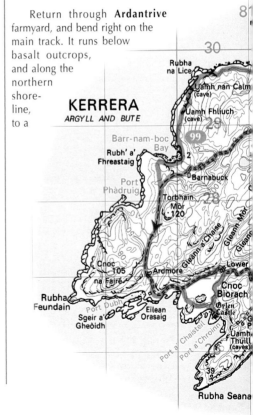

shingle bay **Oitir Mhor** with a small island Eilean nan Eun (Isle of Birds) just offshore. ▶

As the track bears left, keep ahead along the shoreline, between the bracken and

The shortened route joins here: see below.

the beach stones, to Rubha Redegich point. Continue along the shoreline, over some tussocky moor but mostly fairly comfortable going, to reach the sandy **Slatrach Bay**.

At the bay's western end is a roofless ruin. Here a grass track continues along the shoreline, which develops into a raised beach backed by low cliffs. The track follows the top of the cliffs, though the former

293

beach below is short-cropped grass for walking as well. After 1km the track ends at a fence gate. Here turn down right to the shoreline, to pass below a former sea cave Uamh Rubha na Lice (Cave of the Point of Slabs). Floored with sheep droppings and old bones, it's not a suitable wet-weather picnic spot.

Continue along the shoreline, above wave-cut rock platforms, and past a former sea stack pinnacle sticking out of the grass. After 400 metres the cliff projects towards the sea, with a rocky little path. Around this corner, a little sheep path passes up left by a rock ledge, for a continuation along the tops of the low cliffs. The going gets a little rougher, with long grass and soft ground. A wheelmark track forms below the cliff line, leading to the next bay, **Barr-nam-boc**, below Barnabuck house.

From the bay's west corner, cross the grass to a track behind a broken wall. Turn right, passing around the base of a crag, then up to the left. The track disappears, but keep ahead (south) to find the Classic Track, here a wide path, just before it passes through a broken wall.

This is the best bit of the Classic Track. It follows the wandering path south, across a flat little valley and through a pass, to descend to **Ardmore**. On the right, a textbook-style basalt dyke sticks up out of the grass. ◄ In 400 metres the track reaches a rocky bay: ahead through a little col can be seen the top of Gylen Castle. At the bay corner turn off right on a faint green track through a gate. It crosses wet ground, then goes through the narrow little col. Pass around the head of Port a' Chaisteil bay, and take a path up through a rock-sided gap to **Gylen Castle**. ◄

Return through the rock gap to the head of Port a' Chaisteil, and take a path alongside a stream to a gate. A green track leads up to join the Classic Track circuit beside **Upper Gylen** tea garden.

Turn right, on tarmac track that reverts to gravel at the slope top. It descends past a house to the eastern shoreline, and follows it for 2km to the ferry slipway.

Its steeper end makes a tempting scramble, an airy Grade 1.

Gylen Castle is open to human visitors; small but atmospheric, with exciting interpretation boards.

To leave out the northern part of the island
This slightly shortened walk saves 3.5km (1hr). From the ferry slipway, follow the track ahead for 250 metres, past a red phone box. Take the track forking up right past the old schoolhouse. After the farm at **Balliemore**, a gate ahead is signed as the track for Gylen Castle and Tea Garden – that is the 'Classic Track' route.

The **Classic Track** is a pleasant and easy 6.5-mile walk whose drawbacks are that it is mostly away from the shoreline, and is very busy and popular. Take this track to pass just below Barnabuck, and up between two basalt craglets to a gate. Now a wide path, the route runs south across a flat little valley and through a pass, to descend to Ardmore. It passes to right of the house to reach the shore. Short-cut to Gylen Castle (as on the main route) or follow the clear track ahead to Upper Gylen Tea Garden. A signed gate on the right is the side-path to Gylen Castle. Return to Upper Gylen, and continue on the main track to the east coast and the slipway.

However, stay on the main track bending right, and passing through the col of the island watershed. After 300 metres, take the right-fork track, running under a basalt embankment. The track descends, turns right, and passes through a bracken col, before descending again to **Oitir Mhor** bay. Here turn left around the bay to Rubha Redegich point, now continuing on the main walk.

ROUTE 100

Beinn Lora

Start/Finish	Benderloch (NM 905 381)
Distance	6km/4 miles
Total ascent	400m/1300ft
Time	2½hr
Terrain	Paths, good but steep, then peaty and small
Max altitude	Beinn Lora 308m
Maps	Landranger 49 or Explorer 376 (both 'Oban') or FC walk leaflet
Parking	Forestry Commission car park on the east side of the A828 road, or village parking (with café, and path to the 1km-long sandy beach) on the west side of the A828.

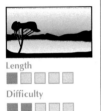

Length

Difficulty

Although Beinn Lora only just makes it to the 1000ft contour, its quality is indicated by the way various institutions in Benderloch below have adopted its name; notably the Ben Lora café, convenient and comfortable and also sells books (no muddy boots). The walk is short and on mostly good paths, but surprisingly steep. The hill itself is basalt, the views have a lot of intermixed sea and landscape, and the broadleaf woods at the bottom are pleasant.

A Forestry Commission map is available locally, and on a board at the start.

◀ Just inside the wood the path divides. To use the steeper path for the ascent, turn left here, following red/blue waymarks. A broad, smooth path runs along the foot of the wood, then turns right and steeply uphill. At the 100m contour it levels into a col, now in evergreen plantations. At a fork, the right branch has a viewpoint bench and will be the return route. For now, fork left, with blue waymarks, climbing gently and then (after a viewpoint bench on the right) more steeply alongside a stream ravine, its

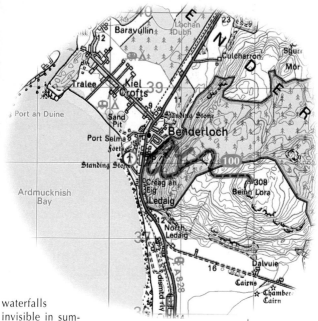

waterfalls
invisible in sum-
mer behind beech leaves.

The path zigzags up through clear-felled ground to meet a forest track. The main route turns right, but first, a branch path across to the left leads to a viewpoint. It's worth visiting for its steep view down on Benderloch.

Return to the forest track, and follow it left (east) to a T-junction. The path ahead passes around **Ron's Lochan** (Lochan nan Ron, not named after me). It's just a reedbed swamp. Then the path rises to the forest edge at a picnic table.

A kissing gate leads onto open hill. A peaty path, slightly downhill to start, leads through some boggy ground – its wet patches are reinforced with stones, so go across rather than around them. Around 500 metres and 90m of ascent lead to **Beinn Lora**'s summit with its trig pillar. Continue 100 metres south for a sub-summit with downward views.

Descend the same way, back into the forest, to the path junction at 100m altitude. Turn sharp left (red and

The forest path up Beinn Lora

blue waymarks) past a viewpoint bench and down under tall firs. The path bends down right, into beech woods, soon regaining the car park. For the beach, cross the A828 into the car park opposite. From its back left corner turn right on an untarred track, then turn left away from a former railway bridge down to the sea.

APPENDIX A
The long routes

West Highland Way crosses Rannoch Moor

West Highland Way

The territory of this book is where the West Highland Way finally escapes the traffic noise of the A82 and sets out into open country. Even so, it remains a broad pathway or track, busy, and it is very hard to get lost. As the first wild hill since Conic Hill, the short crossing between Bridge of Orchy and Inveroran is enjoyable. The edge of Rannoch Moor is crossed on a comfortable track, below the great hill face of the Black Mount; as the map suggests, this can be used as the return leg of a crossing of that high hill ridge (Route 86).

The crossing of the Devil's Staircase to Kinlochleven, on a well-graded and mostly smooth path, gives very fine views and beautiful woodland; it is not part of any plausible day walk. The Lairig Mor has more fine views on the high track above Loch Leven, but ends through forest. The final roadwalk along Glen Nevis can be mitigated by a riverside path (Route 4).

According to your temperament, the crossing of the Devil's Staircase is the 'bad bit' or the 'good bit' of the West Highland Way. If the latter, then you should enjoy the more challenging, wilder, and very much quieter 'through routes' here.

Through routes

The through routes are mapped on the overview maps near the beginning of the book. In the Introduction I've tried to persuade you that if you haven't tried this strenuous but satisfying form of hill fun this area is a good one to start off in.

Even more strenuous and satisfying is the game of hauling the heavy rucksack, with the tent and so on, right up onto the tops. Any high ridgeline that looks plausible on the overview maps will usually be covered by day-walk routes in the book, though you may have to reverse some of the route description. Here I'll mention specifically just two high passes. Walking from Dalmally to Loch Etive, after the first high pass of Route 77 (Dalmally variant), a splendid continuation on fairly good paths runs through the pass immediately east of Ben Starav (Routes 88 and 73). From Kinlochleven to Fort William an even higher pass crosses the Mamores, over Sgurr an Iubhair (Routes 37 and 28) – but even better to my mind is the old path around Binnein Mor's east and north flanks.

Dalmally or Taynuilt to Fort William in three or four days: good. If you don't want to stop there, the overview maps indicate where you could be going next. The first escape off the overview map is at Bridge of Orchy, where a track along Auch Glen leads into Glen Lyon. The continuing walk will be on quiet roads more than paths, through the great green hills of Highland Perthshire.

From Kings House, across Rannoch Moor over A' Chruach is better than the plantation track along the lochside. After Rannoch station and the Black Wood of Rannoch, walkers could head for Blair Atholl and the path network centred on Pitlochry.

From Corrour station a very fine pass north of Ben Alder, the Bealach Dubh, leads to Culra bothy on well-maintained paths through very remote country. The continuation to Dalwhinnie is on a rather harsh Landrover track alongside Loch Ericht.

Fort William is the start of the Great Glen Way to Inverness – a smooth and waymarked way, with too much track and towpath for my taste. However, at Gairlochy it leads naturally into the foot of Gleann Cia-aig, a fine crossing to Glen Garry, with onward paths to Knoydart (see below) or Cluanie Inn, Loch Affric and Wester Ross.

The better way out of William is by the passenger ferry across Loch Linnhe, when a good track by Cona Glen leads by a high path to Glenfinnan station. Stop there, or continue under the 'Hogwarts' viaduct for some really wild and rough country through to Glen Dessarry and Knoydart. In the far west, Inverie is reached only on foot, or by the ferry that takes you out to Mallaig. For those with the legs, this is what Scottish backpacking is all about!

The Three Ridges

Of the area's 44 Munro summits, 27 lie along three 'super-ridges' – these are easily seen on the two overview maps, where Munros are marked by solid triangles. Each of them makes a superb high-level traverse for any extremely fit walker.

Nevis to Grey Corries (8 summits)

This is possibly the best of all. The long haul up Ben Nevis can be done in the dark, for sunrise on the summit. After getting the thrilling Carn Mor Dearg Arête all to yourself, the serious descents and reclimbs on either side of the Aonachs are the make-or-break section of the day. Then you get the whole of the Grey Corries without any of the preliminary forest trudge. Carry overnight gear and end at Lairig Leacach bothy, or else hike out under the moon to Spean Bridge. (Glen Nevis to Lairig Leacach: 25km/3100m or 15½ miles/10,000ft – about 14hr.)

The Mamores (10 summits)

Although it has the most Munros, this traverse is possibly the least excessive of the three. Once two loose hills at the eastern end are sorted out, it's just narrow ridges down a bit, along a bit, and up a bit, all the rest of the way. The range even allows a circular walk, returning to a start-point in either Glen Nevis or Kinlochleven. Just don't get caught in the dark in the forest above Polldubh! (Start and end Glen Nevis, 35.5km/3400m or 22 miles/11,500ft – 17hr).

Etive to Black Mount (6–9 summits)

This is the wildest and least frequented of the three. It's also the most inconvenient; I approached it from Dalmally by way of Loch Etive side. In parts it's pathless, and needs skilful route-finding. A descent of Sron na Creise leaves the outcome in doubt right to the end. (Etive Shore to Kings House, 6 Munros without outliers, 30km/3000m or 19 miles/10,000ft, 15hr).

Completing any of these ridges, in a day or as a self-sufficient trip with tent or bivvy bag, is something to be proud of. At the same time – modesty! The first two of them are linked into Tranter's Walk, the UK's ultimate one-day trek. That's 18 Munro summits, starting and finishing in Glen Nevis, between midnight and midnight. Too much? Well, the Tranter Walk has been achieved in 19 hours in full winter conditions (Gay, Gay and Manson, February 2009). Hill runners attempt to go 5 Munros further (Beinn na Lap, Chno Dearg, Stob Coire Sgriodain, Stob a' Choire Mheadhoin and Stob Coire Easain) in a 24-hour circuit of 90km/8250m of ascent, the Ramsay Round. Though the distance and climb are similar to England's Bob Graham Round, the length of the individual climbs, together with the rough terrain, mean that this is a bit more than a standard superfit human can actually manage – but over 200 have achieved it.

Back in the 19th century, mountaineer WW Naismith achieved all three of the Glencoe biggies (Bidean and the two Buachailles) in one wintry day at Easter. The kind of runners who not only enjoy getting very, very tired but scared as well have extended this into the natural horseshoe by returning along Aonach Eagach; the Buachaille is ascended by the Grade 3 scramble of Curved Ridge. The inaugural 'Glen Coe Skyline' in 2015 was won in just over 7½ hours.

APPENDIX B

Access and deer stalking

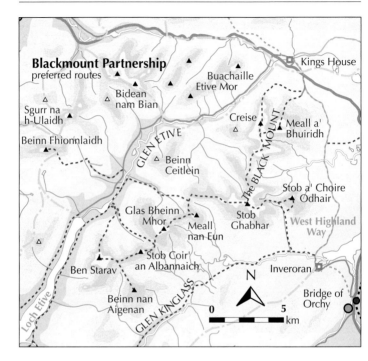

Since 2005 Scotland has a legal right of access to almost all open country and farmland (the main exceptions being growing crops and land around buildings). Footbridges are explicitly included in the access rights, as are non-damaging cycling, and wild camping – though this doesn't mean roadside camping. Access must be taken 'responsibly', which basically means with consideration and care for other hill-users, land managers and the environment. Full text of the Scottish Access Code is at www.outdooraccess-scotland.com (or from NatureScot).

The long linear routes are on established customary paths, marked on Scotways' Hill Tracks map (apart from the Leum Uilleim variant on Route 46). Most of these are rights of way, with an absolute right of access. On Route 77, the Lairig Dhoireann north of Dalmally and the Etive shore path north of Glen

Kinglass are not actually listed as rights of way, but it shouldn't make any difference. Scotways, formerly the Scottish Rights of Way Society, kept these lines alive during the long century before the Scottish Land Reform Act and erected the green 'SRWS' signposts on several routes in this book (www.scotways.com; 24 Annandale Street, Edinburgh EH7 4AN).

In parts of this area, from August (sometimes July) to 21 October, responsible access includes avoiding disturbance to deer stalking. (Stalking does not take place on Sundays.) Useful guidance is 'Heading for the Scottish Hills' found at www.outdoorsaccess-scotland.com (search 'heading Scottish Hills') where many estates give general guidance or contact phone numbers. In the absence of such specific information, you can minimise the risk of disturbance by using established paths (such as the 'standard Munro routes') and following ridges. Take account of reasonable advice that you receive on the day, for example from a sign or a stalker.

Areas without stalking-season issues, including John Muir Trust, National Trust for Scotland, and Forestry Commission, are listed below. The boundaries of the estates are on the overview maps. Find latest info and email/phone contacts at the 'Heading for Scottish Hills' web page.

Grey Corries Mamores West (GCM West)
There are no limitations on access on Ben Nevis, the Aonachs. Mamores: main stalking area is Sgurr Eilde Mor eastwards.

Grey Corries Mamores East (GCM East)
Including Grey Corries, Sgurr Eilde Mor: early August–20 October, not Saturday or Sunday.

Black Corries
Including Beinn a' Chrulaiste: stalking mid-September to 20 October

National Trust for Scotland, Glencoe (NTS)
No restrictions.

Forestry Commission (FC)
No restrictions. Take particular care not to start fires.

Blackmount Partnership
Stalking mid August–20 October. Map boards at car parks and path ends showed requested routes but are now illegible: those routes were the popular ridge routes to the Munros. Phone contacts on 'Heading for Scottish Hills' website.

Glen Noe Estate (Noe)
North side of Ben Cruachan; no stalking issues.

APPENDIX C
Information, accommodation and facilities

Accommodation

Hotels, B&Bs
Visit Scotland
www.visitscotland.com
(or individual tourist information
centres below)

West Highland Way website
www.westhighlandway.org
(for walker-friendly accommodation
near most sections of this book)

Hostels
Hostelling Scotland (formerly Scottish
Youth Hostels Association)
www.hostellingscotland.org.uk
tel 0345 293 7373 or 01786 891 400

Independent Hostels
www.scottish-hostels.com or
www.independenthostels.co.uk

Campsites
www.UKcampsite.co.uk

Travel

Journey planner
www.travelinescotland.com
and Traveline Scotland app
tel 0871 200 22 33

Air
Glasgow International Airport
www.glasgowairport.com
tel 0844 481 5555

Trains
www.scotrail.co.uk
tel 03457 484 950

Coaches
www.citylink.co.uk
tel 0871 266 33 33

Buses
Stagecoach Highlands
www.stagecoachbus.com
tel 01397 702373

Weather and snow
Best weather forecast is at
www.mwis.org.uk, posted at youth
hostels etc daily. The site has links
for snow conditions under 'Mountain
Blogs'.

Avalanche forecast
www.sais.gov.uk
(December to April) and posted
locally. Also BAA (Be Avalanche
Aware) app.

Snow conditions
Nevis Range (Aonach Mor)
www.nevisrange.co.uk

White Corries (Glencoe)
www.glencoemountain.co.uk

Webcams
Ben Nevis
visitfortwilliam.co.uk

Nevis range, Glencoe Meall a'
Bhuiridh
www.winterhighland.info

Summit panoramas
Views from Nevis, Binnein Mor,
Bidean, Cruachan
www.viewfinderpanoramas.org

Fort William and Glen Nevis

Tourist information
15 High Street
Fort William
PH33 6DH
tel 01397 701801

Glen Nevis Visitor Centre
Glen Nevis
PH33 6PF
tel 01397 781401

www.visit-fortwilliam.co.uk
www.lochaber.com
ben-nevis.com

Pubs and restaurants
Many in Fort William. Nevisport has
a hearty café and a bar underneath.
Ben Nevis Inn at the foot of the
Mountain Track (NN 125 729) has
great food, atmosphere and views,
real ale (also bunkhouse), www.ben-
nevis-inn.co.uk.

Supplies
Morrisons supermarket, many gear
shops and all other services. Small
interesting West Highland Museum,
Cameron Square.

Hostelling Scotland (SYHA)
Glen Nevis (year-round)
tel 01397 702 336

Independent hostels
Six, including Ben Nevis Inn

Camping
Glen Nevis

Local transport
Jacobite steam train mid-May–
October
tel 0333 996 6720
www.westcoastrailways.co.uk

Spean Bridge

Pubs and restaurants
Café and chip shop; bar meals at the
unassuming Aonach Mor Hotel

Supplies
Spar shop

Independent hostels
Station Lodge Tulloch; Aite
Cruinnichidh, Roy Bridge; Grey
Corries Lodge at Roy Bridge Hotel

Local transport
Nevis Range gondola
tel 01397 705825
www.nevisrange.co.uk
First gondola 10am summer, 8.30am
winter (depends on weather); last
down 6.00pm or dusk; closed mid-
November to mid-December

Corrour Station

Restaurant
Corrour Station House ('Britain's remotest restaurant')
tel 01397 732236
www.corrour.co.uk

Hostelling Scotland (SYHA)
Loch Ossian
tel 01397 732 207
Now open (with some restrictions) through winter

Kinlochleven

Tourist information
Post office
www.kinlochleven.co.uk
(Local walks leaflet also available)

Pubs and restaurants
Several including late-opening café at the Ice Factor and chip shop. Tailrace Inn is on the West Highland Way and very walker-friendly, with singing of 'Loch Lomond' on Thursday and Friday nights in summer.

Supplies
Late-opening Co-op; hill gear at Ice Factor

Indoor climbing
Ice Factor – UK's only indoor winter climbing wall
tel 01855 831100
www.ice-factor.co.uk

Independent hostel
Blackwater Hostel
tel 01855 831253
www.blackwaterhostel.co.uk

Bunk cabins at Macdonald Hotel
www.macdonaldhotel.co.uk

Local transport
Buses to Ballachulish and Fort William

Glen Coe

Tourist information
Ballachulish Information Centre
tel 01855 811866
discoverglencoe.scot

The National Trust for Scotland
Glencoe Visitors Centre
www.nts.org.uk

Pubs and restaurants
East of Glencoe village, Clachaig Inn with its big and busy bar serves good food and beer until 9pm (tel 01855 811252, www.clachaig.com). At the top end of Glen Coe, the Kings House, even more historic than the Clachaig, has a vast and somewhat soulless new bar but equally good food and drink (tel 01855 851259, www.kingshousehotel.co.uk).

Supplies
Grocer's in Glencoe village, late-opening Co-op at Ballachulish village, and a tiny folk museum.

Hostelling Scotland (SYHA)
Glencoe (all year)
tel 01855 811219

Independent hostels

Glencoe Hostel & Bunkhouse
tel 01855 811906
www.glencoehostel.co.uk

Kingshouse Hotel
surprisingly pricy bunkhouse

Camping

Invercoe camp site (all year)
tel 01855 811210
www.invercoe.co.uk

Glencoe camp site
(at Visitor Centre on A82)
tel 024 7647 5426

Red Squirrel Camp Site
(east of Glencoe Village, open all
year)
www.redsquirrelcampsite.co.uk

Glencoe Mountain Resort
(the ski centre) tel 01844 851226
www.glencoemountain.co.uk

Informal camping at Kings House and
along Glen Etive opposite.

Orchy and Inveroran

Tourist information

Tyndrum iCentre has closed
www.lochlomond-thetrossachs.co.uk

Pubs and restaurants

Good bar meals at Bridge of Orchy
Hotel. (Current staff shortages mean
no bar meals at the nearby Inveroran
Hotel.) Tyndrum has three contrasted
eating experiences: Tyndrum Inn
(basic bar meals); Green Welly
Stop (quiche and coffee), and Real

Food Café (chip shop – with hippie
ambiance, odd but excellent).

Supplies

Two well-stocked shops at Tyndrum

Independent hostels

Bunkhouse at railway platform
www.westhighlandwaysleeper.com,
and By the Way at Tyndrum
(tel 01838 400333,
www.tyndrumbytheway.com).

Camping

By the Way, Tyndrum; informal
camping across the river at Bridge
of Orchy, and at bridge north of
Inveroran Hotel.

Dalmally and Taynuilt

Pubs and restaurants

Bar meals and reasonably-priced
B&B Glenorchy Lodge Hotel,
Dalmally (tel 01838 200952, www.
glenorchylodge.co.uk and Taynuilt
Hotel (tel 01866 822437, www.
taynuiltinn.com); Hollow Mountain
Café at Cruachan Power Station.

Supplies

Small grocers Glenview Stores,
Dalmally and in Taynuilt

Oban

Tourist information

tel 01631 563122
www.oban.org.uk

Supplies
In abundance

Hostelling Scotland (SYHA)
In seafront villa, all year
tel 01631 562025

Independent hostels
Three in Oban; Kerrera Bunkhouse
(and tea garden) at Lower Gylen
(tel 07951 964231,
www.kerrerabunkhouse.co.uk)

Camping
Two camp/caravan sites southwest of
town and one at Benderloch

Local transport
Ferry timetables
www.argyll-bute.gov.uk

Kerrera Ferry
tel 0800 066 500
www.calmac.co.uk

Ferry Oban to Oban Marina, North
Kerrera
kerreramarina.com

APPENDIX D
Further reading

Walking the Munros Vol 1 Southern by Steve Kew (Cicerone Fourth edition 2021): if you simply wanted the convenient route up each of the Munros you should have bought Kew's book rather than the one you're reading now.

Scrambles in Lochaber by Noel Williams (Cicerone 2nd edition), 1996: covers 72 routes, many of them down to the author's own explorations. Good routes lucidly described, with the occasional geological insight as a bonus. Out of print but available second-hand.

Ben Nevis: Rock and Ice Climbs from the Scottish Mountaineering Club (SMT): includes the Aonachs and areas east.

Glen Coe: Rock and Ice Climbs from the Scottish Mountaineering Club (SMT)

Winter Climbs Ben Nevis and Glen Coe by Mike Pescod (Cicerone 8th edition, 2022): the routes graded 1 are accessible to competent walkers with ice axe and crampons (or look at the pictures and get scared!)

Lochaber Geotrails: Glen Nevis and *Glen Coe* by Lochaber Geopark Association: these two leaflets (from TICs) are good introductions to the 'collapsing caldera' formation special to Ben Nevis and Glen Coe. See also the informative website www.lochabergeopark.org.uk.

Ben Nevis – Britain's Highest Mountain by Ken Crocket (SMT, 2009): the history of climbing on Ben Nevis.

Glencoe by John Prebble (Penguin): a passionate but scholarly account of the Massacre without any of the usual easy myths, placing it in context as the first chapter in the destruction of the Highland way of life. Buy it second-hand or on kindle (it's out of print) and skip the visitor centre.

Mountaineering in Scotland by W.H. Murray (1947, currently published by Vertebrate): Bidean and the Buachaille should not just be walked up! Places hillwalking in its wider context of rock, snow and ice-climbing, while being the greatest work so far of Scottish landscape appreciation.

Hostile Habitats: Scotland's Mountain Environment (SMT, Second edition 2019): takes your knowledge a bit further on everything from rhyolite to ravens.

APPENDIX E
Geology

When Dorothy Wordsworth drove down Glen Coe in 1803, she remarked that the place reminded her of the Lake District. She was mocked for this later; Bidean nam Bian is a whole lot bigger than Great Gable. But Dorothy was onto something. All around Glen Coe are mountains which are magnificent in various different ways. Among them, it's Buachaille and Bidean that are magnificent in Lakeland-style volcanic rocks, andesite and rhyolite: Bessyboot, but bigger.

Meanwhile, Cruachan is magnificent in granite; the Grey Corries are magnificent in pale grey quartzite; Stob Ghabhar is magnificent in schist. The area of this book is a hands-on sampler of four of the main mountain rocks of Scotland (the missing two being Torridonian sandstone and Skye gabbro). Let's start with the schist.

Mica Schist (Mamores; Beinn a' Bheithir; Blackmount)
Schist is the ancient basement. It's Precambrian, which makes it older than life as we know it on earth and before all the main geological periods, Cambrian to today. It formed the roots of the great Caledonian mountain chain that rose at the collision of Scotland with England 400 million years ago. With those mountains now worn down to the mere stumps of today, this basement schist becomes the default rock of the Scottish Highlands.

Schist is like the ancient curry my father made on mountain holidays: recooked and stirred about until the original ingredients really don't matter any more. Schist is streaky, grey, and wrinkled. For scramblers, the holds tend to be bumps and wrinkles, rather than anything you can grab onto. Its typical mineral is mica, which comes in shiny flakes. Where the mica flakes lie flat on the surface, they can give the rock a sparkle in the sun. They can also make it quite slippery, especially in the rain. Schist is one reason why the Aonach Eagach of Stob Ghabhar isn't so satisfying as the 'real' Aonach Eagach of Glen Coe.

Quartzite (Grey Corries)
If you make a curry out of a single, simple ingredient (turnips, say), then no matter how you stir and reheat it, it's never going to be quite like other curries. The simplest rock is pure white sand, which is made of the silicon-oxygen mineral quartz. When you crush pure white sandstone 20 miles deep in a mountain crumple zone, the sand grains fuse together; the result is called quartzite.

Quartzite is off-white, smooth and brittle. It's so smooth that even a gentle slab of the stuff can be hard to climb; the scramble called Giants' Staircase, at the

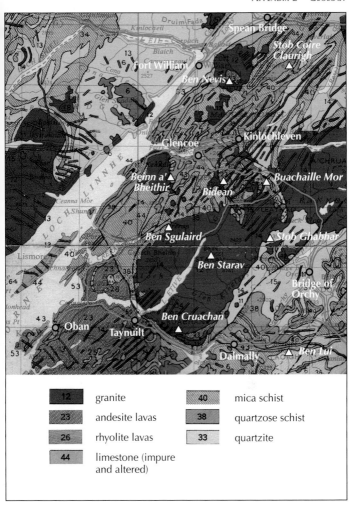

	granite		mica schist
12		**40**	
23	andesite lavas	**38**	quartzose schist
26	rhyolite lavas	**33**	quartzite
44	limestone (impure and altered)		

eastern end of the Grey Corries, appears on the map as a normally-angled hillside. But where quartzite cracks, it cracks angular: quartzite climbs have small but sharp-edged handholds. Giant's Staircase is a first class bit of scrambling!

311

Granite (Ben Nevis mountain trail, lower part; Ben Cruachan, Ben Starav)
Mountain building involves one continental plate overriding another (or an oceanic one). This generates vast amounts of friction heat deep underground. Magma melts its way upwards; when a crack opens to the surface, the magma chamber can empty itself via a volcano.

Often, though, the magma just solidifies in a lump, tens of miles across, several miles underground. When erosion finally digs down to it, the rock revealed is granite.

Because of the slow way it has cooled, granite has big speckly crystals of shiny quartz, grey or pink feldspar, and black biotite. Where its jointing is horizontal, it breaks into huge rectangular blocks like giant masonry, with rounded off corners. The Carn Mor Dearg Arête is a fine example. Where its jointing is sloped, granite forms the wide, wide slabs seen on Beinn Trilleachan above Loch Etive, and the east side of Stob Coir' an Albannaich.

The projecting quartz crystals mean that granite is superbly rough to scramble over. But the rounded corners mean few useful handholds.

Andesite and Rhyolite (Ben Nevis north face; Glen Coe)
The volcanic lavas emerged way up above the granite, where they were the first to be eroded away. At two places, though, a happy accident has preserved them for us to climb on. Where a granite magma chamber empties completely, the ground above can fall down: a cylinder of country rocks and lava drops in what's called a cauldron collapse. As it descends, a ring of granite, like a lubricant, rises around the edges.

Two such structures, at Glen Coe and at Ben Nevis itself, can be made out on the geological map. At Ben Nevis, dark-coloured andesite lavas form the summit and the magnificent north face. Andesite takes its name from the Andes, and is crystalline and rough, splendid to scramble and to climb. In a ring around it, granite makes Carn Mor Dearg and its Arête, and the lower part of the Mountain Trail.

At Glen Coe, the sunken cauldron contains andesite, but also the paler, reddish rhyolite. Rhyolite is even rougher than andesite, and being more compact, it shrugs off vegetation. Enjoy the rhyolite on Buachaille Etive Mor and the Aonach Eagach.

NOTES

NOTES

NOTES

LISTING OF CICERONE GUIDES

For full information on all our guides,
books and eBooks, visit our website:
www.cicerone.co.uk